IGN🕯TE
HAPPINESS

Additional International Best-Selling
Compilation Books by Ignite for you to enjoy

———————

Ignite Your Life for Women

Ignite Your Female Leadership

Ignite Your Parenting

Ignite Your Life for Men

Ignite Your Life for Conscious Leaders

Ignite Your Adventurous Spirit

Ignite Your Health and Wellness

Ignite Female Change Makers

Ignite the Modern Goddess

Ignite Love

IGNITE HAPPINESS

THE SIMPLE YET PROFOUND JOY THAT
COMES FROM WELCOMING PURE BLISS
INTO YOUR LIFE

INTRODUCTION BY **JB Owen**
Founder of Ignite and JBO Global Inc.

PRESENTED BY

ABBEY RICHTER • ADONIE S. • ALBERT URENA • ALEX GONTKOVIC • ANA CUKROV
ANA MARÍA PELAEZ • AURELIE BUSOLLO • BEEJAL COULSON • BELA FAYTH
CLAUDIA PATRICIA PÉREZ DELGADO • GABRIELA TRAUTTMANSDORFF-WEINSBERG
HANNA WICKSTRÖM • HEATHER DALTON • JANICE MULLIGAN • JASON B. FLORES
JB OWEN • JEREMY LAUE • JORJA GIESIN • JOYE MADDEN • KARLA ROSE WEIHE
KRISTIN KURTH-KOELZER • LESLIE LEE • LYDIA SACALLIS • MARGIE ABERNETHY
MEGHAN HUTHSTEINER • MELODY D. BYRD • NICOLE ARNOLD • POOJA S. LANKERS
REBECCA BLUST • SARAH CROSS • SHREYA LADVA • SIMONA SABBATINI
STACEY YATES SELLAR • SYDNEY SCHUBBE • TEHNIYET AZAM
TRACI HARRELL • TRACY STONE

PUBLISHED BY IGNITE AND PRINTED BY JBO GLOBAL INC.

Publisher's Note: We are delighted to offer the eleventh compilation book in the IGNITE series. Our mission is to produce inspiring, motivational, and authentic real-life stories that will Ignite your life. Each book contains unique stories told by exceptional authors. They are of the highest caliber to offer engaging, profound, and life-changing examples that will impact the reader. Our mandate is to build a conscious, positive, and supportive community through our books, speaking events, writing workshops, Ignite experiences, podcasts, immersions, and product marketplace. We always welcome new book ideas and new authors onto our platform. Should you desire to be published and featured in an Ignite book, please apply at www.igniteyou.life/apply or reach out to us at support@igniteyou.life.

Published and printed by JBO Global Inc.
5569-47th Street, Red Deer, AB
Canada, T4N1S1 1-877-677-6115

Cover design by JB Owen
Book design by Dania Zafar
Designed in Canada, Printed in China

ISBN# 978-1-7923-4171-7
First edition: August 2020

Ordering Information: Quantity sales. Special discounts are available on quantity purchases by corporations, associations, and others. For details, contact the publisher at the above address. Programs, products, or services provided by the authors are found by contacting them directly. Resources named in the book are found in the resources pages at the back of the book.

Dedication

This book is dedicated to everyone!!! Yes, authors contributed their stories to this book and shared their joyful tales; however, hundreds of people were a part of these stories and those hundreds of people touched hundreds and hundreds more. It is our hope that this exponential expansion will be multiplied over and over — across the globe — until each and every person has been touched by the glorious essence of happiness. That happiness, although sometimes preceded by difficulties, will be transformed into something greater, more self-defining, and more exciting. The change — the shift in oneself to claim happiness in their life — is the gift beautifully wrapped up in this book and it is now a part of you.

May your heart, spirit, and soul bask in a swirl of happiness from this day forward and always. Happiness unto you!

"Before I wrote my story, I thought I couldn't write. What I discovered through Ignite was a magical and cathartic journey of support and coaching. I am so grateful to be part of the Ignite family."

~ Rebecca Blust

"Having the opportunity to share my story by being an author for Ignite was very special. I got to share my story with the world and I will hopefully inspire others to do the same. I know that someone out there really needs to hear my story and I'm glad I get to give that to them. The process of becoming an Ignite author is amazing."

~ Jorja Giesin

"I have loved every moment of the journey with Ignite, from the spark of an idea to the shaping and then metamorphosis of my story. It has been an incredibly supportive and empowering process, enabling me to accomplish a lifelong dream. Building amazing connections with other authors and being part of a bigger mission has led to a truly uplifting experience — one I will forever treasure in my memory bank."

~ Sarah Cross

"Writing my Ignite story was a lot different than I expected. The whole community was so welcoming and helpful. Every time I went on to the Ignite calls, I was so interested in other people's stories and experiences that it even inspired me to write more. I highly recommend everyone write their Ignite moments."

~ Lydia Sacallis

"Writing the Ignite Happiness book has been one of the best experiences I've had in my life. The community and people were so nice and energetic. They helped me through the process and allowed me to further myself as a writer."

~ Shreya Ladva

"As a first-time writer, I was nervous when I was selected to write the chapter in a book which is part of an Amazon best-selling series. My life story will be coming to the world for the very first time. The Ignite team made everything so easy for me. Whether it was brainstorming or polishing my chapter, they held my hand so that I am confident enough to share a dark secret about my life. I was so lucky to have found Ignite to give me the courage and the necessary tools to share my story with the world"

~ Tehniyet Azam

"My experience with this project was absolutely amazing. It has been one of the most confidence-boosting, fun, and eye-opening things I've ever experienced. I sent a message to JB Owen about an idea for a book centered around happiness and expected no response, but I received an invitation to discuss the idea with JB Owen. During the meeting, she was excited and passionate about my idea, and it inspired me to share my story with the world. One message gave me the best experience I've experienced in life, and that is the beauty of Ignite."

~ Sydney Schubbe

"Expanding my horizon. Sharing experience, strength, and hope even when it's difficult and challenging. Reflecting, looking within, sitting, listening, hearing. The thrill and self-confidence that came from putting pen to paper has Ignited this sleeping Phoenix. This is an experience you don't want to miss!"

~ Janice Mulligan

"I thoroughly enjoyed the entire Ignite process and how it brought together different people from around the world and united us to empower the lives of others. Although I didn't consider myself a writer at first, the Ignite team and community gave me the tools and encouragement I needed to share my story with others."

~ Jeremy Laue

"When presented with the opportunity to write a chapter about happiness, I immediately said "Sign me up!" Not knowing any details, I soon thought what did I just commit to? I have ZERO credentials to write and who would care about what I have to say? I combatted my thoughts with this is your greatest fear, running from truly being seen. Why not take this opportunity and conquer it head on! How thankful I am for getting such wonderful support from a group of individuals I've never met! In this process, they walked alongside me, not in front or behind me. They encouraged, guided, and cheered me on, which allowed me to reexamine and decompartmentalize myself to a degree that has rekindled a fire inside me! Forever grateful to JB and the Ignite team!"

~ Meghan Huthsteiner

Contents

PREFACE
THE PURPOSE OF IGNITE

IGNITE was created to Ignite others and impact humanity. Our mandate is to do more, share more, and spread conscious positive messages to as many people as possible. We believe in human connection. We believe that power comes from being heard, being seen, and belonging to something greater. We invite people to Ignite others. To let their stories be heard, share their experiences, and find their voices. We pride ourselves in bringing people together, offering a solution, giving back, and doing something good for humanity. That is the mission and purpose behind IGNITE. There is power when one person touches the heart of another and sparks something new. Be it inspiration, love, support, encouragement, compassion or belief — each of us deserves to be Ignited and we hope these stories Ignite you.

May you have many Ignite moments that transform you into the amazing person you were meant to be.
— JB Owen

Why Compilation Books Make People Happy

We know that many people read compilation books to find light-hearted content that inspires them. They want easy reading and something not 'too deep' or challenging. We like to believe that although Ignite books can be considered easy-reading, we take it to the next level of storytelling. We curate profoundly inspiring, deeply entertaining, and wildly touching stories that go beyond light reading. These are the true stories of people's Ignite moments — those moments that have changed them in new ways. Ignite experiences are where vast learning, inner awakening, and true transformation took place. Ignite stories are the authentic realizations that each and every person can relate to because they hold values we all identify with: perseverance, determination, commitment, courage, and strength. These are universal qualities; human qualities. No matter where you live in the world, what age, color or creed you are, you feel these emotions and recognize them in other people the same way you also recognize them in yourself.

Our Authors' Stories

This book is a collection of magnificent moments told by authors of all ages. The youngest author is 12 and the oldest author is into their 60s. It is a broad span of real-life experiences that despite age, we all can relate to. Each story is told as it truly happened; unfolding as the writers' describe it. It is also deeply authentic; shared in a way that is honest and from the heart. Not all the authors in this book are 'professional writers; in fact, many are sharing their writing for the very first time. Some have written before and others are acclaimed for their writing in different ways. All of them are just like you and me — people dedicated to sharing in a way that will inspire more happiness on the planet for everyone.

Stories like theirs have been around for eons. In fact, since the beginning of time, individuals have learned from and gained wisdom from the honest, life-changing stories of others. Stories that show progress. Stories that take you on a journey and allow you to intimately feel the highs and lows of the hero or heroine in the process. People love listening to and reading those moments. In fact, stories create positive endorphins and raise levels of joy and happiness in the reader. Laughter, joy, understanding, compassion, and human connection can be both created and strengthened through storytelling, and this book is filled with those and more.

As you dive into the pages that follow, you will find each story starts with a *Power Quote*. It is an inspirational self-activating proclamation. Every writer has one at the top of their story to motivate and encourage you. It is a phrase designed to get you thinking, questioning your ideas, and then charging forward in life in your own amazing way. It is what you might find at the bottom of an email or shared amongst friends joyously at a dinner party over a sumptuous meal. Power Quotes are suggestions you can use when you need some extra confidence or when there are tears of happiness flowing down your cheeks from both conquering life's hardships and enjoying its rewards. Every Power Quote is designed to remind you of what you have inside, what you know you can do, and how your life is your own to do whatever you wish for.

Next, you will read each author's caring *Intention*. These are the joy-filled insights and new ideas they wish to inspire in you. They are personal, heart-felt messages filled with meaning and purpose. The authors want to IGNITE YOU in living your happiest life, and they share in their intentions with the hope their story will indeed spark happiness in you.

Their Ignite *Story* follows. It is an uplifting account of how they found the true meaning of happiness and made the most of it. Their stories exemplify finding joyful acceptance, discovering personal bliss, and redefining the meaning behind their inner contentment. These are some of their most vulnerable recollections gathered into authentic accounts of consciously awakening to the *Ignite* moment that led to a magnificent sense of feeling happier. We each have *Ignite* moments in our lives that change us, define us, and set us on a new path or trajectory. These stories are those moments told in the most honest and heartfelt way.

Once you have finished each story, you will find a list of doable and enjoyable *Ignite Action Steps*. These are the tangible things our authors did to overcome their challenges and rise above any fears, worries, or doubts, and ultimately led our authors to finding, living, and radiating happiness. Each author shares their easy-to-do and effective tips and suggestions for you to experiment with and implement immediately. These are the processes and practices that worked in their lives. Each step is different and unique, just like you are, and each has proven to yield fabulous results.

We all know actions speak louder than words; never is that more important than when it comes to feeling happy. You must take action for happiness to blossom. Action IS the key. To move closer to your true source of happiness, we encourage you to explore each author's action steps and then pick one you can do each day consecutively for 30 days. There are many to choose from, so find those that resonate deeply and will yield the most results for you. Each one is potentially a step that could change your life forever.

Our hope is that something you read within these pages will *transform* you; that one of our stories will have a profound impact and catapult you in a new direction. We want something within these pages to resonate so strongly within you that you just *have* to take action. This is the most important thing — that one of these stories inspires you into a new conscious realization and you feel transformed, inspired, and profoundly happy.

If you feel that your story is still unfolding or that you are still trying to figure it out, we are with you. We all have been through difficulties and go through them numerous times in our lives. Our stories show transformation *in spite of* that. We push ourselves to go forward. We offer encouragement to rise and flourish. We support each other in as many ways as we can. The enthusiasm behind each of our authors' transformations is now behind you. We support you unconditionally and are cheering you on as you uncover your own amazing life. We extend our hands should you need a bit of support, some advice, or a friend to confide in. We offer our services should you ever want to reach out because something we said resonated with you and what we shared was exactly what you needed to hear. We are all accessible and eager to connect; please feel free to find us wherever we are in the world. We are happy to support you as you undergo your own amazing self-exploration.

We are Ignited by the idea of you turning the page and reading the many stories of igniting happiness. We want you to be excited to read how others stepped into the very essence of happiness. Some of those stories may begin in pain and grief. Others might be loaded with joy and accomplishment. All of our authors show a fierce determination to step into the next version of who they were willing to become. Their stories are a guide to the unlimited possibilities that are before you in *your* life. Soak in what they have to share and then decide to go out and do more. Live more. Feel energized. Venture forth with a smile beaming from your face and a spring in your step. Claim your freedom! Love your life and embrace the wonderment that is right around the corner.

What Makes Ignite Unique

Every word written in this book, every letter on these pages, has been crafted with fondness, encouragement, and a distinct clarity not just to inspire you but to transform you. Many people in this book stepped up to share their stories for the very first time. They courageously revealed the many layers of themselves and exposed their weaknesses, fears, and discomforts as few do. Additionally, they spoke authentically from the heart and wrote what was true for them, infusing love, compassion, and a desire to inspire happiness in every word.

We could have taken their stories and aimed for perfection, following every editing rule. Instead, we chose to leave their unique and honest voices intact.

We overlooked exactness to foster individual expressions. These are their words and sentiments. We let their personalities shine through so you would get a deeper sense of who they are. We focused on authenticity, honesty, and personal expression. That is what makes IGNITE. Authors serving others. Stories igniting humanity. No filters. No desire for perfection. Just realness between them and you.

Come turn the page and meet our authors up close and personal. We know you're going to love them as much as we do. Enjoy!

Happigraph

"What an honor it is to take the experiences of these 37 authors and dedicate their stories to you for the benefit of your greatest happiness. You have in your hands a multiplicity of journeys about true, authentic happiness that was curated from deep wounds and painful memories along with joyful moments and exciting experiences. These authors are people just like you; they are moms, dads, sons, daughters, teenagers, students, employees, athletes, friends, and dreamers. Just like you, there was a period when they were going through a trying situation and dreamt of a better time, a better feeling. You are about to peek behind the curtain of their lives and discover how they found happiness without holding back. While their stories are all different, with no two paths similar, every conclusion is the same: they found a life full of happiness, bliss, and joy. One common message is that it takes work. These pages are dense with a summary of the most valuable tips, tools, and techniques every happy person knows and lives by. You also have the added bonus of interactive exercises to jumpstart you right now — today — before you even leave the comfort of the seat you are sitting in right now. Because when we know better, we do better. So let's get you IGNITED because this book is the beginning of the rest of your happier life."

~ Stacey Yates Sellar

INTRODUCTION BY JB OWEN

Founder and CEO of Ignite

How can one find happiness? It's a question that has been pondered throughout the ages. Many have spent a lifetime thinking about it. Others have crossed great lands in search of it. And there are those who have amassed great fortunes with the belief that they could buy it outright. Happiness has been the grand illusion hidden behind the desire to acquire, obtain, have, hold, and revere. And yet, happiness has been found in the simple and the uncomplex. It has been shared in a single moment and felt in a single second. As much as happiness has been the greatest quest for mankind, it can be found around every corner and in every home. Happiness is a state we find when our soul is living the way it was designed to. It is when all the stars align because the body, mind, and spirit have found their calling — the ONENESS we all seek. The true state of happiness has nothing to do with wealth, status, or accolades. Happiness is the contentment that is found with self, with stillness, with knowing thyself completely.

All you need is to trust your own true guidance system. Life will lead you in many different directions. It will tug endlessly and pull feverishly at your wishes, wants, and whims. It will dazzle you with fandangles and entice you with thingamabobs. It will poke at your deepest emotions and prod at the flagrant ego within. All these things will toss you like a paper boat amidst an ocean storm, taking you off course only to demand you find the most valuable destination of them all; your direct path to happiness. There will be a time in your journey where the confusion will subside, the trinkets will lose their luster, and the confirmation of others will mean nothing. Instead, you will follow your own desires and all the distractions in the world will not be enough to take you off the course that you have set for yourself: YOUR real happiness.

P erseverance will be the key to your happiness. You will have to push harder and farther than ever before to obtain the feeling that has been valued throughout the ages. This will require some pushing and grinding. It will not be all roses and rainbows. Instead, it may come laced in hardship and riddled with difficult choices. The journey to truly feeling happiness definitely involves work, but it is the kind of work that — once you've been dipped in the beautiful feeling and filled with the sweet nectar of joy — you will eagerly go after. What was once difficult will become easy. Struggles will give way to devotion and, before you know it, all the hardships will become the hum of happiness forming on your lips when you didn't even know you were humming. There will come a time when all your efforts have paid off and, despite the pain and suffering it took to get there, you discover you love being there. You know it was all worth it and, looking back, you are grateful you made it to that very spot.

P urpose will now be what leads you. What once drove you tirelessly will shift and your deepest happiness will come in new ways. Indescribable ways. The simple touch of a hand tucked snugly inside yours, from a lover or a child, might be the best feeling you have ever had. A flavor will unfold on your tongue — not from the yummiest of foods, but from the juiciest moments of freedom, accomplishment, and success. Your successes will tickle you silly because you obtained them your way, through your own fortitude. Your feet will move to the rhythm of your own inner music — music crafted perfectly for you. Your eyes will drink in the gems in nature, the wealth in friendships, and the richness in stillness. Happiness will be a conviction, a cause, and an all-encompassing feeling that you hold tight to the very core of your being because what now matters to you is your *purpose*. Your reason for being here on Earth is the wellspring of your happiness and with each step you take along your journey, you will step deeper into the very essence of *you*.

Inner knowing will guide you to finding your personal happiness. We have all had 'that friend' or that 'supportive' parent who has tried to guide us along *their* path to happiness. Society, social media, the government, institutions, and an endless number of other things have wanted to steer us in the direction of 'real' happiness as defined by their book or their stereotype. Yet all the forces in the world are not enough to knock you off course when you stop to listen to the inner voice — that magical feeling of your own soul's knowing — that tells you what happiness is to you. Your divine knowing is the only opinion you need to guide you directly to the fruit of the happiness tree. You don't have to go down the yellow brick road, past the polka dot house, or over the bridge patrolled by the troll to find the answers. You need only to listen from within. There, you will hear the precise message that will inspire you to venture forth down the exact road you are destined to walk, for however long it takes, in the direction that is perfect for you.

No turning back. That must be the mantra you hold in your heart, for the quest to find happiness can be long and arduous. We all know that anything worth anything is worth working for. Happiness is no different. Although happiness is a gift, it is not given lightly or gifted without merit. It isn't doled out like candy canes at Christmas time. Instead, it is like a cloistered soothsayer moving its way mysteriously through a dense crowd. You must seek it out, find it, maneuver your life to include it. Its elusive nature tests you to make sure that you are determined and devoted to the quest. Once the quest is begun, your heart must be filled with the knowledge that part of the happiness comes from the journey, the trials, and the tribulations. These are the precursors and appetizers to the banquet of life. In them lie the morsels of what happiness is all about. Go after it. Put in the effort. No turning back.

E is for excitement, for happiness is attracted to energy, high vibrations, and positive emotions. And why not be excited? Other states of being are practical and pragmatic. If you want to feel grounded, you choose calm. Feeling safe requires concern. Happiness is the state of lightness, freedom, and pleasure. It swirls in the uncontained expansion of possibilities and skips through the wonderment of opportunities. You must turn a frown upside down to be happy, and that takes the concerted effort of one ready to embrace its gift. Happiness is a state we enter into when we have worked through the human emotions on our 'to-do' list and stepped into the divine right of just *being* that we were given at birth. There is an infinite vortex of ALL that is available to us when we find the happiness we know is ours. It transcends emotion and becomes the knowledge that happiness is found deep within.

S ome people find that when happiness permeates their soul, their feeling of total self-worth skyrockets. Those once heavy feelings that were holding us back lift and dissipate. We find an inner sanctum in our existence and everything around us seems brighter and more vivid. Our inward sense of contentment shines out like the biggest lighthouse light. We beam from the inside and lift our spirits to feel more of what the Universe has to offer. This raises our self-love, self-knowing, and self-acceptance. We emerge from the chrysalis that confined us only to find the greatest treasure — the love we feel for ourselves. A deep unbridled admiration for the road we took unfolds and, in our vast feeling of happiness, we find the love, compassion, and self-belief that we had forgotten. In our joy, we enter the state of absolute knowing that tells us our human journey on this planet is one we take in order to move our spiritual experience to the highest level. Happiness brings us back to ourselves.

S o now what? Now you get to live in the bliss of the infinite Source of happiness. You are invited and welcomed, at any time and for all times, to live in the overflowing well of loving, happy, Source energy. It is a state of being that, once you find it, you know unequivocally that you are rooted in it. Source joy is yours to have and, like all beautiful things, it takes seasons and reasons to unfold. Love that time. Cherish those moments that question your strength but build your character. Bask in the many sunrises and sunsets of your life and be willing to traverse the terrain that will take form where you are today to the highest peak of your happiness. Happiness is a journey that *wants* to be experienced. It's an inner compass that is found within you. It is meant to be discovered, and you are meant to discover it. You - and only you - can find your Happiness.

Anything worth anything is worth working for.
~ JB Owen

JB OWEN

"Only do what makes you happy."

My hope is that this story awakens in you the knowing that you are both allowed to and given the right to be happy. This joyful state of being is what you were divinely born with. Interestingly, the human condition often removes this blissful enjoyment from us so that we go in search of it once more. That journey back to happiness is a process that ensures we learn, know, and define happiness on our own terms. In losing it temporarily, we appreciate it so much more. May you rediscover your happiness and bask in all its treasures.

THE HAPPY QUOTIENT

Most 'good' stories follow a pattern. They outline the rise and fall of the main character only to have them rise to victory once more. In many epic tales, the journey of the hero or heroine is defined by the need to overcome numerous personal struggles. What makes the story interesting is the admirable qualities of fortitude and perseverance required to traverse the hardships and prevail over the difficulties. It is this process of loss and gain, work and effort, unknown to known, that feels both titillating and comforting to everyone who reads it.

My story is no different from this classic plotline. It has the successful business accomplishments, the big house and fancy cars, only to have that all lost in a painful divorce and the slippery slope to bankruptcy. That downward spiral forced me to move back home with my mom and had me desperately counting my pennies to survive. Just when it looked like it couldn't get worse, a new man came into my story — a character whose presence resulted in abuse, assault, robbery, and tremendous emotional pain. My body started to suffer with illness, stress, and debilitating back pain. My world became shaky, rigid, and fragile, ready to crack like frozen glass.

That was the dark time in my story; when I felt so lost, broken, and humiliated. The sun felt as though it had hidden behind the moon and a darkness crept in like a foreboding fog. For a long time, I was numb. I was meandering through the motions, not able to see what was in front of me. The two most important main characters in my life were my adoring children. My son, the eldest at 11 years old, was thrust into the role of caretaker and supporter. In my illness, I needed him. I leaned on him when my back became unbearably sore and counted on him to take over the many chores that had previously been mine. His little world — one that should have been filled with childhood friends and joys — became one of adult tasks and worries. And more often than not, when he wasn't up to the task, he felt my wrath as the brunt wrath of my frustration and fear thrust upon his loving young heart.

My daughter, just 8, became the entertainer; a jester of sorts. She painted on her smile, cheered up her voice, and made sure to do everything she could to make Mommy happy. Her world was filled with artificial emotions and sing-song answers just to ensure I felt better. She took on the role of protecting my emotions while making sure I was taken care of. In the midst of it all, she felt hollow, pained, and lost in her desperate need to please me.

If you could have pulled back the velvet curtain on the life we were trying to lead, you would have seen three amazing people tip-toeing around one another to avoid triggering the land mines of sorrow that had encased our lives. I felt as if I was permanently wearing a snorkeling mask, submerged under a sea of sadness and loss and never able to fully catch my breath. I watched my kids bottle up their stress and suppress their true emotions as they navigated life on their own, determined to not add their stresses to mine. Our home was a somber one. We had become the paper cut-outs of a life that once was.

Yet, in most good stories, there comes a point when the main character feels compelled to make a critical, life-changing decision. When the situation becomes so grim and unacceptable that they can bear it no more, our hero wakes from their slumber. The hero is forced, by their own account, to do something — anything in fact — to better themselves in any way possible.

With my kids ashamed by our circumstances, I knew things needed to change. The classic arguments over unpaid child support were a monthly battle I had become tired of fighting. Calculating our groceries while we pushed the cart through the store stopped feeling like a fun-filled game. With our diminished financial situation, keeping the kids in private school meant applying for a subsidy and I could feel the weight of judgment from prying eyes turning what should have felt like a helping hand into a burden of reluctantly doled out charity. The theatrical masks of happiness we once wore had turned to the permanent faces of tragedy and we were all suffering.

Of course, my story is not the worst of the worst. Many of us have similar and even more devastating tales to report. In fact, most of us have some sort of tragedy, difficulty, and hardship in our lives. The human experience seems to be one where what goes up must come down; where goodness needs to feel sadness and a whole gambit of emotions demand to be felt even when we try to push them away. I have often held the idea that we are all born with a list of emotions pinned to our birthday suits and, despite the maneuvering we do in our lives, we cannot *outmaneuver* any of the emotions on the list. We are required to experience them all and life will twist and contort to make sure that, despite our best human efforts, we feel each and every one of them fully.

Anger, frustration, and betrayal were just a few of the emotions topping my list at that point in my life and their constant presence was wearing me down and chipping away at any happiness that tried to sprout a tiny seedling in my life. I had lost the luster — the carefree nature and ease — that was once bestowed upon me. My life felt like living in a dark tunnel where neither end looked like it would lead to anywhere good.

Fatefully — like any good story with a fairy godmother, helpful hooded stranger, or colorful, mystical force — I felt the surge of an outside influence start to steer me in a new direction. I began to pluck out the thorns that were plaguing my life and look for the sunshine and rainbow that had once been present. I knew no one could shift me out of the spot I was in but me. I had to do some deep inner work and become my own rescuer. I had to fight the dragon that was living in me and climb my own castle wall to gain my freedom once again.

For many, deep meditation is a portal to the land of inner knowing. It awakens the state of self-reflection and allows personal introspection to help find responses to questions whose answers are elusive. I had taken to meditation as a form of inner healing and used it daily to help bring me back to finding myself. Often my sessions would be riddled with questions. I was begging for answers and insights on how to better my life and further cherish my children. I sat for hours at a time, daily, without exception, concentrating fiercely on the search for peace. It was an important part of my process and, in hindsight, a valuable stage in the journey. Not many traditional stories include this process, but like the bite of the apple, the prick of the finger, or the taking of the blue pill over the red, I used meditation to help me regain my resolve and decide the next important steps I needed to take.

As I struggled to make my way back above water and heal internally, my exterior life was filled with the necessary and the mundane. In my effort to return us to a better life, I witnessed both my kids looking for happiness in outside influences, material things, and living what I called the 'fridge-door' life. They would open the fridge door and unappreciatedly take out whatever food was there. They would eat it gluttonously, only to open the fridge door a few hours later, ready to consume more. They had no clue of what it took me to fill the fridge each week. They just assumed it would always be full. All too soon, they started expecting *everything* to be as abundant as the fridge was. Shopping, sports, entertainment, and time with friends suddenly became a revolving door of what they wanted and simply expected to be provided. It seemed they had no awareness of how lucky they were that they even had a fridge with food and that it was full month after month. An expectation of receiving everything preceded them and I was feeling burnt out.

In my faithful meditations, I began to search for deeper meaning for the reason my life looked as it did. I began to examine every aspect of my journey — the doors I walked through, each crossroad I came upon, and every path I chose. I saw a pattern of pleasing, presuming, and perfectionism emerge. In my quest to scale the great mountains of my success, I noticed I was always taking the billy goat's path — the narrow, harrowing footpath which meanders precariously to the top versus the wide, well-worn, and expansive road the maharaja travels joyfully with his entourage. It seemed I was always picking the treacherous road over the easy one.

I had taught myself that if it was hard, it was worth it. *Difficult* meant *I earned it*. Struggles led to admiration. Perseverance showed true grit. All my perceptions of how a hard life equaled a worthy one had laced my road with broken glass and riddled it deep with harrowing potholes.

With that profound and vivid insight into my patterns, I began to ask myself different questions, ones that would poke holes into my old ideas and shine light on a new way of thinking. I started to find ease and joy in my actions. I looked for more connection with others, more helping hands, and ways to include myself versus excluding myself. Over time, flickers of light began to shine like fireflies in a farmer's field and I followed the new crumbs of learning down paths I had never taken before. Over time, I felt better, lighter, stronger, and a glimmer of happiness began cresting over the horizon. If I wanted things to be different, I knew I needed to make a radical change. *I needed to wash away everything I had done in the past to allow something better to blossom.*

Like Frodo, Luke Skywalker, and Jack with his beanstalk, many successful characters feel compelled to set forth on a life-changing inner exploration — the unknown journey to find meaning in their life. After deep consideration and hours of meditating, I felt a similar compulsion. The fridge door of westernized life had been opened and closed one too many times. The kids also seemed ready to shed themselves of the old burdens they were carrying. Despite the naysayers and worrywarts, I decided to remove the children from school and go traveling. I wanted them to see the many colors of other sunsets, taste the foods flavored by other spices, and meet the people who lived in different cultures. I knew there was a big wide world out there for them to enjoy, play in, laugh in, and broaden their minds in.

For a full year, my two kids and I wandered to new places and submerged ourselves in unique and diverse cultures. We explored 11 countries in 12 months while living like the locals. We ate yucca in the Domincan Republic and souvlaki in Greece. We helped the baby sea turtles at the turtle sanctuary in Costa Rica and taught English to kids at an orphanage in Mexico. We did charity work in every country we went to and raised money for causes my kids chose themselves. We humbled ourselves, gave generously of ourselves, and let go of the old selves we were hanging onto.

Over time, the life we had been trying to reclaim became utterly unimportant. A new way of living was emerging and it was filled with deep feelings of self-contentment and happiness. The fridge door was replaced with trips to the seaside to get the 'catch of the day' right off the boat, buying oranges out of a burlap sack from a man on the roadside, and plucking avocados straight from the tree. Material things were limited to what we had in our luggage and what we could carry. Our choice of 'things' was driven by practical decisions instead of a compulsion to acquire. Life became simple. Actions became intentional. Appreciation for everything was flowing and bountiful. And so was happiness.

In our new story, life had slowed down to include the things that truly mattered: connection, closeness, and caring. We turned our hearts toward one another and began to share how we were feeling. We paid more attention to our honest emotions. We listened to each other and valued each other more genuinely. What mattered most was what would make us happy; that became our new family code. Positive, joyous, and excited emotions ruled our days and guided our spirits.

With this new freedom, more commonly than not, our days transitioned into an easy flow of helping others, learning while teaching, and giving as much of ourselves as we could. With no 'have to's' and 'must do's' holding us back, we took to a new habit of only doing what truly made us feel happy. Each morning while enjoying breakfast, I would ask the kids what would make them happy that day. I wanted to inspire their minds to think of ways for them to generate their own inner happiness. It was important to me that they consciously thought of what would bring them happiness and then worked toward making that happen. Some days, it was swimming in the ocean. Other days, they would suggest staying indoors and reading a book. Often it was as simple as finding ripe fruit at the market or seeing the colorful sunset on our evening walk. Most of the time, the kids suggested simple, heartfelt ideas, family bonding suggestions, and easy-to-accomplish activities they wanted to do. For me, simple pleasures and quiet moments were the happiest things I asked for. No matter what else was planned, we made sure to do what was on our happy list.

Over time, this became not just a habit but our way of life. When we returned home a year later, we continued the practice as it had become engrained in our hearts and vital to our day. The idea of doing things we didn't enjoy out of a false sense of obligation was no longer an option. We held true to the notion that each morning we would share what was going to make us happy that day and commit to doing that. It didn't mean that was the *only* thing we did that day, but it was something we did for sure. Putting gas in my car made me happy because I would get to drive to watch the kids' sporting events. Getting groceries made me happy because it meant I would eat a great meal. Cleaning day made me happy because it resulted in a tidy house. All the chores that were once unfun became happy activities because we shifted our thinking to find what about those things made us happy.

Mornings were the happiest times because we'd share with one another what was going to make us happy that day and then enthusiastically support one another in making sure that it happened. If getting a high mark on a school test made one of the kids happy, then supporting them with study time in the evening was what I did. If a new pair of shoes or clothes from the mall was a happy request, then I'd be the one helping to make sure allowances were earned and research was done about how much the items cost and where to find them. Some days, a happy request would be family game night or raspberry scones for breakfast served in bed. Other times, happiness meant visiting friends, seeing grandparents, and even having alone time just to relax.

When I inspired the children to think about what would make them happy, they made their own diligent effort to have it unfold. They associated all the beneficial feelings that came with acquiring their wish with the effort involved, and that reinforced more positive emotions to keep working toward making sure what they did was surrounded with happiness.

I do this happiness practice every morning to this very day. Before I open my eyes from my slumber, I ask myself what will make me happy. I wait for the answer, trusting that my inner spirit and higher consciousness will share what is for my highest good. Some days, going to yoga will make me happy. Other days, having a decadent dessert or relaxing cup of tea while watching my favorite TV show will be high on my list. Sometimes finishing an assignment or completing a project will be the happiness order of the day.

The most important part of this ritual is that I listen and trust. It is important to be open to the wisdom of the soul and then honor it. Over time, my connection has become so solid that it doesn't take long for the happy message to arrive. Some days, it is sweet and charming, motivating a sentimental phone call to a friend or inspiring me to dig through my craft drawer to find a project that will generate relaxing feelings. Other times, I receive the beginnings of a bigger dream. I hear the suggestions of a plan ready to be set in motion, like researching a trip I want to go on or calling a colleague to get some business advice. I make sure to be open to the messages that come and not negate anything; even if they appear unobtainable at the time. I trust my inner desires and exit my bed knowing in some way I'll take some step in that direction to make it materialize that day.

The truth is, we all should be doing what makes us happy. All the time! In fact, the real practice is the happiness with which you view everything you do and in *only* doing what makes you happy. I know it sounds contrary to what we have learned and many will say, "What about the things I *have* to do?" That is the point of only doing what makes you happy. You begin to shift your life so that the 'have to's' and 'musts' simply fade away. The goal is to restructure your actions so that everything you do and the way you live your life is all about what makes you happy. Your job and the obligations that come with it make you happy. Your responsibilities make you happy because they lead to doing more happy things. Your chores fill you with happiness because they ultimately get you what you want. The social events you participate in are only the ones that create more happiness. The people you talk to, spend time with, and share your life with make you blissfully happy. There isn't a thing you do or time you spend without infusing it with happiness. The rule is, if it doesn't make you happy, don't do it; and if you must do it, then only do it when you can inject happiness into it.

For many, this concept seems foreign and unrealistic, but I can assure you from one who practices it daily, it is doable and possible. Seeing the good, the benefits, and the gratitude in everything you do grows true inner happiness. Finding ways to make responsibilities and requirements a happy activity moves them from feeling forced to fantastic. It is all in the mindset and the perspective. Fine-tuning your viewfinder to hone in on the happier side of things empowers you to infuse a happy attitude in all that you do. That happy quotient manifests more happiness. Your dedication to only doing what makes you happy tells the Universe that you are committed to what you enjoy and that invites more and more enjoyment to come.

Ignite Action Steps

Step into your happiness quotient.

Tomorrow, before you get out of bed, ask yourself what will make you happy. Don't even open your eyes and definitely do not reach for your phone. Stay in that perfect state of subconscious and conscious connection and delve into your mind/heart and ask yourself what will make you happy..

Once you get your answer, make sure to do exactly that! Get out of bed and orchestrate your day in such a way that you maneuver things and do what your spirit told you would make you happy. Be true to yourself and honor your inner needs. Say yes to you and to your happiness by welcoming more happiness. Putting happiness on your agenda each day and listening to the messages from inside will help you become attuned to exactly what makes you happy.

Soon enough, you will graduate to *only* doing what makes you happy and everything you do in your life will be sprinkled with love and happiness.

JB Owen – Canada
Speaker, Author, Publisher
www.jbthepossibilityqueen.com
www.igniteyou.life
www.lotusliners.com
f *jbowen*
📷 *jbthepossibilityqueen*

IGNITE

HAPPINESS

Stacey Yates Sellar

"You'll find happiness when you stop being the victim of your old story and become the hero of your new one."

Come on a journey with me to release the stories and beliefs that no longer serve you. They only hold you back from venturing out into the exciting unknown.

Once Upon an Old Story

Every Tuesday evening at 5:00 PM for a year, I would drive a few blocks from my office to sit on the edge of a faded red velvet couch, some ugly mismatched orange and brownish pillows at my sides. A large floral-print Kleenex™ box sat patiently on the small wooden coffee table in front of me. Another sat on a glass side table between the couch and a small window that hadn't been opened in years. Dr. Julia, my therapist *du jour*, always made sure there was plenty of Kleenex ready for me.

I had an on-again off-again relationship with therapy since I was a teen, trying to solve the *one* problem that had kept me from being successful, famous, talented, confident, stunning, rich, and happy. I couldn't believe I was back on another couch, still searching for the cure 20 years later.

She sat across from me, legs crossed, with a sharp number two pencil sitting gently between her fingers, at the ready to document something profound — or telling — on her yellow legal pad. I thought it was interesting that she used a pencil, as if she could record and then erase what I said. And if she erased it, did it mean that it didn't happen? Or that it wasn't important?

On this day, 18 minutes into this session, she was going to put her pencil down and say something that would change my life.

First, let me take you back in time to a dusty farm in northern California. My parents took us all to the house of a friend of a friend who had made a custom 'haunted house.' As my cousin and I crawled our way through the dark, small, cramped maze, we laughed when a fake claw tried to grab our legs from a hole in the wall. The design of the narrow corridors successfully made our slight 12-year-old frames feel Alice-In-Wonderland big. We maneuvered our way through hallways that seemed like a string of large cardboard boxes but made of plywood, twisting and turning, surprised by strobe lights around one corner, a fog machine in the next, and another arm reaching out to grab us beyond the fog. We scraped our knees as we made our way up a makeshift ramp and came upon my 3-year-old cousin Peter at a dead end. We had all gone into the maze two at a time, yet my younger sister, his 'maze buddy', was not with him. Because there was nowhere my sister could have gone without running into us, as we were behind her, finding him alone was the scariest part of the feeble haunted house so far.

Just as we approached and asked Peter where cousin Kimmie was, a hidden door barely big enough for the three of us to crawl through opened. We were amused that they had decorated the walls of this miniature hallway with tiny antique photo frames and faded Victorian wallpaper. But eight feet into this passage, there was another dead end. As little Peter and my other cousin bumped up behind me, the door we had just come through slid shut. There was no way back and no way forward.

Peter began to cry and I could immediately feel the air getting thinner. I had a quick thought that, "Of course we aren't trapped; I just need to find the trick door in front of me." When it didn't appear, my neck stiffened and my mouth felt like I had just eaten a pack of cotton balls. Whatever the temperature was when we entered, it had just gone up by 20 degrees. The light was faint, but I could clearly see the fearful face of my young cousin, his tears streaming down his cheeks as his loudening cries expressed the panic we were all beginning to feel. There was no way to adjust our positions in the tiny space, but I tried to put my hand on his back, getting moist with sweat. I banged on the wall in front of me and yelled, "Help! How do we get out of here?!"

Just then, a deep voice came into the confined space through a hidden speaker. "Is everyone OK in there?"

"No! We are trapped in this tiny hallway, the doors on both ends are closed, and we can't get out!" I tried to temper my anxiety so as to not add any more to the rising tide.

I banged on the wall ahead of me so hard that I am surprised I didn't break through the cheap plywood. Peter's cries got louder and the feeling that his tears were taking up valuable space in the shrinking room added frustration to my escalating fear.

"We hear crying, so we want to make sure everyone is OK," the mysterious male voice piped in again.

"No, we aren't OK. He is crying because we can't get out! How do we get out?!" My tempered fear was not so tempered anymore.

"But is he hurt?" The mysterious voice asked with less concern than I would have expected in this circumstance. If I had been a swearing kid, I would have let loose worse than a sailor who had just gotten their arm bitten by a shark.

I screamed, "He just wants to get out. How do we get out?!"

Anxiety, crying, frustration, and anger filled the pseudo-hallway like water rushing into a room with no exit. Fear replaced blood and it pumped through every vein. At the peak of both flight and fight, the floor opened up beneath us and we fell six feet down into a pile of soft foam blocks.

My mom came running into the room, laughing, and swooped up the little cousin who had stopped crying but wasn't sure what had just happened. She looked at him and said, "Wasn't that fun? You're OK, sweetie, that was a fun ride."

She carried him into the control room that was just beyond the foam pit and sat him down in front of a small black and white TV monitor that could see into the maze of mini halls. She sat next to a man who must have been the mystery voice. He shot me a big wasn't-that-awesome smile. My other cousin dusted off her pants and ran on to the last section of the haunted house apparently unphased.

I stood up, light-headed and confused. I felt an odd sensation. What I didn't know then, but came to realize many years later, was that it was the feeling of debilitating anxiety seeping into my neural pathways like a milkshake spilled onto a keyboard. This was the starting gun of a lifelong uphill marathon with no end in sight. This would be the protagonist of my story for years to come.

Anxiety crept into my life slowly — and then quickly — over the next 10 years until daily panic attacks made me too afraid to leave my apartment. I couldn't go beyond my front door for six months. Anxiety consumed my life. If I could have had the parasite of panic surgically extracted with a butter knife and no anesthesia, I would have done it myself. I knew that if I could just stop the torture of the panic attacks (and maybe stop eating so many cupcakes), I would be happy.

But that's the problem with happiness. It is conditional; destinational — "If I can just get to _____, then I will be happy." That was the story I kept telling myself.

Other stories about happiness were being written into the margins of my life story as well. I knew they were there, but it was as if the words were written in invisible ink and they weren't as obvious as the panic. If the story about anxiety was a horror, the story about happiness was a fairy tale.

Chapter one: Happiness comes from 'nice' things. It wasn't stitched into a sampler or calligraphed on a sign above any doors in our home. It was my interpretation from living in a big house complete with a pool, tennis court, and horse barn; having fancy cars, and only wearing name-brand clothing. [reference: big castle, glittery carriage, fancy ball gown, glass slippers]. Dad always warned, "You get what you pay for; get the best."

Chapter two: Giving and receiving gifts will make others happy [reference: fairy godmother, aforementioned luxuries]. If happiness was the commodity, gifts were the currency. My mom's subliminal messaging was, "More was better" — if one chocolate made you happy, then a whole bag of chocolates would make you happier.

Chapter three: Making other people happy was more important than our own happiness, even if that meant we had to suffer. [reference: every Disney® heroine willing to give up her own life for love moments before the beast/prince/ sister dies] My mom was that mom who would selflessly wait until everyone else had eaten before she served herself; giving up her comfortable seat, her warm coat, her last bite, her only spare minute to make other people happy. To worry about and even take responsibility for other people's happiness was so incessant that it became ingrained into my genetic code.

My teens and twenties were spent traveling through an allegorical dark forest chased by an evil nemesis called panic, seeking a happiness worthy of cartoon bluebirds landing on my shoulder during musical interludes. I sought figurative glass slippers from abusive boyfriends (a string of princes arriving on high horses rather than white ones). Relationships with them gave me false purpose as I tried to buy them a way out of their own poorly written stories. Unconsciously, I sacrificed my self-worth, my dignity, and my trust fund to buy their love and my consequential happiness. 'Nice things' drained my bank account and my exhaustive efforts to make other people happy offered pathetic returns on both financial and emotional investment. I didn't know who I was or where I belonged. I was stuck in the quicksand of anxiety, uncertainty, and insecurity. I was mummified in the duct tape of doubt and blind to my value and worthiness. Each mistake, rejection, and humiliation I suffered added another layer of tape, a little less air, and no hint of happiness.

I spent the next 20 years chasing happiness with the help of an extensive cast of characters and via a myriad of means, including therapists, spiritual practices, self-help books, medications, 12-step meetings, a dabble in white magic, personal development workshops, psychics, acupuncturists, hypnotherapists, past life regressionists, hair stylists, and even a soul retrievalist. Although I never came upon a genie in a bottle, I did come out on the other side of the forest with the anxiety tamed and a real 'prince charming' (whom I married in a castle in Scotland — insert wink emoji). We have the big house, fancy cars, two beautiful children, and way more 'nice things' than we need.

And they lived happily ever after. Record screech… Not yet.

There was still something missing. The subtitles didn't match the story. There was another audiobook on constant repeat in my head. It was a story of a heroine who was still held captive by anxiety, blame, and old beliefs about how happiness comes from 'nice things', more is better, and being responsible for other people's happiness.

Let's go back to the scene on the couch in Dr. Julia's therapy office. I was not actually crying about my own suffering this time. I went into an 18-minute monologue lamenting about how worried I was about my parents, their relationship, their lack of happiness, and all the tactics I had tried to help rekindle their 50-year marriage gone stale. They had grown apart, but the deep need and responsibility to help them be happier has always been an unspoken, yet understood, part of our family obligation. I shed tears for their individual pain and the pain it was causing my siblings.

Dr. Julia cocked her head in confusion and asked, "Aren't your parents on a four-week cruise around the Greek isles? Have they said they are suffering? Why are you the one crying on a couch about their unhappiness?"

That question hung in the air like a 3-day-old helium balloon slowly being pulled to the floor by gravity. In my head, all my manic beliefs about happiness paused for the answer. My face flushed, my neck felt stiff, and my breathing began to quicken. I wasn't sure if I was having a panic attack or if 35 years of illusions were cracking open… or both.

"Well… because I love them, and I don't want them to hurt. I want them to be happy," I responded with a tone of obviousness.

She leaned toward me and spoke slowly, as if she was speaking a language

I didn't understand, "You do know that you can't feel enough love or pain to relieve someone else of their suffering, right?" Clearly, I did not. "You can't want them to be happy more than they want it for themselves."

With a rather annoying hint of don't-you-see-how-crazy-this-is, she continued, "Everyone has to do their own work on happiness. And that time you spend worrying about other people is valuable time you could be spending healing and improving yourself. Then when they see how far you have come, they may ask what you are doing and then you can share it with them." (Like… in an *Ignite* book many years later.)

Always known for being very talkative, I got quiet. I have spent the last 10 years studying intensely. I meditated. I listened. I journaled. I studied some more. With a full-time job and two boys under the age of six, studying became my side hustle late into the nights. I earned certifications in *Applied Positive Psychology, Positive Psychology Coaching,* and *Conscious Parenting Coaching.* I learned so much, but most importantly, I learned the power of being either a slave or master to our thoughts. It is not events that define who we are; rather, it is our thoughts about those events that define and direct our lives. When we repeat a thought enough times, it becomes a belief. Unfortunately, we are wired biologically and conditioned socially to build up an arsenal of negative beliefs. The negativity we carry about every moment in our life — and about ourselves in those moments — is what leads to unhappiness. And that becomes our story.

The stories we create about beauty, money, health, respect, love, marriage, education, God, parenting, and literally everything around us, even happiness itself, come from our society, our family, our religion, and especially great product marketing. Those stories are all powerful, like Oz, until we pull back the curtain and see those stories are just an illusion. Happiness isn't found in anything or anyone outside of ourselves, and neither is **un**happiness. It finally sank in that neither hero nor villain was coming for me. As long as I kept searching for the Disney ending or blaming anyone for causing my suffering, I would stay an unsatisfied victim. I learned how to deepen gratitude and focus on what's good. I became maniacally aware of my thoughts and my stories, and consciously held back my habitually triggered responses.

Stripped of fairy-tale fallacies, happiness was a naked word void of a solid definition for me. It took 30 years of research and 50 years of experience to bring me to the conclusion that happiness is simply an expression of inner peace. Sometimes it manifests as joy, sometimes pride, sometimes awe; often in laughter. It is a sense of worth regardless of external approval and confidence that is needless of an award, degree, or certification. It is a knowing that you are having a human experience with a range of human emotions, and that you can survive — even thrive — through the worst ones. Happiness is not the absence of challenges but rather what you feel when you can convert grief into growth and pain into power. Happiness is not the binary opposite to unhappiness but rather a deep, internal optimistic essence. While we can enjoy 'nice things,' happiness never comes from them; it is blind to money. If suffering is being attached to unmet expectations, then happiness is being attached to nothing. Happiness knows that success is capricious and has fickle meanings, and so is not dependent on it. It denies denial and rejects rejection. Happiness enjoys the process, not the perfection, without engaging judgment of the self or others. Because the past and the future are an illusion; happiness is being grateful in the present moment. It does not come from loving another or being loved by one (or a million and one). It is instead a manifestation of how much you love yourself.

There is no 'happily ever after' when we search for happiness because whatever you find outside of yourself will never be enough. The truth is, happiness isn't about enough of anything other than feeling that YOU are enough. I found happiness when I exchanged my volumes of victim-led stories with one simple short story: "I am enough."

IGNITE ACTION STEPS

1. **Make a conscious choice** that you no longer want to be a victim. You truly can't move forward without this step. This is the ability to look back on everything that you thought was done TO you and see that it happened FOR you. Now that you know, you can't unknow.

2. **Smoke out the old stories.** If you TRULY want to move from where you are now, you must pause (stop doing so much and being so busy), get quiet (literally stop talking so much), and listen (really hear the voice in your head). With no distractions, get a clean new journal and write down all the negative beliefs, judgments, and stories that repeat in your head. Take note of who and what you blame. Any justification that begins with 'Because she/he/they/it' carries blame. Write it down. Spend a few days carrying this awakened consciousness journal around and every time you have a negative thought about yourself, someone else, or a situation, write it down. Become AWARE. You will not find happiness if you are asleep.

3. **Bring in the new story.** I believe 100 percent that visualizing and vision boarding my happiness supercharged my dreams and manifested them into reality. I was able to achieve all of the material 'nice things,' but they don't mean anything (I promise). The real key to a vision board that results in greater happiness is building it around the FEELINGS you want to feel. Find pictures in magazines or online that represent how you will feel when you are living the life of your dreams one to three years from now. Don't put a Mercedes on the board because it reflects success or status; nor a fit body or wedding ring because those will make you happy if you manifest them. When you align with an authentic state of happiness, those material possessions and socially-driven markers of success truly do not mean what you thought they would. When you have made your board, post a picture of it and tag me IG/@ happierbyminute or FB/happierbytheminute to proclaim your vision! #yougotthis #happierispossible

4. **Do the work.** One journal plus vision board will not create lifelong change. It takes work. There are a myriad of ways to work on letting go of distorted past stories, anchoring lies, and unserving beliefs. (I know; I have tried most of them.) A few practices that are well-known to ignite change are: meditation (I like Transcendental Meditation), online courses (*The Year of The Awakened Heart* with Dr. Shefali), a Positive Psychology Course (free online from Yale University), a coach (happierbytheminute.com), a therapist, exercise, yoga, hypnosis, or books (look for books about awakening consciousness). Pick one (or all) and start today! One last reminder: You are the sum of the five people you spend the most time with, so find a positive tribe of friends and let the rest go.

5. **I am good enough. I am worthy.** Take the following page of affirmation cards and put/tape/glue/cement them around where you will see them frequently throughout the day. This could be your nightstand, bathroom mirror, car dashboard, or your refrigerator. Repeat these short stories often to yourself and your children!

Stacey Sellar – United States of America
Happiness Hacker, Child Whisperer, Conscious Parenting Coach
happierbytheminute.com

I AM GOOD ENOUGH!	I AM GOOD ENOUGH!	I AM GOOD ENOUGH!
I AM GOOD ENOUGH!	I AM GOOD ENOUGH!	I AM GOOD ENOUGH!
I AM GOOD ENOUGH!	I AM GOOD ENOUGH!	I AM GOOD ENOUGH!
I AM GOOD ENOUGH!	I AM GOOD ENOUGH!	I AM GOOD ENOUGH!
I AM GOOD ENOUGH!	I AM GOOD ENOUGH!	I AM GOOD ENOUGH!

I AM WORTHY!	I AM WORTHY!	I AM WORTHY!
I AM WORTHY!	I AM WORTHY!	I AM WORTHY!
I AM WORTHY!	I AM WORTHY!	I AM WORTHY!
I AM WORTHY!	I AM WORTHY!	I AM WORTHY!
I AM WORTHY!	I AM WORTHY!	I AM WORTHY!

IGNITE HAPPINESS

Sydney Schubbe

"Happiness is a fire inside you and the hardest thing to understand is that you are the match that can light it."

I hope that by reading my story you see how living a fulfilled life is accomplished by first finding fulfillment within yourself. The only way for us to feel this is by learning how to find happiness and joy from being who we are. We must embark on a journey of self-discovery and appreciation for ourselves. Know that we have to go through the difficult roads to be led to the amazing ones that shape who we will become. At some point in your voyage, you will discover who that beautiful soul inside you *truly* is. Never let that go. You can manifest joy and gratitude every day just from being who you are. You have to discover the happiness inside before you can generate it in your daily practices. Finding happiness within yourself is how you can experience it in all areas of your life. The only thing you owe to yourself is love and happiness.

A Switch

From a young age I always felt incomplete, almost as if I was missing something inside of my heart. I didn't realize until years later it was self-acceptance and love that I was yearning for.

What made me feel sad is how society looks the other way when young people like myself plunge into an endless abyss of self-hatred. I hated myself so profoundly, so severely. I questioned my own decisions because I didn't fit a mold the world had set for me. I was plagued with self-defeating thoughts everyday, and it affected me so harshly. I hated going out or being photographed, all the things I should enjoy. All those activities only reminded me of the pit of discontentment I hid inside. I was not happy. That is not to say I hadn't experienced moments when I *was* happy, but I hadn't experienced true happiness.

True happiness. It's a funny term to be fully honest. What is true happiness? Is it being happy for a moment, or being happy in *every* moment? When I started to ask that question, I began to change my perspective on so many integral parts of my life. I later discovered that true happiness holds a different meaning for every person. For me, it's being able to stay positive in the hard times and enjoy the good ones to the fullest, despite anything else crowding my life.

It took me a very long time to learn these things. Sometimes we have to go through the difficult roads to be led to the amazing ones that shape our lives.

For me, the path to finding happiness was a total transformation both physically and mentally. I have always been a bigger girl. I inherited those big hips and that broad chest my family carries, and I had always hated them. That's where the envy planted itself, in my insecurities. With enough negative thoughts as fertilizer, a pot of absurd self-standards, and deep roots of masked emotions, I had set up that weed to splinter my soul. Let me tell you, it was planted there for years, and I just kept feeding that insidious vine of foul thoughts with no consideration for what I deserved as the amazing person I was... and still am.

My freshman year in high school, everything began to change. Friend drama and school stress had pushed me to the edge of a breakdown. I was so harsh on myself that I wrote a self-detrimental paragraph about every hate and every resentment that I was feeling. Those hurtful words ended up haunting me and sent me down a spiral of deep self-reflection. I didn't realize how sharing my anger would not only harm me but eventually release me. As I finished typing those painful words, I paused and took a breath, and then something changed.

A click.

A switch in my head had been flipped for the first time, and I thought to myself, "I don't want to be sad anymore." Those words held so much power for some reason. They made me realize how unfair and cruel I had been to myself for so many years. In that moment, I decided I was no longer going to be bitter toward myself anymore.

My path began with focusing on how I felt about my body. At the time, my mom was getting a certification in Nutritional Psychology and she shared with me so much information I wish I had known before. A relationship with food is so incredibly important for our well-being as humans, and I hadn't the slightest notion about it before I received a crash course on the nutrition she was studying.

I learned that food doesn't just fuel our bodies, it has emotional and bio-chemical effects on us as well. I cut out all junk food, outside of a cheat meal every week. After I started eating clean, I realized how rotten my body had felt on the junk and processed foods I had lived off of before.

Food was an outlet for my emotions before I changed my eating habits, but with my new lifestyle, I wasn't chained to guilt or pain from eating a burger or pizza. I also realized when I ate how my digestion was no longer in immense pain due to the lack of chemicals pumped into our unhealthy food.

Exercise also impacted my livelihood dramatically. After the rough bumps of adjusting to a difficult new habit of going to the gym, I found myself actually craving going and feeling successful and powerful when I did. Even my mood and irritability changed with these new habits.

It was nothing close to perfect. During my journey, I had days I was plagued with depression spells or feeling terrible about myself again. But, I started play-ing a game with myself. Anytime a negative thought entered my head, I said "No, Sydney, that's not who we want to be," and I'd replace the thought with a comment of positivity. Every time I faltered and said, "Oh gosh, I wish I had her body… My hips are so big… I suck at my art… Maybe if I were smarter, I would've gotten a higher grade..." When those thoughts flooded my head, I changed it to, "She's pretty but so am I… My hips show my femininity… My art is filled with passion… I'm smart, I just had a rough week."

My thoughts aren't always my friend; sometimes the subconscious enjoys spurring negative thoughts. When my mind lies to me, it's hard to understand how to react. So I do what I would with a bully, brush off what they said and walk off without a doubt that I am magnificent.

After applying all of these new attitudes toward life, I soon felt reborn. I felt freed from my own expectations and from the cage that I allowed others to build up around me. By the time I reached my 15th birthday, I had been through a very long and rough year. It was filled with overcoming mental and physical barriers but, despite that, I lost about thirty pounds.

The one thing no one tells you about losing weight is how the process is not smooth and consistent as a female, as it is for a male. I had days of bloating randomly or just not being motivated to go work out. It was in all senses a rocky road. I want you to understand that mental and physical changes take time and effort and you can't expect automatic results — remember that when, and if, you decide to change habits.

Halfway through the weight loss, I was finally confident and truly happy for the first time. Not because I was changing my body, but because finally, since childhood, I liked who I was. I didn't feel the need anymore to wear mascara or dress nicely when I went out. I no longer cared about the judgment of other people or myself. I finally felt beautiful.

Judgment was the root of my self-hatred and the negativity that ghosted my life before this immense change I went through. It has such a tight grasp on us; we fear judgment irrationally. When we feel insecure about an outfit or our body it's because we are afraid of judgment. I want to let you in on a secret. No matter what you do, you are going to be judged, so stop caring about the irrelevant opinions of someone else.

I've learned that by caring about anyone else's opinion you give them control of you. By changing the outfit you put together, you are letting their negativity win. By being afraid to speak your truth, you let other's voices drown you out. By hiding behind a masked persona, you allow your personality to be trifled with.

Be who you are! Unapologetically!

Dianne Vreeland, a French-American columnist and editor in the field of fashion, once said, "You don't have to be pretty. You don't owe prettiness to anyone. Not to your boyfriend, spouse, or partner, not to your co-workers, especially not to random men on the street. You don't owe it to your mother, you don't owe it to your children, you don't owe it to civilization in general. Prettiness is not a rent you pay for occupying a space marked 'female.'"

That quote holds so much power for me. As women we feel obligated to look nice when we go out, or be lady-like as if it was an abomination if we do not follow those rules. Guess what, honey? You don't owe anyone anything. You don't owe the world makeup. You don't owe mainstream society the face they interpret as beautiful. You can have my big hips, chubby cheeks, and frizzy hair and still be absolutely stunning.

The only thing you owe is to Yourself, and that is Love and Happiness.

I've always hated how confidence is mistaken for vanity and pride. That's why some of us fear being confident and showing who we are; we fear being called narcissistic or even just someone thinking it to themselves. Confidence is believing in yourself, and pride is believing you are better than others — these are two very different ideas.

This journey in finding beauty in who I am, overcoming self-loathing, and sparking the idea to write this book has taught me that I must understand where the line is drawn, or else I may never be on the side I want to stand on. People who don't understand this line will judge you; it's inevitable. So, when you walk down the street, do it with confidence in your step and happiness in your pocket and don't care what they say about you.

Confidence has helped me build happiness within me. I find happiness in simple activities, just reading a book or walking up a flight of stairs is filled with my happiness. I am so thankful for my life that I am the bright-minded and strong, young woman I am. That is what makes me happy.

After I stopped judging myself, I realized how unique and beautiful I am in my own ways. You have the power to be happy. Stop feeling pity for yourself for not winning every competition. Stop hating your body. Stop thinking you are a failure. Stop being negative. Start thinking positive. Start trusting your intuition. Start following your own ambitions. Start believing you can do it. It's hard, believe me I know, but you have to decide for yourself who you want to be.

In India, to trap monkeys, people put bananas inside a box with a hole in it. Once the monkey comes along and grabs the fruit inside the box, he realizes the banana doesn't fit through the hole. The monkey feels trapped not wanting to let go of its beloved dinner and gets captured. The funny thing is, the monkey is never trapped; all it has to do is let go. Don't be the monkey. Don't hold onto the negative thoughts and pain you feel so attached to. Stop holding your banana. You have the power to let go. You have the power to be happy. Happiness isn't found in just things and experiences; it's found within that beautiful heart and soul your body carries.

I live every day drawing happiness from the gratitude I feel in my life. I am where I want to be with my body and work out to improve my strength and accept every unique imperfection I have. My thoughts about myself are filled with positive admiration and encouragement. I try every day to uplift and inspire others. I may just be a teenager, but the one thing I know is, my happiness comes from being thankful for who I have become.

The best way I can explain happiness is a great extravagant fire within you. Blissful moments will light it, but sometimes the wind of emotion will blow it out. At times, you will feel helpless and won't understand how to light it back up. You are the key to your happiness. Happiness is a fire inside you, and the hardest thing to understand is that you are the match that can light it.

Sydney Schubbe – United States of America

Ignite Action Steps

Go do something, or be with someone, that makes you unconditionally happy! After that, I challenge you to think about *why* that thing or person makes you so happy and just reflect on it for a moment. Write down the emotions or thoughts you have when doing this activity.

_____

_____

_____

_____

_____

_____

_____

_____

_____

_____

_____

_____

_____

_____

_____

_____

_____

_____

This will help you figure out what fuels your fire. Channel that in your daily life for a week.

Then, do one thing that makes you joyful every day even if it's just petting your dog or sitting in the sunshine. See if you notice a difference in your thoughts or mood. Write down the top three things that make you feel the most joyous.

1. _____

_____

2. _____

_____

3. _____

_____

Remember to be grateful for every moment you have in the life that you have been given, even if it is not always easy! Write down 10 things you feel grateful for.

_____

_____

_____

_____

_____

_____

_____

_____

_____

_____

_____

Gratitude can be hidden in the smallest places of life; we must seek them out to truly give thanks for them.

Aurelie Busollo

"Keep it light. Keep it fun!"

Abracadabra, dear Ones. May this story free you from what you believe 'happiness' should be. The 'magic word' is not 'please', it's 'thanks.' Live in gratitude and things will unfold naturally. Stop chasing happiness. Let go of your expectations. Follow the flow. Life is pure Magic.

Happiness is Magic, Just Like Mike. Enjoy the Unfolding.

Do you remember your teenage years? You know, the horrible haircuts, those not-so-fashionable outfits, the guy every girl dotes on, and the boring school lessons. Yes, all of that plus one thing: the rebellion against any form of authority. Conflicts often highlighted with doors slamming or insults as the single answer to any parental question... at least according to the movies. I never experienced that firsthand. Not that my parents were the super tolerant hippy type who would approve of any comings and goings. No, I was just a head-bobbing doll without a social life. I didn't make waves and simply followed the rules, doing what I was told.

True, I wasn't a popular kid around the age of 13, when I got braces and started wearing my first bras. However I didn't mind the social outcasting much because I had a few close friends, not the older, cool ones who would skip classes to roll a joint or sneak out to go clubbing. My Saturday nights were spent in front of the TV, charmed by three sisters with magical abilities and vampirized by a blonde teenage slayer. These fictional characters were living lives I fantasized about. Meanwhile, I fitted perfectly in the TV program grid, a mere zombie going through the motions.

Magic may have been *on* the air then, but certainly not *in* the air of my sloped ceiling bedroom in the South of France, where I went through my uneventful teenagehood. I was bored to death, but when I saw other kids who seemed far less privileged, it felt unfair to complain. I was a middle-class white girl with good grades and a nice family. I had a pet cat. I wasn't bullied, and my mother always bought my favorite biscuits when she went grocery shopping. I should have been happy. I had no reason not to be... yet, my secret diary revealed the contrary *"I'm so bored here, nothing ever happens. I hope I can go around the world soon."*

As comfy as I was, I couldn't help but dreaming of the day where there would be some rumble in my cozy monotony and I would finally experience something out of the ordinary. My idea of happiness seeded in traveling. What a foreign concept for someone who grew up spending all her family summer holidays in the same resort year after year. It must have come from the clever marketing teams of Thomas Cook and Co.™ who seduced me during each commercial break.

An entire decade and a half later, which felt like a s...l...o...w...l...y... moving century, passed before I dared making my first bold move, a series of them in fact. I enacted my own 'Lord of the Rings' trilogy, except that I broke ties rather than going on a quest for a ring or any other type of stable commitment. One after the other, I left my partner of three years, said a teary goodbye to my soul sister (and former flatmate), and quit my job as a high-profile headhunter. I had a new land in sight, Australia. According to the saying, 'The destination doesn't matter; it's the journey.' In my case the most important was neither of them; the whole point was that I was finally getting a hold of my life. It was perfect timing; having just turned 29, I had only a couple of years left to benefit from an Australian working holiday visa. Finally being brave gave me the chills, halfway between throwing up and wetting my pants with excitement. Consequently, on the day of my departure for Melbourne, I went to the airport with butterflies in my belly!

When I kicked off this trip in koala land, I followed four different guide books to make sure I wouldn't miss out on anything. I believed that in order to have a blissful vacation I would need to check all the boxes. My travel plans were well defined and perfectly timed, almost to the point of including toilet breaks. The first months touring around the country were great fun: marshmallows and music jams by the campfire, and plenty of people to meet. Overall I caught up on most of the classic teenage activities I had missed, including couch-surfing in a foreign land. Yet, boredom poked at me. I smiled, all teeth out, like in the toothpaste ads; happy on the surface, I felt somehow blasé. Following a fixed schedule and predetermined route, there was only little playfulness and spontaneity involved. I had the freedom to do whatever I wanted and yet I felt like I was trapped in a Discovery Channel program. Beautiful fauna and flora. Stunning landscapes. Perfect weather. But, no drama. No action. Ok, a little romance but PG-rated (at least officially — what happens in kangaroo country stays in its pocket!) I was missing out on the feelings of true joy. My delight was then conditional; roaring high when all was well and surfers were in sight but noticeably low the days with a mechanical failure or when facing a shortage of iced coffee.

Aware of my control issues and aiming for a change, I gave up my Excel sheets of must-do activities. This was the beginning of me feeling a deeper happiness. Finally, I started enjoying the moment. The momentS! The perfect ones and the bloopers, like slicing my toe on a shell while strolling on a gorgeous beach or wandering, lost in the rainforest, devoured by famished mosquitos. Who would have guessed that these quirky random *(mis)*adventures would spike up the fun? Over time, a deep change percolated in me. I peeled myself off from my mental restrictions and self-limitations and a miracle happened.

Only by letting go, I started to regain control over my life!

Still, I didn't fully appreciate this mindset shift until early on the first Saturday of fall, when a lightbulb went 'on', even brighter than the rising sun. I was at a condominium in Townsville — not a fictional name, despite appearances — on the Australian East coast, standing on the edge of a turquoise swimming pool, still wet from the dive I had just made. I hadn't gone into the pool as part of a morning fitness routine nor led by a desire for physical activity. Nope. I simply had to jump in because my ID was at the bottom of the pool. Right in the center, at the deepest point (thanks to Murphy and physics). How did it get there? Well, the previous night had been a bit wild. Clear evidence that I was coming out of my control-freak chassis and lifelong role as a well-behaved daughter... but mind you, at a city-zone speed limit and without the influence of any psychotrope.

Under the moon's first crescent, my travel mate and I, along with six others (a group summing to a total of eight, in an equal number of males and females) had jumped fully clothed in the pool (technically, I got pushed!). In the spur of the moment, still sweaty from a night out dancing, we disregarded the most basic hygiene rules and skipped showering. Not following the rules made me feel frisky... but not as frisky as my friends. Less than ten minutes in the water was enough time for couples to form. Six dark shapes blurred into three. As the remaining single guy approached me with broad strokes, I demonstrated my reluctance by climbing up the metallic stairs. I twisted my green dress to get rid of the excess water and yelled to the group, who couldn't care less, that I was going back to the flat. Seemingly unwilling to stare at the pool's mosaic designs while everyone else cuddled, the man followed me inside.

The young man grilled me over my rejection. He was quite charming and fit, a 'Down Under' Captain America in the moonlight glow, but I simply wasn't wooed. My mates seemed thrilled to have paired up, but I knew that just like following travel guides, copying others' ways wasn't my own route to happiness — so I stood firm. Kinda... I was stumbling to find the right words. Only my gaze was steady, fixed upon the military name tag around his neck, avoiding his pleading cub-like eyes at all cost.

The situation was awkward enough; I dripped water over the living room carpet, my soaked outfit sticking to body parts I would have wished to remain more mysterious. Nonetheless, things worsened when, amid my explanation, the three couples rocked up to the flat in dire need of privacy. They requisitioned the two bedrooms and living room for their 'mature audience only' activities, forcing the two of us to retreat into the kitchen. Our desperate attempt at conversation failed to cover their moans. I have rarely felt as uncomfortable in my life, and not merely because I was clumsily seated on the kitchen bench between a toaster and the sink, wiggling to avoid the greasy patches. Time dragged until my resigned suitor exited, politely avoiding glancing at the couple in the living room (turned out he was a fine gentleman!). I was then left to read the back of a cereal box until the couch where I crashed was free.

Surprisingly, the previous night, when I jumped in the pool at three in the morning, I had felt almost immune to the cold. It was maybe because my five senses were so engaged from playing water volleyball, singing, and dancing in the pristine liquid. My brain had no opportunity to process the bone-numbing water. Too bad no one else was there the next morning to entertain me or, even better, fetch my ID for me.

The hair on my skin raised up in bumps like the walking dead as I dipped a toe in the tranquil water. Chilly! And not the spicy hot Mexican kind. Quite the opposite. More like what a bald polar bear would feel in the melted Arctic ice caps. I really didn't want to, but I had no option, so I dove in. Short of breath, muscles contracted and heart pumping loud, my first few seconds in the pool were distressing with a freezing of my eardrums and a numbness in my toes. I retrieved 'my precious' almost instantly. I can't explain why, but I lingered in the water. Against all odds, I was enjoying myself. I was having so much fun that I swam around as if I was Nemo exploring the Great Barrier Reef.

Once out, standing on the peach tiles, all my body parts decided to join a tap dancing competition, without me signing any waiver form. The winner of the hammering? Likely a tie between my teeth and my knees with my ass cheeks as close second. My body looked slightly blue and in mild distress, yet, a massive grin parted my lips. For a split second, I feared that the cold had created some neurological damage before I grasped the root of my happy feelings.

After months of implementing a gratitude practice, I had finally received proof that this daily exercise had successfully rewired my brain. For a long time I wondered if the effort was worthwhile, having not yet manifested the winning lottery ticket and the perfect boyfriend, despite listing my blessings each and every night. But all doubts cleared up as I, still groggy from a short sleep, floated in a freezing cold pool, appreciative and with an everlasting smile plastered on my face.

As I stood there shaking, waiting to dry some more before returning indoors, 'something' got hold of me. My chin raised a few inches taller, my pulse slowed down, and I felt softness regaining my flesh. I was joyful, only not jumping up and down with excitement. Instead, I radiated calmness. Standing motionless, my mind went to another dimension. I found myself expanding into a universe entirely painted white, filled with millions of sparkles, my soul absorbing the surrounding stars. Nothing intruded in me. Quite the opposite in fact: I got rather out of my shell in an out of body exploration!

Then, all of a sudden, I sensed wetness in my eyes. Outburst of emotion or wet hair dripping on my face? I couldn't be sure. Reflexively, I patted my eyes dry. This movement got me out of my trance. Now, I knew the tears were mine. I looked around. It felt odd to be surrounded by buildings. I squinted, bothered by the intensity of the sun, several yellow shades darker than the translucent light I had just emerged from. I raised a hand toward my forehead. Was my brain still in the fog, despite the dive? Or, did I just have a glimpse of what some call 'Nirvana'? How did such a mundane activity lead to 'that', whatever 'that' was?! I wasn't under the influence of Ecstasy or any other type of drug and yet, what I had just experienced was a serotonin release totally out of this world.

I didn't dare tell anyone about this, not even my travel mate, but when we left Townsville, I knew that the version of me traveling in the car wasn't the same who had started the journey. By having to retrieve nothing else but the item acknowledging my identity in a pure body of water (sanitized by chlorine, instead of blessed but still), the Universe had led me to go through a true cosmical rebirth!

From then on, my spirituality grew and I became more mindful of the consequences of my positivity on my outer world. I would beam at the sight of similar digits on a number plate or feathers on a trail, sure that these were mystical signs. Yet the most striking manifestation happened roughly two weeks after my episode in the pool. I was still high on life, despite a persistent drizzle over the past couple of days. Nevertheless, I didn't complain; looking at the bright side (without sunray), I explored alternate activities to keep me dry until being able to resume my adventures in the wild. I fully accepted the weather as an uncontrollable parameter and basked in the rain's fresh smell. I appreciated the tiny things and at the same time marvelled at the massive constructs that life had to offer.

Without a couch-surfing confirmation, we reached Maleny, a cute town inland of Brisbane, an hour before dusk. We felt doomed to have to put up our tent in the pouring rain to sleep that night. Rather than immediately setting up camp, I went to the town's biggest supermarket and placed an ad begging for a dry shelter. My travel mate was anxious, for her we were only delaying the inevitable, resulting in us having to pitch our tent in the downpour, but also in the dark. I remained hopeful. Forty-five minutes later, my phone rang. A woman with a soothing voice, mother of three teens, was willing to host us. Bonus, we were also invited to share their dinner... Had I inciendently mastered the witchcraft of mind control? I started to believe so, as while in this state of 'happiness-induced flow', I received impulses, inspired ideas, and profound thoughts, introducing effortlessly good things into my life and impacting other people's behavior for my benefit (no sociopath tricks involved)... I tell you: pure freakin' magic, without mushrooms! In a way, the 13-year-old me had known this all along. Magic exists in real life too; however simply watching HBO fiction doesn't teach how to unlock it.

Stepping forth from my time capsule a few years later to the present day, I'm stuck for weeks at length in a room. I have an odd feeling of deja vu, a draft from the past recalling my teen years as a channel surfer. Few notable differences though; this time the room has an uneven flooring in lieu of a sloped ceiling and the TV has gone, replaced by creative distractions, like painting and writing. Also, the lengthy downtime is now praised, being the perfect excuse for meditating, doing yoga, or assembling puzzles. I could still be bored as there are many hours to fill in a day, yet I am pleased. I get a chance to relive my 'ungrateful' years with an attitude of gratitude. Not expecting anymore than what is and enjoying the basics I once overlooked, like a simple window with a view on the street or a laughter-filled call with a friend.

Finally, I have gone full circle: finding bliss within the routine, like a hamster playing in its wheel rather than a rat squandered in the maze... In other words, I became both the magician and the happy bunny, and I must admit that this 'live performance' is pretty hot stuff!

Here's a little trick from one wizard to another. If I were to give you a golden envelope filled with words of wisdom, it would reveal, "You are the leading character in your own journey; nobody can steal your spotlight, so take it easy and stay cool as you play along with life. Good things will come out of the hat as if by magic and without you having to wave your wand in a particular direction. Simply follow your joy and be grateful for all these experiences. Happiness will automatically follow!"

IGNITE ACTION STEPS

Close your eyes and vaguely point at the table on the following page. Follow the prompt. Repeat this game whenever you feel like it.

Aurelie Busollo – World Citizen and Avid Traveler
Writer and Life Adventurer
🄵 *aureliebusollo*

IGNITE HAPPINESS ACTIVITY

Meditate

1. Put on some relaxing music.
2. Breathe deep.
3. Relax.

Create Your Mantra

- Your power quote
- A haiku you like

Dress Up

- Dress fancy
- Dress dancy
- Dress crazy

Throw-back Time!

1. Remember what you loved as a kid.
2. Do it as you did then, or bring a new twist.

Art Day

- Go to an art gallery
- Make your own creation at home
- Appreciate beauty

Make Your Own

Surprise yourself

Sweet Talk

- Compliment someone
- List things you like about yourself

Dinner's Ready

1. Choose a recipe.
2. Follow it, or not.
3. Enjoy the process.
4. Enjoy the dinner.

Take a Look Around

1. Pick an object.
2. Bring back good memories about it.
3. Repeat.

Pamper Yourself

• Take a hot bath
• Cuddle your body
• Go for a manicure
• Scrub'n'Rub

Move Your Body

• Shake your booty
• Follow a yoga class
• Imitate your dog
• Dance crazy

Sing Along

1. Choose a YouTube playlist with lyrics.
2. Karaoke time, baby!

Treasure Hunt

1. Stroll in the 'hood.
2. Smell at least one flower in each garden you encounter.

Go Social

• Call a friend
• Wave at a neighbor
• Smile at a stranger in the street

Bless You!

Share all the things you are grateful for in a diary or with someone

Sane and Sound

1. Set an alarm for each hour of the day.
2. When it goes off, identify sounds you hear nearby.

ALBERT URENA

"Happiness is not something external, it is already within us; we just need to tap into it."

My intention in writing this story is to give you the awareness that, no matter the pain and circumstances you've been through, Happiness is available to each and every one of us. I want my story to empower all individuals to express the best version of who they really are.

TAP INTO YOUR HAPPINESS

My life is a blessing. Every morning, I wake up with the feeling that life is good. I'm living some of my dreams and manifesting many more of them as my soul travels its divine journey of the human experience here on planet Earth. Traveling the world with friends from all over the globe; writing chapters in two compilation books and becoming an international best-selling author; having direct access to my role models and mentors who I used to watch on my laptop; it's more than I could ever have imagined. I've found myself having lunch and dinner with extraordinary people, putting myself out there as a Transformational Leader, and enjoying life to the fullest. It wasn't always this way; there was a point in my physicality where all I knew was sadness, anger, hate, and resentment. I literally believed I would never be able to be happy, no matter what happened, and no matter what I accomplished. Let me take you into the deepness of my walk through the valley of the shadow of death.

My soul manifested on this planet Earth in the northeast corner of the gorgeous Caribbean island of the Dominican Republic. Living in a third world country, my grandparents had immigrated to the United States back in the early 1970s; however, my mother went back to our native island in the 1980s, where she ended up meeting my father. I arrived in this world on August 9, 1989, a moment that brought so much joy for my family. I was the firstborn child of the family's only girl, for my mom had five brothers and she was the only one who didn't have a child until then. Just a few months later, my mother moved us to Lawrence, Massachusetts in the United States so I could have a brighter future. I became an American citizen, something many people would consider a source of happiness.

My first few years of life happened in Massachusetts. I was learning both Spanish and English at the same time. I experienced snow for the first time in America, and I can still remember my eldest cousin teaching me how to form a ball with my hands and throw it at my other cousins — a playful game that always filled me with delight. In my early years, I went through phases of being bullied, just because I spoke and looked different. My sister Michelle was born in 1991, but this new sparkle of joy brought by her birth would soon fade away, as my grandmother, my mother's mom, passed away from cancer. I was still very little, but I was devastated. I couldn't grasp how my sister just got here and my grandmother was no longer. I was confused, scared, and lost.

Needing a change of environment, my parents moved us and my grandfather to New York. On December 9, 1993, a few months after my baby brother, Jose, was born, my father was robbed and killed with a single shot to the head. I was four years old. It seemed that for every new life our family was blessed with, another was being taken away.

The back-to-back deaths of two of the most important people in my childhood extinguished my innocence. I was mad at God, I was mad at life, I was mad at everyone I saw who still had their dad and both grandmothers. My mother was paralyzed with the pain of it all. She couldn't move forward with life. She needed to get rid of everything that reminded her of all of the tragedy. Attempting to shake off the sorrow, she moved us back to the island to be close to my father's side of the family. That move worked to heal most of our pain.

Some of the happiest moments come from my childhood memories in Licey, a small town in the Dominican Republic with little houses surrounded by palm trees and mangoes, and people all around. All the cousins, uncles, and aunts gathered every Sunday at my grandparent's house to spend time together. What a beautiful tradition that was. Christmas was even better as we all played with our new toys given to us by Santa Claus, who we soon discovered was our own uncles and aunts blessing us. I remember one time we all received bikes as a gift and immediately went out to ride them. I fell so hard on the floor, but even though it hurt, I was smiling. It was such a wonderful and joyful time. Being playful is my favorite expression of happiness, and as an adult I do my best to embody that state of being each day.

I think my mother made a genius move in going back to the island. She got a great-paying job and she was grateful. We got involved in the town's sports teams, both baseball and basketball. Playing sports was a huge source of joy for me… at least until I started comparing myself to my cousin. That's when I realized that comparison is the thief of all joy. My cousin was the best player on both our teams and I was one of the worst, at least that was my perception, and it made me really sad. I ended up dropping out and not playing sports for many years, just because I always compare myself to other players instead of focusing on the joy that playing brought me.

We studied in a Roman Catholic School run by nuns called "Colegio Padre Fortin" for what we consider elementary and middle grades. At this campus, I got to discover many things that made me happy just by doing them: playing the flute, singing in the school chorus, and acting on the theater team. Expressing that creative side of me was healing and for many years it helped me let go of the pain I was feeling deep inside.

That happiness didn't last long. I was confused when my mother left us in Dominican Republic with our uncle Joey and grandfather in 2001 while she moved to Florida along with her brother, my uncle Elvis. She was pursuing a new job to set the foundations to take us with her, but I didn't understand that then. My mother was always a determined woman and, a year later, she picked us up and brought us back with her to Florida. Moving back to the United States meant leaving my friends behind and I was terribly angry about it all.

Playing video games as a kid was something that brought me lots of joy, and as an adult, it still does, though I recognize now that it is a temporary pleasure and not true happiness. I was 14 years old, and after a long day of high school, all I had on my mind was going home to play my Nintendo GameCube™. Little did I know that these games would be a gateway to another source of 'happiness' — smoking marijuana. I stumbled upon two of my buddies who lived in my neighborhood, the same buddies I tended to play sports and video games with. They were hanging out at Eric's home and I rode my bike there to join them. When I got there, they lit up a cigarette. I saw my grandfather smoke all the time, which to me didn't seem very appealing as he was constantly coughing and sick. He used to smoke a pack a day and I remember promising myself to never go down that route. But when I smelled the fragrance that came out of my friends' smoke, it wasn't familiar. "We are not smoking tobacco, we are smoking weed — marijuana — and it makes you so happy you can't stop laughing," my buddy explained.

I could smoke happiness? I was sold. Anything that could make me laugh and numb the pain I felt inside, I welcomed with opened arms. All afternoon, I laughed so hard I had to lay down on the couch. I felt like I was flying and on cloud nine at the same time.

A few days later, back home in the DR, my grandfather passed away. We didn't have enough money for all us to go bury him and my mother had to go by herself to say goodbye to her father. Here I was, 14 years old, going through another grief; I didn't know how to feel or express what I was feeling. I was crushed, weighed down by a mix of grief for my own loss and a terrible knowledge of my mother's pain. I quickly decided I needed to find another way to be happy, and that I did. My next thrill came from going into stores to steal video games and movies on DVD… until the day I got caught in the Coral Square Mall. I was walking out of a store when I felt someone grab me by my shirt and push me to the wall. The cops came, big and intimidating, and still to this day I can see the face of the officer, filled with compassion when he asked me why I did it. Instead of sending me to jail, the cop saw greatness in me, and gave me volunteer hours to serve the community instead. His words were, "Next year, you will be old enough to work and buy your video games and help your mother with money."

His words inspired me. When I turned 15, I immediately got my first job flipping burgers at McDonald's. That was my first exposure to customer service. I loved working and helping customers. And I loved making my own money, buying my own stuff, and helping my mom in the house. The more I worked, the more my self-esteem went through the roof. Slowly after, I made a dream come true and purchased my first vehicle with cash money: a gold Honda Accord. I felt powerful! I enjoyed going to school and working at the same time. I suddenly was giving myself better experiences than others around me in the form of new clothes, new shoes, and new video games. Before I knew it, I had become addicted to material possessions and had become a workaholic. I had two jobs and I was going to high school at the same time.

Yet, with all this professional and financial growth, I still had a deep void inside of me. I was still unhappy. I craved connection, to belong to something greater than me, and that's when I joined a street gang and made it my new family. My new family meant having more friends to party with and more bad ideas of how to be happy. At that time, we had all-ages parties at several night-clubs, going after the sexy ladies, getting into fights with rival gang members, smoking weed, and getting drunk — it was all part of the thrill of my pursuit of happiness. And yet I still felt miserable inside.

Around this same time, the gang lifestyle became an obviously unhealthy one for me, and I converted into Christianity and transformed my life around my newfound relationship with Jesus Christ. I was the happiest going to the services more than once a week, attending spiritual retreats, and even enrolling in Bible College. I was becoming a young leader within my church family and it felt good. But then, still a young teenager, I slipped off the path and relapsed into drugs.

Watching movies, I noticed that the gangsters and drug lords always had fun with women and cocaine. That intrigued me, and my curiosity attracted the opportunity to try that drug. One night, when two friends knocked on my window around one in the morning, I snuck out of my house and we went to sniff cocaine. I went down the rabbit hole of partying and taking ecstasy pills at raves; living young, wild, and free.

And then my freedom was taken away from me in a most dramatic fashion. One night, we were inside a car on our way to a party, smoking weed, when we got pulled over by the cops. That landed me in Florida's 'Drug Court,' a six-month program for drug users. One month in, I failed a drug test and ended up in jail for 30 days.

Jail should have been the least happy moment in my life, but it wasn't. I had lost my freedom, but in that loss, I ended up finding everything that mattered. In jail, I had an encounter with my calling as a Spiritual Teacher. Every night, we had a prayer circle and, on my second week of being locked up, I was given the honor of bringing the 'Word for the Day' through the Holy Bible. I was so happy and grateful for the responsibility. Each morning, I prayed for guidance to deliver the message the inmates needed to hear. The best part was that it wasn't hard at all. I was simply expressing myself and watching the reactions of the other inmates. And what I saw was magical.

When I read the scripture and gave a lesson on it, I saw drug addicts and criminals begin to cry. They began to pray and ask for forgiveness. They started to get along with each other instead of fighting over every little thing. It was divine. The Universe was giving me a small glimpse of what was in store for me as a speaker and writer. In those moments, I knew that this was what I was here to do. This is what I was meant to do in my life. I had finally found something meaningful.

And I was happy. Now, I understand that Happiness is something I get to tap into and that is within me. It never came from the outward things I lusted after or the chemicals I put into my body. It came from the essence of the divine within me. It came from me.

During the worst pandemic in history, we chose to rise up and Ignite the Happiness of the planet, and the only way to do that is to draw on what's within. The way I personally choose to express that is by writing this story to inspire you. I also launched my home-based business where I Ignite people's happiness by giving them a 'boomerang,' an opportunity to be able to explore the world within their budget by accessing a platform that helps them save money on travel. I love making a living giving so much that it doesn't feel like work. That's because it aligns with who I am and with why I do what I do. I love EMPOWERING each individual to expand their horizons and express the best version of who they really are. To live a life free of debt and experience the abundance that is our birthright.

I used to always be in the pursuit of happiness. Getting the money, the girls, the promotions at work, and having flashy things was, I thought, the key to a happy life. I was dead wrong. I have realized that material possessions will only give you a boost of dopamine and endorphins and then eventually it will become familiar and not Ignite the same feeling. In other words, the happiness we feel from stuff is not happiness at all.

As human beings, we have been taught the "Have-Do-Be" model of life. That mindset says, when I have 'xyz,' I will do what I want to do and then I'll be happy. Today, I invite you to embrace a new paradigm: the "Be-Do-Have." This new model empowers us to choose what we want to be beforehand. I choose to be happy; therefore, I do what happy people do. And, as a result, I have what happy people have.

One of my recent mentors, Lisa Nichols, taught me that our life won't go anywhere that our mind doesn't go first. When you choose to *be*, you are able to get into any state of being you desire. I learned a simple exercise from my favorite author, Neale Donald Walsh. It's called the 'Beingness Grid.' It goes like this... You take a sheet of paper, create a column for each day of the week, and write morning, afternoon, and evening. Next to each of these, you write the state of being you choose to be for that day at that time. This is really fun and playful. It takes the seriousness out of life and you can test it to see if you can be what you set out to be regardless of what's going on around you that day.

My favorite state of being is *Playful*. I choose it over and over again. I choose to be playful, therefore everything I do is with a playful heart. The result is that I get to enjoy life and have fun just by choosing to. This is what I mean when I say you can tap into your own happiness. Whenever you wake up, or any occasion of the day, take six deep breaths to reset your nervous system. Once you are still, choose how you want to be. If happiness is your choice, choose to be happy. I choose to Ignite the happiness of every person I come across, and I am honored to be able to share this wisdom with every reader today and every day.

Be happy. Join us in elevating the vibration of the planet with our contagious joy by simply tapping into your own happiness. I believe in my heart that we are the happiest when we express who we truly are and make space for others to do the same.

IGNITE ACTION STEPS

- Be YOU.
- Breathe. Take six deep breaths. On each inhale, mentally say, "I inhale positivity," and on each exhale, mentally say, "I exhale stress and overwhelm."
- Use the *Beingness Grid* by Neale Donald Walsh that I describe in this chapter. Choose to be happy at the start of your day, every day.
- Move your body. Go for a walk, for a run, or dance. Shake off stress and find joy.
- Travel the world with your family and friends and expand your horizons.

Albert Urena – United States of America
Entrepreneur, Author, Speaker & Transformational Leader
alberturena.com

Karla Rose Weihe

*"I can only know how full my life is now because
of how vacant it was before."*

**I hope to bring light into your darkness. No matter how dark it gets, how
much pain there is, and how insurmountable the wall seems, life can and
does get better. If life has shown me anything, it's how incredibly strong
and resilient you can be and how it is the internal battles that forge our
compassion, love, and faith.**

From Darkness into the Light

One of the key ingredients in my life for experiencing joy is surrender,
allowing what is, to be. I learned this lesson on my first 10-day silent Vipassana
course, a meditation retreat that honestly saved my life because it made my
life worth living again. It brought me back into my existence by showing me
that my happiness is up to me.

I had hit rock bottom in my third year of university. Academically, I was
doing well and I had a beautiful group of people around me but old trauma had
reemerged and I could no longer keep it locked in the 'do not enter' corner of
my mind. I was suffering from full-blown post traumatic stress disorder and
emotional pain that few words can describe. It felt like someone had taken a
shredder to my soul. I discovered that the blackest pits of hell exist nowhere
but inside my own mind.

Eventually I was so worn out that all I wanted was out of this game. I had been thinking about and planning how I was going to end my life for a week, when I realized that not once had I thought about leaving behind a note. I was so deep inside my own pain and grief that it hadn't even occurred to me to think about my family and how I should leave some kind of explanation for them. I thank God for that important realization. For one second, it took me out of my own pain and allowed me to see the dire reality of my situation. It gave me enough time to realize that I didn't actually want to die, that a part of me still wanted to live. I had people in my life that were worth living for. I finally reached out for help and started on medication.

Antidepressants brought me a measure of stability; they took the edges off the pain and allowed me to open the door to brief experiences of happiness again. I remember crying on my way home from my Grans one day because I felt happy. It had been so long that I couldn't even remember what that emotion felt like; I had almost written off my life because I never thought I'd feel it again.

Meds anchored me enough to be able to attend the Vipassana course. I still wasn't in a great space mentally but I wasn't about to crumble from the softest of winds anymore.

The course came into my life as one of those inexplicable things, like those moments you find something you hadn't even realized you'd lost. I didn't know anyone who had done the course or ever heard of it before when I somehow stumbled upon it online. As I read the first line of the description, '10-day silent Vipassana meditation course', my soul somehow knew this was fated. There was just a knowing, a silent stillness of recognition. Immediately, I checked dates for the next courses and, as fate would have it, the dates fell perfectly over my winter break.

When I arrived at the Dhamma Pataka center, two hours outside of Cape Town, South Africa, the air was clear and the ground still held puddled remnants of that morning's rain storm. Men's and women's residences and common areas were separated. My room looked out over the valley below to the Cederberg mountains beyond it. Ringed by mountains on all sides, the center sat in its own little basin of seclusion and stillness. The usual sounds of traffic and urban hustle were replaced with bird song and the occasional roaring of lions in the neighboring hills. I delighted in my decision to bring along my newly-purchased sheepskin boots as it was only early afternoon but already bitterly cold. The silence hadn't begun yet and people were talking around me, but I didn't want to engage in conversation. I wasn't concerned about making connections with others. I was there for myself and I didn't have the energy or inclination toward faking interest in anyone else's story.

Honestly, I had hardly done any research on the course prior to my arrival, which was very unusual for me. I was the kind of person who will read a million reviews before committing to events. Upon arrival, I was informed that I would be sitting for 10 hours of meditation a day. Any sane person would have had at least a reaction of surprise and apprehension but still the inner knowing and calm carried me through. Like coming home.

For the next 10 days, I was bereft of any external distractions, no reading, no writing, no eye contact, no speaking, no exercise. Meals became the highlight of my day, the only external stimulation, like pamphlets in a waiting room before the days of smartphones.

Days felt like years with some passing easily and others feeling like an uphill battle. Sometimes the meditation was easy and I could sit in stillness for ages while other times it felt like whole parts of my body were on fire. It was one of the most challenging experiences of my life but it gave me so much.

I had to sit with my boredom, my anger, my anxiety, discomfort, and pain. I had to drop the habit of trying to control or choose the experiences I wanted and surrender to what came.

I keenly remember a day where my anxiety was so severe, it felt like I had bees crawling under my breastbone and an iron vice wrapped around my chest. This feeling carried on for the whole day and all I could do was sit with it. I couldn't escape or seek distraction and relief; all I could do was observe it. Finally, I let go of the resistance I felt toward my anxiety and truly just made peace with its presence. The physical feelings were still there but suddenly they didn't cause me anguish anymore. I was able to see them as physical sensations that would pass in time. Suddenly, my mind was free, as if I'd realized I could breathe underwater.

The course gave me firsthand experience of the transient nature of life. Sensations arise and then they pass again. *This too will pass* was etched into my brain. I realized I cannot hold onto anything; everything moves and changes. Holding onto or resisting an experience is like trying to take a child's favorite toy away; it will only end with frustration and a power struggle. However, give the child time to grow up and naturally they will give up the toy themselves. Movement and change is the inherent nature of the Universe.

Along with the taste of equanimity of mind, the experience also gave me knowledge of the power that I had always held — power to determine my inner responses. I now understood that I had the power to make peace with my thoughts and experiences or resent them. I could choose to be miserable or to be content. I had been living much of my life as a victim, at the whims of my external and internal experiences. I had expected my life to improve through a change in my external environment.

My Ignite moment came in one of the evening lectures. As the Vipassana teacher, Goenka, explained, "You are the only person responsible for your own happiness. No one can give it to you; you get to choose how you will respond to things." It was on hearing Goenka's words that I realized I didn't have to be miserable. I didn't have to carry all of my old baggage with me. I had felt powerless in the face of the memory and pain of having been molested as a little girl. The experience had already robbed me of so much joy, light, and trust. At that moment, I decided to choose happiness and I decided to choose forgiveness. Forgiveness for the sake of my own joy. I wasn't going to let my past steal any more of my future. I was no longer a buoy being thrown around in the waves; instead I chose to be a leaf floating on the top, allowing the waves to wash over me. Taking personal responsibility for my state of mind gave me the wings to leave the nest of victimhood, to decide to be more, and no longer be defined by my past trauma.

Spending 10 days with myself took me to some of my deepest places, both high and low. As much as I had faced challenging experiences, I also felt some of the most profound joy. The kind of joy that made me weep, it was so overwhelming. The joy that comes from the sheer pleasure of being. This joy was the experience of knowing the purity of my own soul and it brought me to my knees before its splendor. I didn't know what it meant to be alive until I felt that kind of joy.

The thing about that kind of joy is you can't chase it. There's no add A to B = C equation. It comes to you in the moments that you let go; you let go of all that you think you're looking for and just be with what *is*. Then you realize what's really there, how you are full — life is full and there is nothing you need to add. If I'm only ever looking for gold, I'm not going to spot the diamond. How often in life do we miss the beauty that is there because we don't see the pretty picture we're looking for?

I walked out of that course having taken tons off my shoulders. My body felt like it had taken a beating; I felt stiff and sore from hours of sitting and yet I walked out more erect and with a lightness of step. I felt fully grounded in my body with a newfound consciousness of the contact between the ground and my feet. The sounds, smells, and colors in the world, even the feeling of the steering wheel in my hands, felt richer and I literally glowed with an inner radiance. So much so, I was described afterward by someone I had just met as shiny. I felt stronger than I ever had because I finally understood my own resilience. I knew that nothing could break me. I was the master of my own well-being. My life existed in that moment. I was no longer a ghost unable to step out of my own past.

The person who walked out was a 180-degree change to the person who walked in. I no longer needed therapy or medication. My life was no longer controlled by the darkness and misery of anxiety and depression. Rather, I felt fulfilled in the simple moments of day-to-day life. The gift of warm sunshine on my skin. Music was a fully immersive experience, as if hearing it for the first time and every cell of my body called out in response.

For six months, I rode the post Vipassana glow and didn't sit to meditate once in that time. I was in such a good place that I just enjoyed it; I lived in the moment. Slowly, with time, the high wore off and I returned to a more 'normal' state of being. I never went back to that deep hole of despair but my life has had its ups and downs as all lives do. I've had times where I've been happier and times where I wasn't but the knowledge that I'm responsible for my own happiness has stuck with me and put me onto an incredible path.

I realized I wanted more than a corporate job and financial success. I've spent the last two years traveling the world. In that time, I've seen 12 countries and lived in three. I've met some of the most beautiful souls who have enriched my life beyond words. I've been able to heal and enjoy my sexuality in a way I didn't ever think would be possible after my trauma. I've resided in ashrams and had the opportunity to make spirituality and growth my core focus.

Two years ago, I trekked in the wilderness of Kyrgyzstan, in central Asia, with people I had only met three days before. People who took me in and became like a second family to me. We followed old Soviet maps through valleys that hadn't seen tourists since the days of the USSR. We made camp next to glaciers 4000m above sea level. I clearly remember one of the highest peaks we climbed. As we reached the summit, my chest still heaving from the exertion, I took a few minutes to sit with only the sound of the roaring wind for company and the air whipping the cool sweat of the climb from my face. Green and brown valleys furled out below me and the sun glinted off glacial peaks in the distance, obscuring the horizon. At that moment, I knew what it meant to be on top of the world. Sitting there, I could not believe how far I'd come. From scaling emotional mountains to physically climbing thousands of feet, I had traveled to places of healing and wholeness I could never have imagined would be so beautiful.

Throughout everything, I have been brought back, time and again to the lesson of surrender. Of letting go and being present. It's been in those times that I've been able to experience the most happiness. Happiness as a state of joy, a state of contentment, of peace and stillness, unaffected by the changing nature of my experiences. Ironically these times of joy and peace have often been during times of external hardship, where surrender allowed me to embrace and grow from the experience rather than put all my energy into resisting it. It is through internal changes rather than external changes to our lives that we can find complete bliss. One of my favorite reminders is...

Before enlightenment: fetch water from the well.
After enlightenment: fetch water from the well.

Pain, hardship, and suffering are both our jailer and our greatest paths to freedom. I now understand that we turn these experiences into a cage of our own making instead of seeing them as the key that shows us that true freedom and liberation are always present. It is in transcending and not avoiding these experiences that we evolve. Trying to control or curate our lives in such a way as to try and avoid suffering brings only a temporary false sense of security and limits our evolution. We come to earth with all its pain, suffering, and anguish for a reason, because these are its gifts.

One of my favorite stories is of a Buddhist monk, Lopon-la, who was locked up in China for 18 years. The Dalai Lama asked him if he had ever felt fear in that time? He responded that yes, he had feared one thing — that he might lose his compassion toward the Chinese. It is such a beautiful story of what we can be as humans, how our compassion can override even the most terrible experiences.

Struggle and hardship show us our true selves. They show us our ability to be limitless in the face of external limits. How our path can be one of choosing the higher ideal. In the face of pain and suffering, we can choose love, choose surrender, choose faith in the goodness of humanity. It is in making these hard choices that we evolve and it is in our evolution back to our truest self, the place of true love and compassion, that we find authentic happiness.

IGNITE ACTION STEPS

What is something you actively dislike doing? Go and consciously do that thing and while you're doing it, try and observe your mind. Watch it as if you were an outsider observing the experience.

Action is an unavoidable part of life; learning to become the observer of your experiences can help you step out of the misery of the like and dislike toward things.

One of my favorite practices for coming back to a place of relaxation and letting go is Yoga Nidra. It is the practice of psychic sleep. The first stage of the mediation is a rotation of body awareness.

Start by laying down on the ground. Piece by piece, bring your awareness and breath into every body part. Starting with the right hand thumb, index finger, third finger, fourth finger, little finger, palm of the hand, right wrist, etc., up the arm, into your torso then your leg. Repeat on the left side, then bit by bit, the head and back and front of the body. Try and release all the tension you are holding. Let go completely and allow the floor to carry you and observe your natural breathing.

A wise man once told me, "Your natural breath is a representation of your relationship with the world." Is it shallow and restricted or deep and easy? How easily and deeply your natural breath flows is an indication of how much you trust the world around you.

Karla Rose Weihe – South Africa
Human Being

IGNITE HAPPINESS ACTIVITY

Likhita Japa is a written version of mantra repetition. Choose a mantra or symbol that has significance for you. Then, with awareness and focus, repetitively write out this mantra or symbol in lines, patterns, or shapes that resonate with you and with the message of the mantra. The practice can be as simple or creative as you like. The aim is to keep your focus on the mantra and your own resonance with it. As you write, a relationship develops between you and the mantra. This practice can be used to still the mind and connect with your own center and heart space.

TRACI HARRELL

"Stay true to your core values and tap into your 'Bigger Than Me' moments."

Embrace the journey of life fully with the expectation that happiness is your birthright. Happiness is your baseline state of being — it is who you are at your core. Happiness is the greatest gift we can ever give ourselves and we have an endless supply. No matter what is happening in your life, despite any ups and downs, the power of happiness awaits you at all times. It is yours for the taking… yours for the awakening.

THE POWER AND JOY IN OUR 'BIGGER THAN ME' MOMENT®

The last three years have been the most terrifying, traumatizing, dehumanizing, minimizing, sometimes belittling, often numbing, saddening, maddening, and downright awful of my entire 50 years of existence. I experienced fears even worse than dying.

During this same time period, I have also experienced what I can easily describe as the most liberating, optimizing, energizing, redemptive, sometimes restorative, often therapeutic, meaningful, transformative, and downright joyful years of my life. I have experienced happiness greater than I ever imagined.

It was *awful* because I was forced to come face-to-face with some of my greatest fears and my deepest insecurities. You know, the fears and insecurities that you don't typically share with others. The ones you barely want to admit to yourself.

It was *joyful* because I had the opportunity to get to know myself on a deeper level and I was challenged to reconnect with my core values, which allowed me to tap into a wellspring inside that grounded me and allowed me to flourish.

Despite a series of unending challenges, I consistently rose to the occasion and exceeded my own expectations. This is the story of my triumph — overcoming my fears and, in the process, becoming a better woman for my troubles.

One of the deepest fears that I carried with me through childhood and into adulthood (although I hid it well) was the fear of being different. This fear grew poisonous barbs inside me like a sea urchin, all sourced from the same core insecurity. These painful barbs included the 'fear of not being accepted,' the 'fear of not fitting in,' and the underlying 'fear of not being successful *because* I didn't fit in.' The toxicity from the 'fear of being different,' sometimes led to the *lonely* 'fear of not being loved,' and the more dangerous 'fear of not being lovable.'

I've always been different. My differences are a blessing and a curse, but I am what I am. Once I accepted that I was different, I started putting those fears and insecurities behind me, or I buried them somewhere and I tried not to let them control me. I have always been taller, darker, bigger, bolder, and louder than those around me. Fortunately, I was also generally happier, funnier, and 'smarter than the average bear.' I was often bullied while growing up. I was called names like Tar Baby and Count Blackula because of my dark skin, dark hair, and dark eyes. In the media, blonde hair and blue eyes were considered beautiful and clearly I could not meet that mark. But I knew I was special. I was always striking a balance between feeling different and feeling amazing. I knew that I was meant for something great. I believed that my purpose in life was 'Bigger Than Me' and there was something quite comforting in that.

The first time I recall tapping into the power of 'My Inner Superhero' and embracing a 'Bigger Than Me' moment, I was in Florida as a young girl riding home on the school bus. The bully was there, Judy was her name, and she was causing havoc as usual. Whether she was bullying me or someone else, I typically tried to ignore her. I had stuffed my feelings and suffered in silence for years while I was getting teased for being different. I knew that bullies seem to go harder and deeper on the abuse when one would show an emotional reaction or respond in any way, so I had learned to just take it in silence. I stifled my feelings and just held everything in. On that day, Judy had been at the back of the bus yelling at a young girl who was seated in front of me. The girl was new — I didn't even know her name. Judy had been saying some awful things to her and was threatening to 'get her' when we got off the bus. The young girl was clearly upset, although she didn't turn around or make a sound. I could see her rapid breathing, her shoulders lifting in sequence with the faint sound of whimpering.

I had a feeling inside me that I can't describe as anything other than an out-of-body experience. My Inner Superhero took over and my first 'Bigger Than Me' moment was born. I stood up, turned around, and said, "Judy, enough!"

She was shocked. So was I. She said, "What?"

I said, "Enough! If you want to fight someone, fight me. Let's do this. I am sick and tired of you picking on everyone. This must end."

She laughed and said, "Really? Who's going to stop me, you?"

"That's the plan," I replied. Now, full disclosure — there was no plan. What happened was that one of my core values, Justice, had just swelled up inside of me and I could feel it bursting out. I *had* to stop the bully. In that moment, in that 'Bigger Than Me' moment, I knew what I was seeing wasn't fair and that I had to stand up for myself and all the other innocent kids who had been bullied for so long.

As I walked off the bus that day, I felt so proud and strong; so courageous. I felt like Wonder Woman® with cape, boots, and all. I stepped off the bus onto the sidewalk and laid down my backpack. I wasn't afraid, even though I didn't know what I was doing — this was my first fight. Whatever the outcome, I definitely was not going to let Judy beat up on some other little girl. To make a long story short, I got my butt kicked that day.

All I remember was the first punch in my face, crushing my lip against my bottom teeth, causing a warm pool of blood to form in my mouth. I recall wearing a soft white shirt and seeing a stream of bright red blood pour down the front of my blouse as I lowered my head. I generally have a bad memory for negative things; but on that day, I remember feeling both scared and excited at the same time. I was standing up for what was right… and that felt great. From what I'm told, I may not have even thrown a single punch that day, but the victory was in being true to who I am. I had stood my ground. I had never felt more proud or more fulfilled. I had done the right thing. It was an amazing 'Bigger Than Me' moment.

I will never forget feeling like a champion that day. I had stood up for myself and I had taken a stand for Justice, and that was such a rewarding feeling. That experience changed me forever. I learned what it felt like to be true to my core values. That feeling has never left me and it sustains me even to this day. I realized that once I understood my core values and could be true to who I am, whatever actions I take will be the next right actions for me.

From that moment on, I relied on my core values and my 'Bigger Than Me' moments to serve as my source of peace and happiness. I now try to listen to my inner voice and tap into my Inner Superhero as often as I can — for major challenges and even for little things, like resisting a slice of pie or repelling someone else's negative mood or abusive actions. Try it; it works for everything.

I believe that happiness is my baseline state of being… it is who I am at my core — and I'll fight to maintain that inner peace at all costs. And the cost is free. It's free for you and me. All you need is just a little courage and conviction. Happiness is yours for the taking; just awaken to the possibilities. No matter what circumstances occur in your life, the power of happiness awaits you at all times. We activate happiness by pausing to breathe and tapping into our core values. It is the most effective way to help guide our actions. The rewards are valuable and the applications are endless.

Now, I'm not saying that I haven't been bullied since that first 'Bigger Than Me' moment when I found my Inner Superhero. To the contrary, the next transformative experience I'll share also involved a bully, just a different type of bully more than 35 years later. I was now more confident and equipped to handle challenges — although I still had a lot to learn. I had experienced many 'Bigger Than Me' moments since my first one, and my 'Practice of Happiness' was ingrained into who I am. Knowing the true source and power of happiness throughout this time had kept me focused on the positive and feeling like I could overcome anything. Then, one day, everything changed.

The day I got fired was the happiest day of my life. I was shocked *and* transformed.

The three years leading up to that moment changed how I felt about myself and the world. This journey started with me moving across the country from Florida to Seattle for an exciting job opportunity.

My first year with the company went amazingly well. I was thinking outside the box and solving one challenge after the next. I was confidently accomplishing complex projects; and I was building partnerships and getting credit for the work that I did (as it should be). At the end of the first year, I received a large financial bonus as well as major kudos and awards. I also received sincere compliments from my leader. He said, "You are amazing. You have superpowers… you have multiple superpowers! Sometimes I can't even keep up with you." He said I was doing all the right work and that I would be rewarded handsomely if I could apply the new process and system, which I had developed, to more of the programs in the coming year. That, of course, was exciting to me and I enthusiastically charged forward, fully believing that if I worked hard, I would be rewarded for my efforts. My work was great. The results were tangible and undeniable. And I believed that I would receive what I had earned, as promised.

The second year of the project wasn't just a regular work experience for me. I desperately needed to ensure that I would get the promised financial bonus because I wanted to use it to pay for a medical procedure that would save my brother's life. Tony, a veteran, had terminal cancer. He had been told that an experimental procedure was possible, but it would not be covered by the Veterans' Hospital. I knew that, with my bonus, I could pay for his medical procedure and save his life. "What a blessing," I thought. "How cool that I am in a position to help in this way," and I happily shared my excitement with Tony and his wife, Renee. I knew that all I had to do was complete the project and I would receive the bonus to save my brother's life.

As the end of my second year approached, I was feeling tired but excited and satisfied in the knowledge that I had completed the work and exceeded what was asked of me. My bonus was imminent and Tony could have his procedure.

Then came the day of my Year Two review. A new leader had joined the team a few months prior and, apparently, he changed the rules. He didn't recognize the work that I had clearly completed and the bonus that I had understood to be my compensation was no longer coming my way. I was shocked — actually, devastated. I couldn't believe what I was hearing. Another bully. A big corporate bully. They had all the power. I sat there in the chair looking stunned... I was feeling disgusted, betrayed, belittled, confused, minimized, dehumanized, taken advantage of, diminished... I felt violated. I had poured my heart into that project; I called it EARL, the *Eligibility Automated Review List*. It was my baby and it was awesome... I designed it, developed it, and delivered it. By all measures of success, I had exceeded expectations both operationally and strategically. The corporate bullies decided they wanted what I had and they were going to take it. I sat there feeling worthless. Shocked. Powerless. Basically, he said, I just didn't fit in on his team. Well, I *was* different, I can give him that, but I was also amazing. I had just accomplished what they had said could not be done. I was truly traumatized, but I couldn't feel those feelings yet.

Bottom line, I didn't get credit for the work I had done and I didn't get my bonus. My brother Tony did not get his life-saving medical treatment. Sadly, and most devastatingly, he died. I couldn't believe it, but I also couldn't react. I didn't know what to say or do, so I did what we are told to do — show no emotion. No crying allowed; just soldier on. When I tapped into my Core Values of Justice and Progress, I found strength and comfort. Armed with my superpowers, and in Tony's honor, I focused on how to defeat this corporate bully. Given my lack of institutional power, I believed that the only way for me to find justice for the loss of my brother would be to train my leaders and the organization in the areas of Equity and Inclusion. I wanted to prevent the injustice of what I had incurred so it wouldn't happen to anyone else.

I didn't allow myself the time or energy to focus on my sadness. Instead, I focused on trying to make things better. I poured myself into helping the company make progress with our Equity and Inclusion initiatives. I wouldn't allow myself to name or claim the feelings that I had at that time. The only thing that brought me comfort was the idea that this was a 'Bigger Than Me' moment. This was an opportunity for my two core values, Justice and Progress, to unite with a passion. I *could* make things better. I *could* create a culture where fairness and justice were applied equally to everyone.

For 3 years, I continued to allow these corporate bullies to abuse me. I never fully recovered from the trauma and broken promises, and yet I found myself empowered to push through and try to make a difference. Each time I felt vulnerable about an insecurity, terrified due to a lack of trust, devastated by another unjust outcome, or anxious about next steps, I just tapped into my core values. I found happiness in my 'Bigger Than Me' moments. I knew everything was happening to me because someday I would inspire a change to help others. That idea made me more powerful and more resourceful. I continued to push back on the corporate bully with mild demands. I was Happy and committed, believing I could drive positive outcomes for others even though I was still personally traumatized. As I focused on my new *Adaptive Leadership Equity and Inclusion Initiative to Stop Corporate Chokeholds*®, my leadership was supported 'in theory.' They agreed that the principles of equity and inclusion were sound, but they weren't sure how to implement it… or they just didn't have the will to change. I believed that these were good people. I thought they just didn't know any better and I didn't want to give up on them.

On the day of my year-end review during year five, I opened the door to the meeting room and was shocked as I saw the HR manager with a package of documents on the table. I knew that I was in a termination meeting. These corporate bullies had broken my trust; but instead of feeling broken, I truly thought I could make a difference. I believe I did in some way. But I couldn't save my brother and, clearly, I was being fired, so I couldn't save myself.

Halfway through the termination session, my eyes full of tears, God reminded me that this, too, was a 'Bigger Than Me' moment. I exhaled a slow long breath, wiped away my tears, and smiled. I was transformed. It was a breakthrough moment. I started to FEEL my feelings fully for the first time. I could now name it and claim it. I felt relieved, happy, excited, proud, courageous… and calm. It was amazing.

I actually smiled through the second half of the termination session. I realized that I was experiencing a Divine moment — it was like another out-of-body experience. I was crying tears of joy while I was being fired. All the feelings I had repressed and suppressed for so long had now broken free. I cried for my brother whom I couldn't save. I cried for all the other injustices and for all the 'unfelt' feelings. It was such a catharsis. I could barely read the papers through my tears. They were warm, sweet, refreshing tears that ran down both cheeks and into my mouth.

It was in that moment that I remembered how the blood had pooled in my mouth when I faced off with my first bully. Facing this corporate bully felt even more rewarding. What a relief. What a victory! I was ALIVE at that moment. Nothing was held back; no feelings would ever be held back again. I was so grateful for that breakthrough. I felt happiness beyond my wildest dreams. For the first time, I was experiencing PURE BLISS.

Once again, the bully had won the battle, but I had the ultimate victory… Joy prevailed. I was standing up for what was right and that felt great. I had stayed true to my Core Values of Justice and Progress, and relied on my 'Bigger Than Me' moments to serve as my source of peace and happiness. I didn't have to find happiness; it was waiting for me. Waiting for me to let go and to just BE. For the first time ever, I had permission to Just Be Me — my full Authentic self. This was a 'Let Go and Let God' moment, a 'Jesus Take the Wheel' moment, a 'Bigger Than Me' Moment®. It was clear that God had a plan for my life — a beautiful one. I could just pause and be blessed, and He would take care of the rest.

This was the moment when I realized that Happiness is not really a choice. It's a state of being. We can just BE Happy. No matter what is happening around us, we don't have to choose it. Happiness has already chosen us. We just have to take down the walls and open up our hearts. The process of receiving the Power of Happiness simply requires us to just PAUSE and accept it… expect it… and let it wash over us. Let it in. Do nothing. And in that nothingness is your Bliss. Happiness awaits you… awaken to the infinite possibilities.

Ignite Action Steps

- Happiness surrounds you; it's like the air that you breathe. You can't see it, but it's there for you. Pause and just take it in. Simply focus on the positive and embrace pure Joy in all that you do.

- If you find your level of happiness diminishing or your mood shifting, you can quickly rebalance by reconnecting with your Core Values. There is a knowing that will guide you, with peace and joy as your pathway to staying true to yourself.

- Happiness is your most prized possession; guard this precious gift closely. Others can't write your story. Don't let the words or actions of others take you off course.

- Activate your 'Inner Superhero' by doing what all superheroes do. When they see a 'Bigger Than Me' moment or encounter a need greater than Self, they immediately *leap* into action. Happiness is yours when you tap into your Core Values, and use that Peace and Energy to quickly take the next right action.

- In moments of stress and trials, you can immediately shift to a 'Bigger Than Me' mindset by tapping into your 'Inner Superhero' to stay aligned with your Core Values. Slow breathing is key to the shift… take four slow inhalations and exhalations. Each time you inhale, visualize the blossoming of your truth. Ignite your Core Values from deep inside your mind, body, and soul. Each time you exhale, say to yourself, "It's Bigger Than Me… It's ALL Bigger Than Me." It's in these 'Bigger Than Me' moments that you can immediately amplify your personal power to produce happiness at will.

- You can manifest happiness and all of your desired outcomes by tapping into the power of your 'Bigger Than Me' moments. You know what to do. You have always known how to IGNITE the Power of Happiness — the instructions for your truth and your peace were planted like seeds inside of you from birth. It's what feels good, feels *right,* deep down in your soul. You don't think about it, you just do it. You just know. You automatically know what is good for you and good for the Universe.

- Use the Power of Happiness to love every step on the Journey of Life while staying focused on living out all of your dreams.

- Uncover a limitless wellspring of joy, peace, and love until happiness rains over you like the nurturing shower on a spring garden, flowing to you, through you, and to all those around you.

- Embrace your personal bliss. Nourish the seeds of joy inside of you each day and moment by moment. True and sustainable happiness is within your reach. Believe it and you can achieve it. Pause and unleash the possibilities.

Traci Harrell – United States of America
President, It's All Bigger Than Me® Consulting
Founder & Reverend, It's All Bigger Than Me® Ministry
(Positive Psychology – 'A Ministry of the Mind®')
Producer/Host, 'Bigger Than Me'® Action TV®, YouTube & Podcast
Author, 'Loving the Journey & Living the Dream®'
Movement Lead, "Bigger Than Me – Success Series®: Achieving Racial Equity & Inclusion in Business, Education, Wealth & Health"
www.ItsAllBiggerThanMe.com

Ignite Happiness Activity

Happiness Vision Board Activity – Nurture Your Seeds of Possibility

Use this space to draw a picture and build a vision board of how you plan to nurture the seeds of happiness inside yourself to bring everything you desire to life.

1. **Focus Areas**: Label the stem of each flower with an area in life you want to focus on to manifest more happiness. Draw in new flowers to fulfill all your dreams and desires. [Like: Relationships, Career, Health, Home, Family, Finances, Spirituality, Education, Social, Travel, etc.]

2. **Core Values**: Identify which of your Core Values are most important to you in each area of life. Label the center of each flower with one to three Core Values. [Like: Justice, Progress, Achievement, Adventure, Balance, Connection, Community, Contribution, Faith, Knowledge, Love, Service, etc.] Note: Your Core Values can be filled in after you have completed Step 3.

3. **Action Steps**: For each focus area in your life, identify specific steps you will take each day to manifest more happiness and fulfill your dreams. Inside each flower petal, write one action or step.

Your Happiness vision board should be an iterative and evolving activity that you enjoy cultivating, to nurture your seeds of Joy & Possibility.

Happiness Vision Board Activity- Nurture Seeds of Possibility

Lydia Sacallis

"Do the hard things, the things that bother you, the things that scare you the most but that you know are for your greater good."

Each time I am faced with a fear, I always get jittery. I then remind myself that often our fears are there to help us live life to its fullest. You never know how it's going to turn out and you may end up with a fun story to tell. I want to help you realize that even though you're reluctant to do something that scares you, you should go ahead and do it anyway just to feel what the experience is like. Face your fears. Don't think of what could go wrong; think more of the memories that shall come of it. Life is full of opportunities, so take them!

Free Falling into my Fears

I was nine when my Dad took my brother and me to the fair. I sat in the back seat of my dad's blue pickup truck. I could feel the gray cloth seats under my bare legs. It was itchy. All the windows were rolled down and my hair was flying into my face. "Shape of You" was playing on the radio and I was singing along while staring out the window. As we pulled into the parking lot of the P.N.E. in Vancouver — the Pacific National Exhibition, Canada's oldest and greatest fairgrounds — my dad couldn't help but say, "You guys ready to *pee-a-kne* (p-n-e)?" just like he always did whenever we would go to the fair. He used to say that all the rides would make you pee your pants from fear.

The P.N.E was an annual event that took place in the fall. I looked forward to it every year. I usually just ate the delectable fair food which mostly consisted of fluffy pink clouds of cotton candy and mini donuts drowning in a sweet mix of cinnamon and sugar. I always got a stomach ache after but it was worth it.

The night before, I hadn't been able to sleep, so I decided to plan my outfit for the next day. I settled on a yellow button-up shirt, dark washed denim shorts, and my hair in two buns that lay on top of my head.

I was ecstatic because I was finally tall enough to go on most of the roller coasters. The biggest roller coaster was visible from where we parked. It was an ancient wooden one and I could hear a kind of creaking and people yelling as the coaster rushed around its curves and bends. And that was the day that I would finally, after years of longing, be able to ride that colossal ride with my brother.

My brother and I ran eagerly over to the entrance to the rustic wooden roller coaster. It was probably older than me and my brother combined, but there was no chickening out now. We didn't even think twice before getting in line. As we waited for our turn to get into the cart, we stood silently but my body was anxious and excited. We really wanted to be at the front of the train, but we got pushed back and settled for second. I had no worries in the world. This was going to be a fun ride and my brother and I would end up going on this one coaster the whole afternoon. Or so I thought.

As we went up the large looming structure at the beginning of our adventure, I could practically feel my heart beating out of my chest from fear and excitement. There was no going back now. Around the corners and bends, we went until we came to the first big rise. I could hear the clicking of the mechanism as it pulled our cart up the steep hill. As we neared the top, the heads in front of us dropped from my view.

Everything seemed to happen in slow motion, but I still wasn't scared at this point. As we crested the top, I could see us heading straight for the ground. Our cart tipped down the drop and I could feel myself lift up out of the cart. My hands clamped onto the lap bar for dear life, but my body continued to rise. I couldn't breathe and not even a scream would come out of my mouth. Up ahead, where the cart went into a tunnel, I could see a wooden beam holding up the framework of the coaster coming straight for my head and I was petrified. My brother looked over at me with glee, but seeing I was rising high enough to almost stand at this point, he was struck with terror. My brother grabbed me by the hem of my shirt and pulled me under the safety rail just before going under the structure. His rescue unlocked a rush of tears and a scream erupted out of me once I was safe. I stayed there in his grasp, crying and screaming for the remainder of the ride. When the ride came to a stop, my breathing was heavy and my tear-stained face was hot. I was never EVER doing that again.

And... I didn't. For two years, I didn't. But then, about two years after that experience, my family and I decided to take a trip down to Disneyland in California. After three days of driving during which my sister Jorja was puking and car sick, plus countless hours of Netflix were watched, we finally arrived. The long drive down was hot, sticky, and boring and called for some pool time after dinner where we could splash and stretch our bodies after so many hours of sitting in the same position.

I was thrilled for the day ahead of us. It was my first time at Disney and I could not wait to have the adventure. Going through security and taking those first steps into the park, I was ecstatic that the day had finally come. As we entered the park, I looked around in glee, soaking in the bright colors of the flower beds and a sweet peppermint cinnamon smell that drifted through the air. Disney was exactly how I imagined it.

The very first ride I saw was the *Pirates of the Caribbean* ride, an indoor roller coaster, and my heart lit up with excitement because this was one of my favorite Disney movies. Thoughts of the experience I had had two years earlier with my brother were running through my head, but I tried to silence them. I hoped that there was no big drop inside that mysterious building. We stepped into a boat-like cart going through water. The smell of rum and salt water filled my nose. As I rode through the ride looking at all the decorations, I heard something. Screams. Not screams coming from the animatronic fighting scenes that played over the speakers, but real-life screams. I clenched my sister's arm, closing my eyes tightly as I realized what was about to happen. My sister thought the situation was absolutely hysterical. As I saw my life flash before my eyes, she continued laughing. I wished I hadn't insisted on sitting at the front of the cart. My parents sat silently behind my sister and me, and my brothers behind them. As I felt us coming up onto and over the drop, my brain stopped working. My senses were at the top of their levels and everything seemed surreal. I started to calm myself down. I looked around and enjoyed the sets surrounding me as best as I could through the tears that were still in control of my eyes. I was still holding tightly to my sister even though there was nothing I had to worry about anymore.

In the distance, a light was approaching, which meant the end of the ride was near. My sister was still laughing at me. She was folded over the lap bar almost in tears from laughing so much. In the end, as we exited the ride, my mom got close to my ear and whispered, "Are you okay, Lids?"

Tears were still running down my face. I didn't want to be seen by my brothers. They would have mocked me and told me how much of a baby I was for crying. I cuddled up into my mom so no one could see my face. She asked me if I wanted to go get some Mickey Mouse ears from the gift shop and I immediately said, "Yes." After looking for a while and seeing nothing in the *Pirates of the Caribbean* gift shop, we decided to walk around the park. It was Christmas time so the whole park was decked out in fake snow and Christmas lights. The California heat would never let snow fall, but it made Disneyland feel like our home in Canada.

The next ride we took under our wing was the *Nightmare Before Christmas*. I was skeptical. The building looked exactly like the previous nightmare I had just encountered. My emotions took over my body once again and I could feel my eyes getting watery even before the ride began. I wanted to enjoy the moment, but the fear I had deep inside me wouldn't let me. I sucked up my tears and told myself it would be okay. My mom and I were hand in hand throughout the whole line. I sat with her during the ride and she gave me a sense of safety that I didn't have with my sister.

I had freaked myself out expecting there to be another drop, but I trusted my mom when she said that there wasn't one on this ride. She started making jokes about the animatronics on the ride which cheered me up and, in the end, I thought it was a great ride. The walk through the gift shop at the end was my favorite part. I picked out a pair of Mickey Mouse ears that were designed to be like the character Sally from the *Nightmare Before Christmas*. The teal blue ears contrasted with my bright red hair, but I didn't care. The ears brought me enormous amounts of joy. My 10-year-old self was full of exuberance for my new Disney attire.

Roller coaster after roller coaster, my siblings did not understand my fear and would make fun of me for crying. They would try and make me go on rides that they knew I would be scared of just so they could laugh at me. Nonetheless, I had a fun time at Disney. I filled the rest of my day with smaller rides, swapping which sibling I sat with on each one. I could feel in my heart that my whole family wanted to go on the bigger rides and not have to take turns staying with me because I was too scared to come along. I ignored this feeling, but I kind of felt guilty.

That day at Disney was hot and the Florida sun was blistering. Disneyland offered a couple of attractions that included water. After one look at the log flume with its show-stopping drop, I refused to go on it. I wasn't being fooled by that one. My whole family told me that the only water ride that had no drop was a white water rafting ride in the back corner of the park. My skin was sweltering, so I hesitantly agreed to go with them. The wait was long and there were many people in the line. Once again, my sister was cackling at me for absolutely no reason. My family was quieter than usual, but I didn't notice. I was too busy looking over the edge of the wooden bridge that led up to the building labeled 'Waterworks.' It was jam-packed with people.

The rafts departed and came back to a revolving concrete slab that allowed the huge round rafts to stay in the water. The raft seated eight and we got paired with two other people to fill it up. The two girls who joined us had to be in college at the time. The seats were all soaked from previous passengers and the cool of the water felt good against my thighs. We got all buckled up and were sent on our way, winding through the canal of water and hitting the walls at every corner we went around. Water would splash us when we hit it just right. At one point, we slowed to a stop and I could hear the chains trying to grab onto the bottom of our raft. The clicking sound was very familiar and then I remembered that when you go up, you always have to go down. I looked at my family in distrust. There was obviously a drop coming up and it was coming quick. Panic rushed over my body and there was only one thing going through my head:

"I need to get out!"

I struggled to unbuckle my seat belt, gasping for air. Unsuccessful, I then slid myself down in my seat trying to slither out the bottom. I was screaming and crying, and I could hear my siblings laughing hysterically. My parents were tugging at my arms to try and keep me safely in my seat. The screams of the people in the raft ahead of us filled my head once again. I struggled against the tight grasp of my parents as they told me to just calm down. I could only imagine the looks on those two girls' faces. I was definitely causing a scene, but I couldn't help but panic at the feeling of unsafety.

The raft came to the very top of the edge. My heart missed a beat and I squeezed my mother's hand tightly. I could feel the raft beginning to tip as the chain let go, the seat threatening to fall away from beneath my legs. I gulped in the air like a goldfish and squeezed my eyes shut. I felt my body become weightless and opened my eyes to see we were free-falling into a sea of water. I tried to scream but the sound wouldn't come. At the bottom, a wave of water splashed up to meet me, soaking me through to the skin. Goosebumps prickled on my arms and the cold shocked me into breathing again. I wiped my eyes clear of the liquid. My brothers had their faces in their hands in embarrassment. Jorja wasn't the only one laughing at this point; the two girls who rode with us were laughing too. I couldn't help but join in and laugh at myself. I was perfectly fine and safe.

At that moment, I realized that I had just conquered one of my biggest fears. Not only had I overcome it, I actually quite enjoyed it. The feeling of relief and pride energized me and made me feel like I could do this. I could do whatever I wanted. I was at the top of the world. At that moment, I realized that it's better to face your fears than to run away from them, and although I still do hate roller coasters, and anything with a drop in it for that matter, I also love how they help me be able to take more risks in my life. Plus a little cotton candy as a sweet reward after facing your fears never hurt. My family teases me about this moment to this day, and yes, people do laugh about it, but a big part of me is glad that I did it (though I'd never let my family know that).

Since that day, I've jumped into more scary adventures. I've gone white water rafting with crazy Russians tourists in Turkey and both zip-lined and climbed up a waterfall in Costa Rica. And, scariest of all, I've talked to my teachers when I had to, even when it was hard. After embracing the idea that I should do the hard things, the things that bother me, the things that scare me the most but that I know are for my own greater good, it has really made me feel like I am in control. When I do the hard thing, it lets me come out of my shell and makes me feel free and absolutely happy.

Happiness comes from experience. Never be afraid to do something that could be extraordinary, no matter how big or how small. Whether it is just to say "Hi" to someone you don't know or jump in a plane and go skydiving, you never know how life is going to unfold. You should stop fearing the worst thing that can happen and think instead of what *can* become of it. Now, I'm not saying that you shouldn't be cautious; what I'm saying is that if your opportunity comes, take it! You are never going to know if you will enjoy something if you don't try it. Life is full of opportunities for happiness, so take them!

IGNITE ACTION STEPS

Make a Happiness Jar. Go get a jar out of your recycle bin and then clean it out and decorate it. Write on it, stick stickers on it, do whatever you feel like to make it yours.

Each day and every day, write something happy that happened in your life. After a while, you'll start to look in your day for things that you can write in your Happiness Jar. It can even be those little things like someone smiling at you, finding five bucks in your pocket, or getting the last cookie from the box.

At the end of the year, go back and read all of the notes you wrote and recall all the amazing memories you have experienced. Realize how good your life is and how no matter how scary the circumstances are, you can always find a little good in everything.

Lydia Sacallis – Canada
Smart twelve-year-old

JASON B. FLORES

"Go THROUGH the open door to unleash Happiness."

You and you alone can spark that fire of happiness inside of you and know what that means to you. Remaining in the middle of a crossroads is a choice. It is choosing to be indecisive. Happiness is unleashed when you make the choice to step out of the middle and not just knock on one of the doors in front of you, but go THROUGH the door to your left or to your right. The trial and error you experience gets you closer to happiness as time progresses. There is no perfect, so just keep shining!!

CHOOSE YOUR LIFE LENS

When I was in grade school, I would eagerly await each Friday. It was a family tradition to have supper at McDonald's™ after a long week of school in my friendly little Midwestern town. My face could light up a dark stadium at the sight of those Golden Arches™, and my expression only grew brighter at the smell of those fries as they were freshly taken out of the fryer. It was the reward and highlight of my week and could turn any frown upside down instantly! As a child, viewing happiness through that lens was a much simpler formula, but it seemed to become progressively more complex as time went on. Looking back, it's incredible to see that the simple things in life were more than enough to bring me happiness.

As I grew older, that slowly and silently changed. My happiness started requiring more and more. There I was, at my first job, at the age of 13; mowing lawns in my neighborhood for $20 a pop. Little did I know how much the fragrant smell of fresh cut grass would teach me about the importance of money — that having more of it so that I could buy what I wanted made me happy. The formula was born: money = happiness. Thus, the quest to fulfill this equation was now engraved in my mind. It was like I had unconsciously fallen into a trap and was going deeper and deeper with no signs of surfacing. If I buy this, then I'll be happy. If I get that, then I'll be happier. Once this project is done, I'll be really happy. It was like I had taken a taste of something delicious and was now craving more and more of it. But, in the back of my mind, a thought lingered like an unscratched itch: when would this end?!

Nevertheless, through my early 20s I remained on the path, following the passion that would lead me to something that would get me more money… and therefore more happiness. I have been a techie all my life, going from tinkering with tape recorders to spending countless hours in front of a 15" screen, fascinated by hearing the funky combination of squeals and beeps coming from a box below the desk. Those simple noises were a sure sign that, in a few brief moments, I would be greeted with "You've got mail!" Those three words never failed to plaster a smile on my face that could have stretched for miles. The Internet was a doorway; walking through it let me consume loads of articles and data day in and day out, feeding my thirst for knowledge. This further fueled my curiosity about other cultures and places, creating a desire to expand my knowing outside of myself. I knew that I was meant to have technology in my life, and that propelled me to start a career in tech — a career I love to this day.

In my thirtieth year, I felt blessed to have made it far along my path. I had earned everything I could imagine — I owned a three-story loft home, had a great career in the airline industry, had traveled to 25 countries, and had thriving relationships with family, friends, and loved ones. Then the day came where I received a phone call from a recruiter at one of the dream companies on my list — Amazon™. It was a long shot, but sure, why not? I'll give it a shot! From there, everything happened in a whirlwind. I went through a few phone interviews and was flown to the home office for several rounds of intensive on-site interviews. That ultimately landed me a, "We would like to extend an offer," email.

Just like the words, "You've got mail," thrilled me in the early days of the Internet, that one email made me dance like a second grader and feel happiness like never before. That familiar formula, money = happiness, surfaced in my mind with lots of dollar signs. This was it! I had surely made it now. I mean, I was on cloud nine! There couldn't possibly be anything else I needed.

To celebrate my achievement and scratch my travel junkie itch, it was off to Iceland's beautiful landscapes and ice-capped mountains to celebrate with my girlfriend. I remember standing out in the middle of the magical landscape quivering and shivering in one of the most joyful moments of discovery and one of the most beautiful sights I had ever experienced. I distinctly remember feeling I had surely hit my ceiling of happiness. Little did I know of the enlightenment that was upon me.

Feeling exhausted after a long day, I had laid my head down to catch some much-needed sleep. In the still of the night, I was rudely awakened by a pounding jackhammer in my head. I sat up, got some water, and tried to shake it off. Those would be the last movements I would make for a while. I tried to stand up once more, wanting to walk it off, but there was no doing that as my body would no longer move.

My girlfriend, awake now and realizing something was terribly wrong, called for medical assistance. Before I knew it, my life in a limp, immobile body flashed before me. I thought to myself, if this was the end, I was grateful for having lived quite an amazing life. And then my consciousness faded to blackness.

Miraculously, I awoke. I found myself laying under crisp white bed sheets in an Icelandic hospital bed. My loved ones told me I had had emergency brain surgery from a severe bleed known as an arteriovenous malformation (AVM) that instantaneously paralyzed my entire right side. It is estimated that 10 in 100,000 suffer an AVM; of those affected, about half result in a sudden hemorrhage like mine. As I lay there in the hospital no longer able to even add 2+2, denial quickly entered the room. I told myself it was a dream and I tried to get out of bed, only to collapse straight to the floor in a tangled heap of limbs. Well, so much for being a dream.

The next few months were a battle to regain my bearings. What was I to do now? I was at the top and — poof — was now at the bottom. It felt as if I had nothing; not even my health. I reran that familiar formula that I had learned decades ago, money = happiness, but it would no longer compute. That formula was all I had known until that point. I was lost.

My memories of those times are spotty at best, but I vividly remember laying in that hospital bed, wide awake, staring at the ceiling in the dead of the night. Ironically, I — who could no longer move fluidly from bed to bathroom without assistance — was thinking of my next move. The double whammy of the brain and physical impact was more than I could bear. Rudimentary tasks such as naming words that start with the letter 'S' drew blanks in my mind. Drinking a glass of water without giving myself a bath was a struggle. Yet this was my physical reality. My girlfriend, unable to cope, had fled both the hospital and our relationship. Witnessing my parents curled up in hospital chairs and blankets to stay by my side day in and out was both a blessing and nightmare. It was time to recalibrate. And that I did.

I painfully had to learn to value my happiness more than a dollar amount or professional status. For me, that was not easy at all. Here is the thing though: When I put my mind to something, I am committed to making it happen. There is no being in the middle. It was time to get back to the basics of being thankful and happy about the simple things.

I woke up the next day and took a deep breath. That breath, that gift of life, made me happier than any TV or car. Why? Because at its most basic form, it means I'm alive, and that is more than enough to celebrate and be happy about!

It took trial and error to learn that happiness is an intentional choice from within that can be made at any given moment. After living decades here on earth, I have come to find that emotions and feelings are also infectious. If I am on a high vibe among others, I have noticed that they often feel uplifted themselves; if I am distraught, then the energy level is lower across the board.

Over the years, I have found that the middle is often hell. Happiness awaits on either side. When I make a decision to forgo something, I have a clear path that I have committed space for. The inverse is true where I can commit to leaving space open for something else. It doesn't matter which path you choose; both can lead to happiness. Happiness is unleashed when you make the choice to step out of the middle and not just knock on one of the doors in front of you but go THROUGH it.

Walking through one of those doors provided me the prospective I needed. It showed that self-acceptance is a foundational component of happiness to me. It also taught me it's okay — if you like me, great! If you don't, great! Either way, it's great! I accept me. This is me! How you feel and how I feel are both great.

I have so much love and compassion that I give to the world. If I can impact or influence even just one person, then this is all worth it. Loving myself was the key I needed to unlock my happiness, and I found it all starts from within.

Confidence and gratitude for the little things are another key component of my happiness. I am beyond happy and blessed to be able to walk after my AVM incident, even if my steps are not pretty and a little funky. I hobble along with an awkward limp and handshake; but nevertheless, I OWN IT, as I am still me on the inside. That person is someone I can live with and will absolutely adore until my last breath. I know now that I have a bigger purpose here on earth and have no reason to waste any of that time being sad or feeling sorry for myself. Instead, I'm learning to spread the magical gift of gratitude.

My parents, my family, and my friends showered me with love and acceptance when I was in hospital for those many months, and I feel a huge need to continue spreading that love. I have found, given the trying circumstances unfolding around the globe, there is a need for making people laugh; to bring a bit of happiness into their world if only for a minute. I thought to myself, what is something that can be done virtually to touch humans in their homes? Boom! Alongside my good friend Francis, the *High Vibe Reports* on Facebook™ were born purely with the intention of making people laugh. It's the change that I want to see in the world more so than ever before.

For me, happiness is a whole world of doors to walk through. It's a refreshing new x = y formula that has nothing at all to do with money and everything to do with the most fundamental elements of human existence; those simple things that combine to make a life: acceptance, confidence, gratitude, laughter, and joyful enjoyment of each other.

The beauty is that YOU define what happiness is for yourself. Chocolate ice cream may be your haven or your worst enemy. What happiness is for me may not be what it is for you — different strokes for different folks, as they say — and that is quite alright. That is what makes you, *you*; and what makes me, *me*. And that is a beautiful thing.

As much as I feel the societal pressures to conform, forging my own jagged path has allowed me to learn who I am, accept who I am, and be happy with that person. That light had been something that I originally thought was lost forever. Little did I know that I just had to widen the beam so that I could see what I was missing out on and shine.

"I just want you to be happy," is commonly heard from our family, friends, and loved ones. Of course, we all deserve to be happy. It's the meaning and perspective I apply to it that differs. The realization, for me, is that happiness is a not concrete thing. It is fluid and — just like water — will evaporate if you don't replenish it. I learned that happiness is not persistent; it needs constant work. It is not a mathematical formula that, once mastered, is yours forever. Happy today does not mean happy tomorrow, and that's okay. It all starts with awareness and acceptance from within. No*thing* will TRULY quench our quest for happiness; it's a constant belief, passion, and drive that sustains internal happiness. But once attained, be grateful because happiness can disappear.

Letting go brings me happiness. The longer I dwell in the land of indecision, the further I get from happiness. The longer I fight against what is, the longer I stand undecided in front of two doors, the longer I dwell in the land of unhappiness. It's a hard lesson to learn to surrender, but a valuable one that puts us on the right path forward. Getting out of the middle and moving forward has been my rule of thumb. The facade is the knee-jerk easy path to happiness; *that* is not real. It's the temporary quick-fix satisfaction that I had mistaken for everlasting joy. It's ironic, but I believe that pursuit of the quick fix is rooted in our nature and in being not fully conscious. If I know what makes me happy, I know the path; why do I not always take it? I had to learn to get out of my own way. I learned to stop putting up my own barriers and focus on the reality instead of filling the space with wishes and stories.

Today, I still struggle with a significant right-sided paralysis and am unable to do the things I used to love. Nevertheless, I have embraced my situation and learned new ways to do the things I love, and to do new things that I was not able to do before. I realize everything happens for a reason. My AVM allowed me to reveal what is important to me. For myself, the gift of life, friends, and family have replaced mansions and sports cars. My realization is that the end is inevitable for all of us. Why spend even a single moment of this short life in anything but joy? I am not perfect by any means, but I have created my own formula for happiness. When faced with emotion, accepting it, learning from it, and releasing it to get back to my vibrant self is the change I now recognize and practice.

Let's face it, life can be a pile of dog doo-doo. We all go through the ringer. No one is exempt or immune. You never know when something as little as a bleed in your brain might throw everything you thought you had forever into jeopardy. The key is all in how you bounce forward and how you apply the learnings to every day that follows.

I have learned to create what happiness means to me. I have learned what happiness looks like when viewed through a new lens. And that is my message for you: You ALWAYS have the ability to choose your lens. You can have happiness at your fingertips whenever you want it! There is no 'too late.' The time is always NOW.

Go on, don't wait! Create your own happiness TODAY! Let's co-elevate our harmonious lens of happiness and, together, uplift this beautiful gift called Life!

Ignite Action Steps

Happiness, to me, is being yourself and not feeling the need to conform. The small nuggets are often all that is needed to set you on the trajectory of happiness. Own your happiness and choose a door; get out of the middle. What doorway will you choose to walk through today?

- Unlock and enable opportunities to express gratitude around you in your daily life, from the coffee shop to your evening reflections.

- Accept that everything will work out in the end as it is meant to be. Think, what is the worst that can happen? And live unapologetically.

- Surrender to and create the space to *feel* your emotions. This allowed me to lay a clear, conscious path forward to living my best life.

Jason B. Flores – United States of America
Tech Product Solutions Executive Leader, Travel/Transportation Industry
Entrepreneur, Co-founder, President & COO — Resilience Element
⊙ @typejason
jason@jbflores.com

IGNITE HAPPINESS ACTIVITY

Draw your life through a new happiness lens.

Create your own Happiness Formula

Health _____ + _____ = _____

Wealth _____ + _____ = _____

Relationships _____ + _____ = _____

Career _____ + _____ = _____

Success _____ + _____ = _____

Happiness _____ + _____ = _____

Next level happiness ;-)

_____ + _____ = _____

Sometimes eliminating or removing things from your equation is the key to true happiness.

− _____ = _____

− _____ = _____

− _____ = _____

JEREMY LAUE

"You are not alone."

I want you to take away a strategy that helps you get closer to achieving the happiness that you seek. Although learned through particularly emotionally difficult events, these lessons have shaped my interaction with the world and I hope they can do the same for you.

WHAT COULD I HAVE DONE?

I met Ryan at the beginning of my seventh grade year. Coming into a new and larger school, I felt a little lost and scared those first few weeks, as most friend groups had already been established. Seeking to belong somewhere, I joined our junior high cross country team, a group of six boys with whom I bonded over the excruciating pain of long-distance running. Among them was Ryan. Red hair. Freckles. Tall and lanky. Ryan never had a great desire to be the center of attention but any conversation with him had the potential to cause me to laugh my heart out.

When I first met him, I decided that Ryan was an awkward kid as he seemed somewhat uncomfortable when I'd try to talk to him, but I later discovered that his awkwardness was a great part of his charm. His jokes, although unorthodox, were incredibly clever, but you had to be paying close attention to understand them. Although I was occasionally the butt of his humor, it always seemed to make me feel closer to him.

The first day I attended cross country practice, we were tasked with running eight laps around the school track. As a junior high school kid with an endless supply of unearned confidence, I sprinted out determined to be the first to finish. The first lap was okay, the second lap was getting difficult, and by the time I got to the seventh and eighth laps, my lungs were working so vigorously that my breath stirred up the dust on the track. Needless to say, I didn't finish first.

After crossing the finish line, I remember looking back and seeing Ryan, steadily trudging along, step after step, coming up toward the end. All of a sudden, Ryan stopped. He stood there for a moment, doubled over, and threw up his lunch all over the track. Although disgusted at the time, we would tease him and laugh about it later as a team. If only I had known.

Oftentimes during practice, we would run together in a line, our breath synchronized to the rhythm of our feet pounding on the hard asphalt or track. But when we ran with Ryan beside us, we didn't get very far. Ryan's left shoe had a habit of always squeaking when he stepped. This small, high-pitched noise was enough to regularly halt our entire team, all of us laughing at Ryan and his noisy shoe. I never understood why he kept it for so long, but looking back, I am glad that he did even if it was just for the memories. If only I had known.

At the end of the school year, with the running season long-since finished, our team, with many other junior high students, was corralled into the gym on a rainy day. While fellow classmates played games such as basketball and volleyball, my cross-country team decided to put a spin on the most classic schoolyard game: tag. We decided that each person would be allotted two lives, corresponding with the number of shoes they had on. Each time someone was tagged, one shoe was removed until that person was slipping and sliding on the hardwood floor in their socks; they would then join the tagger's team. Being very agile and intensely focused on winning, I was able to dodge most of the tagging assailants coming my way, that was, until Ryan came along.

Toward the end of the round, I was running around the gym, dancing about, evading this hand and that. Just then, I turned around to see who was following me and, low and behold, the red-haired, freckled jokester himself was coming straight for me. With a determined look on his face, he raced at me while trying to cope with the lack of friction caused by the combination of his socks and the slippery floor. The whole scene was such a sight to behold that I laughed. I laughed so hard that I couldn't run anywhere. I was caught and tagged, all the while still laughing at that hilarious scene. If only I had known.

Years passed and I entered my tenth grade year. Now at a different school, focusing on different things, I no longer ran cross-country but instead was a member of the high school tennis team. On my way to the courts one afternoon,

I was met by a ninth-grade friend of mine, Ancel. He and I casually started up a conversation which eventually led to which junior high schools we attended. I told him that I went to San Marcos Academy at which his face darkened.

"So did you know Ryan?" he asked.

After telling him I did, he said softly, "He was a family friend of ours, and I just found out last night." Puzzled, I asked what happened.

Visibly saddened, Ancel shared, "He commited suicide two nights ago."

I fell silent.

This was my first close experience with death. At the time, all of my grandparents were still living, my dogs hadn't passed away, nothing. When I learned about Ryan, I didn't exactly know how to process what had occurred. I kept wondering how it could have happened to someone who I knew. I had heard about suicide in media and television but it never crossed my mind that it could happen to a friend of mine.

The day of the funeral, I slowly walked up the steps to the church. As I entered, I saw friends and family of Ryan's, all teary-eyed or sobbing, showing the scope of how many people Ryan deeply impacted over the course of his life. During the service, they played a few short video clips of Ryan talking to his running coach. Even two years after I had last seen him, Ryan was still making the same funny and clever comments he was known for.

Recalling my personal memories of him, all I could do was hopelessly contemplate what I could have done. What if I had called him the night it happened and just talked? Would the same events have transpired? My head was swimming and I was confused. I tried to remember what I was doing the night that it happened. Had I been too busy to talk? What if I just sent a text that just said "Hi"? What could have been more important than reaching out to a friend?

And then it hit me. I was never going to see Ryan again. I'd never hear him crack a joke or squeak his shoe. I'd never see him throw up on the track or make me laugh again. This reality felt overwhelming. I could have only imagined what Ryan's family felt.

Months passed and life seemed to eventually return to normal. I sat on the living room couch one day with my eight-month-old niece, Lily. TV was playing in the background as Lily bounced up and down in her crib. Seeing that I wasn't paying her any attention, she began to scrunch up her face and cry. Lily had the power to make anyone in my family give her attention when she wanted, and so, succumbing to that power, I rushed over. I grabbed her soft monkey toy and gently touched her face with it while she giggled and grinned her toothless smile. In her face, I saw my niece's innocence and genuine happiness and I realized the value of the life of the girl I held in my arms. And I loved her for that.

My baby niece taught me two of the most valuable lessons I know:

1. As simple as it may seem, life has value. There is a beauty and intricacy in the people and the world around us, but we are so often blind to it. Ryan probably never saw how many people he affected on a day-to-day basis just by being him. Although he had closer friends than me, he always managed to touch my day in some small way with the humor and awkward charm that he brought. I only wish he could have seen his value to those around him and seen that he had family and friends who truly cared for him. He wasn't alone.

I was always under the impression that I should tackle all of life's problems on my own. I figured that since I'm the one in the situation, it should be up to me to get through it. I rarely realized that there were people who had been down the exact same road that I was traveling and there were people who were going down it with me — which brings me to the second lesson I learned.

2. We are not alone. As my niece so obviously demonstrated, we need only ask for help and someone will come running. It doesn't matter who you are, or where you live, there is someone in this world who cares about you and would gladly help you shoulder your burden. As infants we are completely helpless, so we must cry out to survive, but as time progresses, we get so caught up with independence and individuality that we forget that we have people to fall back on. We forget that our happiness doesn't have to solely rely on ourselves. We forget that we are not alone.

The understanding of these two lessons helped tremendously with my ability to cope with the less beautiful parts of life. About a week before I finished writing this story, my grandfather passed away due to complications from a hip breakage. After hearing the news, I don't remember the walk to the car or the drive to my grandfather's house. It hadn't hit me yet. When I arrived at my grandparents' front door, I entered with my mom and dad and saw my grandmother utterly destroyed. This felt really strange to me as I'd never seen her quite so broken down. To me, she had always been a very strong, if opinionated, woman. After hearing her heart-breaking cries of grief and then seeing my mother's tears run down her face, I realized that it was my turn to be giving the help and that I had to be strong for them.

I forced myself to see the good in my grandfather's passing: he was no longer suffering and when he died, he was surrounded by people he adored. His life had love: which I believe, although cliché, is the greatest gift any human could ask for. After putting it in this different light, I became almost relieved that it was his time to go. But I wondered how I could find a way to tell my family this.

That night, we all sat around the dinner table, not saying much. I was trying to think of some way to cheer my family up when my eldest brother spoke up. He reminisced and told little stories about how Grandpa used to play pool and write in his Sudoku books, using the exact same mechanical pencil for years and how he would make silly facial expressions. Immediately, I knew what to do. I began racking my brains for my funniest and fondest memories of him. I spoke of when my grandfather and I had a burping contest and talked about his favorite old-fashioned expressions. I noticed that the gloom was lifting. My brother and I kept going until eventually everyone began chiming in with their own memories. We all spoke and laughed and loved knowing that Grandpa had a place in all our hearts. I saw my family's happiness at reliving our memories with Grandpa and I knew that they were also beginning to come to terms with his passing. We reminded ourselves that we weren't flying solo. We had each other and we dealt with our loss together.

I'm not by any means some spiritual guru but ever since my grandfather's passing, I have found it easier and easier to see the value of the life around me. Life's temporary nature, I believe, is what contributes to its grace. I have learned that we have to make the most of our lives and create happiness while we can, because we won't be here forever.

The world sucks sometimes, but we have our people who will stick with us every step of the way. Knowing that there are people for us and that life is full of value for experiencing, brings us one step closer to self-acceptance.

Happiness is not so much a destination but more so the journey getting there. The tools we acquire while overcoming the problems in our lives are what allow us to reach happiness through our own self-acceptance. If the journey was easy then everyone in the world would be happy and nobody would need this book. But through your acknowledgment that you are not alone, you give yourself the needed ability to achieve the happiness you seek to find.

Jeremy Laue – United States of America
Ignite Teen Project Leader, Fun Uncle, Cinema Connoisseur

Ignite Action Steps

1. Appreciate the life around you. But what does that mean? There is so much to our world that we have left to discover. In the hubbub and busy schedules of our everyday lives, we forget to just stop and have a look around. This 'look around' can mean different things for different people. For some, it is spending more time with loved ones, involving them in your life and taking the time to connect on an emotional level. For others, a simple walk in the woods can bring them closer to understanding the value of the world they live in. These seemingly small experiences allow us to take a break and live in the now, something that we need every now and then while combating the ferocities of modern life. By becoming closer to the world around us, we come to terms with its impermanence, bringing us closer to the true happiness we want to achieve. Take a few minutes and list three places where you could start 'looking around.'

_____

_____

_____

2. Remember that you are not alone. There have been a few times in my life when the world has felt absolutely overwhelming. As I grow up, I'm sure there will be more of these occurrences, perhaps increasing in severity. But I find comfort in the fact that I have people to help me get through these times. I have people who won't leave my side, no matter what. I also know that when the time comes, it will be my turn to stay by their side and they can count on me. Our pride keeps us from crying out for help oftentimes when we need help the most. But if we just recognize that the people in our life are there for a reason and know that they're there for us, we can become more willing to accept help in our times of need. Never, ever forget that you are not alone. List two people who you know you can count on and who can count you.

_____

_____

_____

3. Be open to giving help. We tend to not let on when we're going through a challenging time and we get so good at hiding our pain that the signs often go unnoticed. But just as we must be willing to open up when needed, we must be willing to offer our ears. This requires a little less action as we don't want to force people to accept our advice and help, but we do need to make sure that they know that we're there to talk to. They'll come to you when they're ready and you can help them feel less alone. Take a moment and think about someone you know who needs your help and write down one effective way you can show them that you care.

JANICE MULLIGAN

"More than just one life can be changed in seconds and inches."

If you're stuck in all you've ever known and are terrified of what you don't, maybe it's time to change. Not just one thing but everything! You can always come back to where you're at, but what if there's a way of life unlike anything you have ever known? What if on the other side of that leap there's a way to live unlike anything you've ever dreamed possible? I was a prisoner, locked up from the inside out, and today, one day at a time, I'm free! I hope that you can discover, like I did, that there is another way to live!

UNEXPECTED OUTCOMES

It was a sunny, cool winter morning in California. A Tuesday. I was shopping for a wedding dress surrounded by people who loved me: my sisters, my best friends, and future mother-in-law. They were so excited for me because in July, just seven months away, I would get to marry my soul mate. I wish I could say I shared in their excitement, but at that time of my life, I was incapable of any such emotion. I was dying on the inside, but not from a lack of love. That day, as I walked out of the dress store, I had a moment of clarity. I was just so exhausted. I was tired of my life, of my lies. I sat in the driver's seat and thought to myself, "You'll never make it to that wedding. You're going to be dead by July. You'd better start planning your funeral." A shiver went through my body from top to bottom. In that instant, I knew this to be a fact. I made a decision that day. I came up with this plan of "I'm gonna get sober on Friday."

I don't know why I chose Friday, December 14th; honestly I don't think I am the one who chose it. I now think that it was a divine appointment. But, there were still three days between that moment and Friday. I drove myself home with an unfamiliar relief inside of me. I had made a decision.

Thursday dawned an early cold winter morning. I'm not sure how long it had been since I had passed out the night before; everything was a bit hazy. I had been up late shopping at the mall for Christmas presents. I knew that, come Friday, my life as I had grown accustomed to was going to be over. I was trapped in the thought that I was never going to be able to do anything ever again because I was not going to drink. I do know I was up and down all night; most nights had become as such. But that Thursday morning in particular, I was woken up by my teenage son, Michael. He was standing at my bedside, sobbing, red-faced and with clenched fists, confusion and shock on his face. He was pretty shook up. He told me that his best friend's brother, Aaron, had committed suicide from carbon monoxide poisoning. He was just a teenage boy! "Why, Mom? Why did he do it?" This was a question I could not answer.

I felt as though I was suffocating and this painful feeling was all too familiar to me. You see, when I was just 16 years old, I heard the words, "He shot himself; Ed shot himself!" That was a day I wish I could rewind, that I could change, but I knew I couldn't. Ed was my brother, my Irish twin, my best friend. He was 15 when he was found with a shotgun laying across his chest and a hole in his head. This was a day I'd never forget, and as I heard Michael's words, it felt as if it had happened all over again.

I, too, was pretty shook up… from my memories, but also for a completely different reason — I was still drunk from the night before and had to take a moment to orient myself and figure out where I was. You see, I am an alcoholic mom. I can't remember the last time I actually woke up refreshed and renewed. Most days, still intoxicated and sleep deprived, I had to piece together what was happening every time I came to.

Up until that moment, I had never considered the thought that my drinking was hurting anyone other than myself. That moment though… it was unlike any I've ever experienced. It changed me. Seeing my son's pain at my bedside, something shifted. A mountain was moved. I found myself lost in my son's tears. My cold, dead heart cracked open and as I looked at him, so distraught and powerless, my soul was fiercely shaken. From that moment, there was no turning back on tomorrow.

Michael went off to school that morning and I was left with me. I shuffled to the toilet where I threw up, and then I took a handful of pills and hoped I could keep those down. I needed to level off, so I could gain some composure and gather my thoughts. I reflected a lot that day, more than I had in a long time. I found myself driving the car past the house where this tragedy had transpired; a young man had ended everything all in a matter of a few hours.

As I peered at the closed garage door, I couldn't help but think about the lives that would permanently be rearranged from his decision. And for the first time in my life, as a 36-year-old woman, I realized I was not unique nor different from Aaron or Ed. I, too, was committing suicide, a slow painful suicide. It may have looked a little different from those boys; sure there was no gun, no car in the garage running. Instead there was a bottle of booze and pain pills. These were my weapons, and for all those years it just seemed ok, but that day I saw what it was. I was killing myself.

Standing back at my house that afternoon, it was plain as day. It was as if the clouds had parted and a stream of light passed through my soul. I could see what I had never been willing to see. I had become accustomed to playing the game of Russion Roulette with my life and the lives of my four children and fiancé! Alcohol gave me wings to fly, but then it took away the sky! Yet I did this every day and, for some inexplicable reason, on this day I had awoken and become aware that this was no longer *okay*. Any given day, I could have fallen asleep never to wake up. The thought of my children coming into my room to say good morning Mom, but Mom not being there… to have fallen off to sleep forever by my own hands… what then? A corpse, a shell, my life gone if I kept on. It made me sick to my stomach to think of what could have been. What kind of life would my kids have trying to unsee my demise!

The idea exploded in my head that day, and I can only assume it was by the grace of God. I thought to myself, perhaps there's a different way, a different path. Over the past 18 months, I had been going to a 12 step program, but I was not sober. I was doing everything that was suggested except the 'don't drink or use' part. I really thought I was different. I couldn't imagine life without alcohol. But on that day, I thought, maybe those people in the meetings are right. Maybe this thing *could* work for me. That Thursday was the last day I picked up a drink, the last day I was loaded.

I 'came to' the next morning — Friday — and I dropped to my knees. I prayed a prayer I've never meant more in my life! I begged and pleaded with all the desperation I had in me, mixed in with 20 plus years of chaos, drinking, using, lying, cheating, and stealing. I asked whoever, whatever was out there for help. I'm sure the prayer went like this: "Dear God, help me not to drink or use today! I don't want to die, and I can't live like this anymore! Please God take this, I am willing to do whatever it takes to never pick up ever again! I can't do this without you; this I am certain of. Please God HELP ME!"

The pain and loneliness that comes from alcoholism is unbelievable. I had become so immune to it, I don't even think I realized how far gone I was. My way of living was not living. I had people around me who loved me. People planning for the future. But I couldn't see past myself. I would go to any lengths to get drunk and mow over anyone who stood in my way.

I was 19 years old, and an active duty Marine when I had Michael, my first born. I was a kid having a kid, a single mom. My intentions were always to be the best mom; however, an alcoholic mom who is drinking is not capable of being the best mom. Michael kept me as grounded as possible. He was always there and in the back of my mind; he was what stopped me from pushing to the point of no return.

Over the next fifteen years of drinking, I went from being a pretty happy person who enjoyed a good party, loved happy hour, and always thought that the *sign and sail* card at the cruise ship bar was the best invention ever, to an angry shell of a person. Others around me could drink and still be functional, yet alcohol was eating me from the inside out. My confusion was bigger than I could even comprehend — why was my life not working for me as it once did? One kid turned into two kids, followed by a failed marriage, then three and then four kids... all the while never considering a different lifestyle. There were moments where I would get a nudge; I'd think maybe when they all grow up and move, I can try to stop drinking. No Way! Chances are better of hell freezing over than me quitting drinking. I didn't know it at the time, but I needed all of this to get me to my knees. I Am A Miracle!

The things I did in my addiction that I am less than proud of are my greatest assets today. Those demoralizing things motivated me on a whole new level — a level that only became reachable because of suffering at my own hand. God had a plan for me. A BIG plan. When I was drinking, I couldn't ever comprehend in my soul what a gift my children were to me. Ever since that Thursday when Aaron died, I can't help but have this internal nag that tells me, "I could have missed this happiness!" I have found my purpose, but boy, has it been a journey getting here.

The impact Aaron's death had on me and by extension my children and others who love me was not yet finished. When I was 82 days sober, I was at my regular Saturday morning women's meeting. I was having one of those days where you just wonder, "What's the point?" Changing everything I've ever known was the hardest thing I've ever done in my life. My kids hated me, or at least that's what I thought at the time. I would later learn my kids were afraid of the monster I was when I was drinking.

As I sat in that cold church basement, there were children playing in the room across from us. Their bright, happy colorful selves were a painful contrast to the gray within me. I was seeking a solution that felt impossible to attain. I felt hopeless. Poor me, poor me, Pour me another drink! I was exhausted, feeling lost, questioning my worth as a parent, not connected at home, and just wondering, "Is this all worth it? Why am I here, what am I doing?" At the end of the meeting, it was birthday time and I was caught in my own shit. I was ready to bolt, but I couldn't leave without being noticed, so I just sat there. A woman got up in front of us to speak. She was celebrating a two-year milestone. Everyone was happy it seemed, but me. I was stuck in my head. Little by little, her words trickled into my consciousness. At first I wasn't paying attention so much, until she said that on December 13th, her oldest grandson, Aaron, had taken his own life.

I had chills from head to toe. I popped my head up and tears started running down my face. I leaned over to my friend, who was sitting next to me, and grabbed her hand. I knew I was exactly where I was supposed to be! She talked about what the last year of her life was like. She said her husband had suffered two brain aneurysms. I started to bawl. I couldn't compose myself. I was alive because of what happened to her grandson! I was awakened because on that December morning, Aaron's eyes closed for the last time and mine finally started to reopen. He was gone, but I was finally here. This awful, irreversible event changed the course of both our lives forever!

There's lots to be said for a drunk mom who comes to one day and realizes she has four kids. The next few years, I would embark upon a journey that some would possibly turn their back on. I've heard it referred to as the Path of the Spiritual Warrior. There were lots of tears, fights, fears, and painful days that turned into weeks. I found out at 18 months of sobriety that I was pregnant with our fifth child but something was tragically wrong. We lost that baby four months later. I couldn't understand it. I was Sober. Why, God? But through it all, I didn't drink. I stayed on the path. That tragedy became a blessing, teaching me without a doubt what a God-given miracle my four kids were. They had survived despite my many careless choices.

It was not always easy to be sober. I had no idea how to be a parent and there came a time when I was forced to seek outside help. But then there were days that were magical, enchanting, and in rhythm with a power, a Force I call God.

Those were the days when I would seem to tingle from my head to my toes almost the entire day. What was that tingle, that happiness, you ask? I believe it is God.

I don't recall the last time I truly belly laughed, possibly since before my brother died. But as the days turned into weeks and weeks into months, something started to unfold. Joy and laughter. There were moments when I started to enjoy being sober, laughing with friends, crying over the ridiculous. My belly hurt from the joy of it. And it felt *fantastic!*

At two and a half years clean, Thomas, my sober baby, came into the world and I knew our family was complete. Day by day, I was healing all the relationships around me. I thank God every day for those painful steps. I could have missed what was coming next and now I share a bond like no other with my kids. My daughter and I started to connect through music. When I didn't know what to say to her or vice versa, we turned up the country music loud. We sang and sometimes danced and this feeling of happiness would bubble up and take over. I would remember being a little girl listening to country music with my dad… Patsy Cline, Willie Nelson, all the voices of my childhood bringing joy to my own children now. My middle daughter is really a daddy's girl. He raised her those first five years of her life while I drank; that's the truth. But with this new lease on life, I've bonded with all three of my daughters in a way I never knew possible. They share things with me that I probably never should know, and it makes me so happy! Thomas has known a completely different mom than I was able to be for Michael. My kids trust me now and feel safe with me. That makes me so Happy. Just to think, I could have missed all of this.

There were so many times that I couldn't show up emotionally before, and now I can and I do. Alcohol had blocked me from the sunlight of the spirit. I remember sitting in the theater watching my oldest daughter dance on stage while emotions I couldn't identify brewed within. I felt like crying, but I was not a baby. Crying is for babies. The first time, I fought those feelings and pushed them back. Watching my son play football, the same thing started to happen. What was this feeling? I just wanted to cry but I couldn't understand why! It had been so long since I had felt anything other than dead, but something warm and fuzzy was happening. *I was happy.*

Graduations, dance recitals, musicals, ice skating, cheerleading camps, swim lessons, camping trips, roasting smores, Christmas Eve, Easter Sunday egg hunts, surprise birthday parties, parent teacher conferences, pool parties, concerts, roller skating. You name it, it happened: I was happy! The feelings that arose in these experiences took my breath away and those tears slowly started to come out into the open. As they began to surface, I began to water my roots! I have since come to recognize that those tears are tears of Happiness, pure joy, and delight. The reality and awareness is in me as sure as the sun rises in the east and sets in the west, that 'I could have missed all of this.' That is the most profound thing to me as a mom of five kids today!

The more I let go, the bigger my life got! The more I surrendered, the more I gained. From being almost a stranger to my kids to becoming their person in times of distress, it has been an amazing journey. I had given up drinking and gained the love and trust of my family. The best thing that I can do as a mom today is stay sober. For me, it took a single day of decision, a little poke from God, and a lot of action to show me a world of Happiness unlike anything I ever thought possible.

If you're struggling with any sort of addiction, something that has a hold of you, what if you, too, could break free from those chains? It may not look like you think it's going to look, but it's better than you can ever imagine. Don't leave before the miracle happens. Are you ready to make today your Friday?

IGNITE ACTION STEPS

- Journal. Physically write at least five things down on paper before you start your day! Writing what I call 'God letters' in a journal helped me get through each moment. Put pen to paper and turn your worries over to God. Write a letter to your Higher Power, Spirit of the Universe, Mother, supreme being, *whatever...* every day, ask Him or Her to show off for you today!
- Practice 365 days of gratitude for your kids, husband, wife! Get a journal for each of the people you love. Every day, write something that you are grateful for concerning them. At the end of one year, give them their journal as a gift.
- Addictions strain relationships. For any strained relationship issues, my kids and I had an assignment. My kids listed everything they hated about me, everything they were upset over, things I did when I was drinking. I wrote my own list: everything I loved about them. We sat in a room together as they read their list to me. My only job was to listen. I did not defend myself. Then, I read them my list.

Janice Mulligan – United States of America
DVBE Contractor/ Retired Marine / Loving mother & wife
◎ sobriety_rocks

REBECCA BLUST

"You are responsible for your happiness; in fact, you create it."

My wish for you is that by reading my story you will understand just how powerful you are and that you and only you get to create your happiness. You don't have to wait for that relationship, job, event, or anything else. Stop missing out on your life. Start today and Ignite your happiness.

GENERATING YOUR HAPPINESS

I can remember being so full of happiness that I would look up at the sky, grip the steering wheel in glee, and screech, "I am so happy!" It bubbled out of me and felt effortless. I often had the sense of weightlessness and pure joy like anything could happen. Yes, I was one of *those* people, those 'obnoxiously' happy people — until I wasn't.

I was in my mid-forties and I was convinced I had it all. An easy and content marriage, a career I loved, and two daughters I cherished. I was blessed to be able to stay home with each girl, only going back to work two days a week after they were older. The girls and I spent so much time playing, cuddling, reading, going to the park, and having playdates. It felt like summer vacation all year long. One of my fondest memories was giving them some art supplies and coming back to see that my oldest had decorated popsicle sticks and taped them to their foreheads because they were unicorns. My youngest looked so proud with her fat little cheeks and a popsicle stick taped to her forehead. She beamed up at me and said, "Mamma, I'm a unicorn."

Life was joyful and flowing, everything seemed easy.

Eventually, I went back to work teaching sixth grade part-time. It seemed ideal; I was able to get off work about the same time as my girls, and I had every vacation day off they had. My little family was happy and my working situation was perfect. I was fulfilled and got to spend quality time with my children while still having rewarding adult connections during my week.

Then, what seemed to me like suddenly, but had been slowly progressing for years, my stable marriage ended. This was after 16 years of being together and it felt devastating that I had failed. My parents have been married for over 60 years and I had planned to be married for life. I couldn't believe that my happy home had become a statistic. How were my girls going to handle this? How was I going to cope financially? What were my friends and family going to think? Those were some of the thoughts that spun around and around in my head causing me to feel, for the first time, not so happy, but in fact completely overwhelmed.

Our decision wasn't sudden and we had many, many discussions as our marriage was deteriorating. The one and only conversation that stands out was the day we decided it was over. I will never forget that moment. It was a heart-wrenching conversation. I felt angry, worried, and also a tiny bit of relief. We decided we would tell the girls together, so we could remain a united front.

We brought the girls into the living room and sat them down. Although I couldn't tell you what we shared, I will never forget the emotions that I felt. My brain seemed to be filled with cotton and buzzing like static at the same time. I couldn't comprehend anything that was being said around me. It was like an out of body experience. My heart was beating through my throat, and tears were clouding my eyes, barely being held back by my eyelashes. The whole thing felt surreal.

The only thing I do recall is my youngest, looking at us, her eyes panicked and huge. She screamed, "You are lying! You are lying!" Her dad quietly said, "Honey, we aren't lying." She started sobbing, She wept and wept — her pain like an open wound, while I held her and my heart broke. I felt like a terrible mother. How could I be causing this pain to my cherished baby? The person I would lay my life down for.

It took hours to calm her and we reassured her of our love and devotion as her parents. My oldest acted the opposite, like it wasn't a big deal. Falsely hiding her feelings behind a teenage attitude.

I remember writing in my journal that night, *My heart is broken, My heart is broken...* over and over with tears streaming down my face — salty drops drenching the page. I was raw and broken inside. Not broken for me, broken for her — this innocent, wonderful light of a child, whose whole world had changed. Still, thinking of that moment brings a rush of tears to my eyes and a tightness to my throat. I would have thought that would be my emotional bottom, but it wasn't even close.

As if my separation wasn't enough to deal with — my work stability crumbled at the same time. My school district entered into an ugly drawn out teachers' strike. It seemed as if each side couldn't fling enough negativity at the other. It was in the newspapers, part of every conversation, and community businesses were taking sides. The negativity of it was infectious; it poured out of the people I worked with and into my inner world which was already rocked by a separation and the heartache of my children.

I will never forget standing outside of the school I had taught at for 20 years, side by side with my fellow teachers, picketing the strike. We all stood shocked, looking at the new gate that had been installed. It resembled something a prison would use: tall, silver, with razor wire on top. Soon, armed police arrived inside the gate looking as if *they* were protecting the school from *us*! I don't know what they thought we were going to do. Rush the fence and climb over? We were adored school teachers just wanting to get back to work.

Every morning a blacked-out bus would arrive wheeling around the corner at an unsafe speed carrying the kids heading off to school. It barely missed people, blasting by us and powering through the open gate. At one school, someone actually got run over by one of those rushing buses. It was crazy! Did they think we were going to attack the bus? Filled with children who we loved? I remember feeling so outraged, so angry. How dare they treat us like criminals and act as if we were a danger. How was it that we could go from 'beloved teachers' to 'dangerous criminals' so quickly?

My life had evaporated. It had gone from happy, secure, and flowing to full of conflict, negativity, and insecurity. My school district had painted me and all the other teachers as dangerous people; my husband had moved out and I carried this dark cloud of guilt that I had fractured my children's secure world.

How had I gotten here? What had happened? This is what I was thinking as I leaned my head in the shower against the wet tile, hot water pouring down my face, while sobs punched through my gut, racking my body for the umpteenth time that month. I let my anguish out in that tiny space hoping the water and shut doors concealed the sound of my grief. I didn't want my daughters to hear me. I couldn't be that mom who was losing it. I remember wishing I had a 'Get Out of My Life' card that I could somehow play.

I was done — done with the pain.

I asked myself, "What had happened to that buoyant happy person I used to be? When had the stress become so overwhelming? How had my committed relationship gone from being connected and joyful to full of conflict and eventually ending? How had my fulfilling career gotten turned into an ugly thing that left me feeling like a villian? How had I gone from being a great mom to being one who broke her children's hearts? What had happened to that spark I used to have?" I had moved so far from the happy person that I knew myself to be.

I would have loved to be able to blame something or someone. It would be easier; I could blame the strike, how we were being treated, my former husband, the divorce, someone, something. But I knew deep down it was me and only me who was responsible for my happiness. I knew with a certainty that if I was going to be happy again that it was up to me. No one was going to come along and save me — which felt both empowering and scary at the same time.

I could see that little by little, I had made choices that led me down a path to inner darkness and feeling overwhelmed. I had temporarily lost my resilience because without knowing it, I had stopped the practices that had kept me at a higher level of well-being. I wasn't working out or doing my daily gratitude practice. I had stopped hanging out with connected friends because they were associated with my teaching role or my marriage. I found myself in a life without gratitude, connected relationships, meaningful work, and the feeling of flow. What I was left with was a bunch of DOing and not BEing. I felt burned out and left out. You see, I am a doer and if I am not doing and feeling accomplished and getting kudos, I feel anxious and like I am wasting my time. My worth was tied to my activity and what I could accomplish, and I found myself in the painful position of not seeing my value as a wife, teacher, or mother.

Why did I choose to let this happen? I couldn't tell you. My life slipped away without me realizing it. On that day, in the shower, when I laid my head against that wet tile, I knew I had to change, and I knew it was up to me. I knew if I sunk any lower, I would choose the 'get out of my life card' and end it all. I was horrified that I was feeling so low that I could even contemplate leaving my daughters. I understood that my small decisions had gotten me to where I was. No one was coming to save me.

In that shower I made a conscious choice that going forward, I wasn't going to just *live*, I was going to THRIVE! I was going to reignite my happiness. I was going to overcome the mental turmoil, not crying in the shower daily, feeling stressed and depressed. I was going to have a life of joy and ease with connected relationships, a meaningful career, and a fulfilling purpose in *my* life.

I became determined to pull myself back to the happy, buoyant person I had been. The first thing I needed to do was leave my job. It no longer felt like my calling. That was my first step.

The next step was finding the path back to myself. It wasn't easy and it wasn't overnight. It was hard work. Some days, even several days in a row, I'd feel like, "Yes!" I have this." Then I'd find myself drinking an entire bottle of wine, tears creating rivulets down my face, as sobs hiccupped out of me. Then, the next week or two would be great. It went on like this for about two full years.

What kept me going was my girls. I clearly saw how my moods and well-being directly affected them. Even though I hid the days that weren't so good for me, or thought I was, they often reflected my moods, for better and for worse. As I climbed out of the darkness, they seemed lighter, less negative, and happier.

I diligently kept at the work of rebuilding my inner happiness. I delved into positive psychology, reading books, watching videos, listening to podcasts, and taking courses. Finally, I started to see progress from my daily practices: gratitude, meditation, letting go, exercise, eating well. Eventually, I was happier more often than I was sad. Soon I was mostly happy.

Slowly, my outer world began to reflect my inner world. I've met a wonderful man who is adventurous, smart, and has a vision to help the world. I created a totally new fulfilling career that I love. Now, I travel the globe and meet amazing people who have a big impact and give with hearts of service. I maintained a healthy co-parenting relationship with my former husband as we raise our kids together. We celebrate holidays together, sit together at school events, and he comes over for family dinners.

I learned that it is easy to be happy when things are great and I learned you can reginite your happiness after hardships and trauma. I realized I was empowered and I could create happiness from within and then have that happiness as a reserve to draw on when the challenges come up — because they will.

Our culture leads us to believe that happiness is outside of us and that it is contingent upon others around us, events that are happening, and what we have or don't have, when in reality it is inside of us. Each one of us has the ability to grow that inner happiness so that when challenges come along, and they will, you can build your inner resilience allowing you to move through difficulties more easily — and quickly. That creates a different life.

My passion in life is to help people understand that happiness is not only their responsibility but it is within their reach. Once they understand that...

they are empowered to change. They don't have to wait for anything external to shift. It doesn't take immense bravery, strength, or self control to change the trajectory of your life. It takes one tiny step in a new direction, backed by the belief that you can change and you are responsible for that change. We all can begin to or even reignite our happiness through positive strategies that are simple and only take minutes a day.

Just imagine what life would be like having your thoughts full of gratitude and positivity. Picture having all of your relationships full of calm and ease because you are focused on others strengths and their goodness. Envision choosing your reactions from the best version of yourself.

Here's to the life you love, *all of it.*

Ignite Action Steps

If you want to Ignite your happiness, the easiest thing you can do to shift from negative to positive is to keep a gratitude journal.

There have been many studies about gratitude and its impact on our bodies, mental health, emotional well-being, and our relationships. All of them point to an overwhelmingly positive impact.

Robert Emmons is the world's leading scientific expert on gratitude. He did a study where he had people keep a gratitude journal for three weeks and the results were overwhelming. According to Emmons:

1. Gratitude allows us to celebrate the present. It magnifies positive emotions which is important since we are wired for negativity and we often gloss over positive emotions.
2. There's recent evidence, including a 2008 study by psychologist Alex Wood in the Journal of Research in Personality, showing that gratitude can reduce the frequency and duration of episodes of depression.
3. Grateful people are more resilient. Meaning when a stressful or challenging situation arises, they'll recover more quickly.
4. Grateful people have a higher sense of self-worth.

How do you get started with a gratitude journal?

Rebecca Blust – United States of America
Positive Change Agent
www.positivethinkingrevolution.com

Ignite Happiness Activity

Gratitude Journaling

How do I do it?

Keeping a gratitude journal can be as easy or involved as you want it. You can write complete sentences like, "I am grateful for a healthy family." Or, you can write, "I am grateful" at the top of the page and make lists. All you need is something to write in and something to write with.

How does it work?

Since we are wired to see negativity more than positivity, this practice helps us refocus so we can see the positive in the big and small things.

How long does it take?

If you want to successfully create a gratitude journal habit, tie it to another habit you already have like writing in the journal after brushing your teeth. Make it easy! You won't start something new if it feels like work. Make sure your journal and writing utensil are in a place you can easily grab them. In the beginning, limit yourself to two or three things to be grateful for unless it feels easy and joyful to write more. Make it rewarding by using something that is attractive and feels good to use. Maybe it's a gorgeous journal or a pen that feels like silk when you are writing.

First, find a habit that you can tie your gratitude journal too, preferably at night like when brushing your teeth. Your established habit will become a cue for your new habit.

Second, make it easy to do by having your journal and a writing utensil you like using stored where you can see them.

Third, start small. Research shows us that we won't stick with a new habit if it is hard, so start with only two entries.

Remember, just like physical fitness, your emotional and mental fitness has to be taken care of daily.

JOYE MADDEN

"Each one of us deserves someone who is capable
of holding our sacred space."

My hope is that you never have to feel alone again. When we have a witness to our story, we can find hope and healing. The pain stemming from mental illness and addiction has deeply affected my family, and at times was truly unbearable. I am here to offer proof from my own experience, that healing and happiness are available to us all.

I HAVE WALKED THIS PATH ALONE — YOU DON'T HAVE TO.

My story started 47 years ago when I was born into a family that has suffered generations of addiction and mental illness. We lived in a small town in Alabama, United States where almost everyone knew everyone. My dad worked for my grandfather, a successful businessman, and they were both well known in our community. Very early on, appearances were an important part of my life. Everything looked 'perfect' on the outside. But, on the inside of our beautifully decorated family home, it was very different.

My mom suffered from major depression, which often kept her hostage to her bed for weeks at a time. She attempted suicide many times and experienced many drug overdoses. She and my dad never appeared to be a 'happy' couple. My dad traveled a lot with his job and he spent many months at a time away from home in treatment for his alcoholism. I learned to 'adult' early on — there were times where either my mom or dad would be away at treatment and I was home with the other one. I can remember when my mom would leave, I would be terrified that something would happen to my dad. I often had to wake him up in the middle of the night and put him to bed after being passed out in his black leather recliner. I felt as though I had to always be there to take care of the other parent — cooking, chores, whatever needed to be done. That environment in which I grew up, where depression and addiction took center stage, was also the environment in which my parents were raised. The unconscious conditioning, cultural background, and the genetic disposition were perfectly set for me and my children to carry on the dysfunctional environment. It was like the exact egg and the exact sperm were perfectly matched in the petri dish and the predictable identity was formed — all the factors were there to produce another generation riddled with mental health challenges. And, in some ways, that is exactly what happened.

Growing up, I developed coping mechanisms to face the trauma I was regularly experiencing in my home. There was not a set of values instilled in me to live by or strive for. Most of the time, I was left to my own devices to manage my way through my childhood and young adulthood. I became very capable of taking care of myself, but I also harbored a lot of resentment for not having anyone to take care of me like I witnessed happening in other homes. My childhood consisted of mostly playing alone. I did not have any siblings, so my parents would buy all the Barbie™ dolls, Cabbage Patch Kids™ and doll houses, so that I would just 'be quiet' and play in my room. My room became my safe haven. The walls were a bright turquoise and my bedspread was a rainbow. I had white wicker furniture and I can still hear the creaks and cracks it would make when I opened a drawer or sat at my desk. I learned very quickly to stay 'out of the way' because I thought that would make my parents happy. I was an able caretaker, people pleaser, and perfectionist. I learned that the more I controlled, the more I gained the order and structure that I was regularly seeking. These were coping skills that helped me through my childhood, but didn't serve me when I applied them to parenting or my marriage.

As a young girl, I dreamed of having children. I knew that I wanted more than one and I intensely believed that I would be a better mom than mine was. I can remember thinking that I would get up every morning and make their breakfast, that I would never be late to carpool, and that I would make sure they brushed their teeth every morning and every night. In my small, innocent head, I believed that was all it would take. I would just 'be there' and that would be enough. I thought that marrying the man who would whisk me away, living in our home with the white picket fence with two dogs and two kids would bring me happiness. That was the answer to me becoming happy and getting out of the dysfunction of my family home.

Seventeen years ago, I was blessed with Morgan, the first of my three beautiful children. After several years of infertility, as I approached 30 years old, it had finally become my turn. I was finally a mom! My dream was coming true and happiness was right around the corner. I could just feel it.

As each of my children was placed in my arms at birth, my dreams for them were filled with joy. The look of pure innocence and stillness took my breath away. What I did not realize was that each of these precious souls would struggle with their own individual journey and two of them would face their own mental health challenges. The fight against mental health had now paved its way into the next generation.

On May 2, 2015, early in the morning hours, I received a call that my mom was on a ventilator and they were not sure that she was going to make it. I quickly woke up, threw my clothes on, and went searching for my keys. As I passed through the kitchen, I remembered what day it was. It was Morgan's 11th birthday. She was not awake yet and I would miss her smiling face as she came running down the stairs. We love birthdays in our home. We celebrate big time and always have this special routine on birthday mornings — we have balloons, Krispy Kreme™ donuts, and we throw streamers. A rush of feelings came over me. I was angry with my mom. I had been down this road with her many times before… always rushing to the hospital, only to watch her embarrass herself on the hospital table because she was so 'high.' I was sad knowing that I would miss being present for *my* daughter's celebration. I found Morgan's card that I had not yet signed, filled it out, and left it on the breakfast table for her to see as soon as she sat down. My mom died in my arms, two hours after I arrived at the hospital.

Morgan and my mom had a bond between them that was more than I could ever make sense of. I always remember feeling jealous in a way. I wished that my mom had given me the attention that she so openly gave Morgan. They had special signs and secret messages that stayed between them. When my mom passed, it was devastating for Morgan. The look on her face at the burial will be with me forever. She stared at everyone shoveling dirt on to the coffin, unable to take her eyes off it. My heart broke for her. It was like a piece of her died with my mom. Then there was me. I was sad, but there was a piece of me that was relieved. I had been my mom's 'target' for emotional and verbal abuse for years. I was exhausted. For decades I had felt trapped by my mother's emotional abuse but I hadn't found my voice to speak up for myself or set boundaries. I never could be good enough. I always felt so responsible for her feelings that I didn't know my own emotions. Yet, I blamed her for everything. I blamed her for my unhappiness, my unhealthy relationship patterns, my insecurities, and my deep sense of low self-worth. If she would have been a better mom, then I would be happy. I wondered, with her gone, would I finally be free? Would I finally be able to be myself?

It was around the time of my mom's death that I began to see the signs of mental illness in my daughter. Her death was very traumatic for Morgan and trauma is often a leading cause of the onset of anxiety disorders.

As Morgan and I grieved my mom's passing, we became deeply enmeshed. When she was unhappy, I was unhappy. When she was having a good day, I had a good day. When she was in the depths of her depression, so was I. I didn't know where she began and I ended. We were a big tangled knot, all intertwined with one another. I had no boundaries. To be honest, I was not even sure what a boundary was. Professionals had talked to me about them, but I thought if I had 'boundaries', then she wouldn't love me, or she would feel as though I didn't love her. I didn't learn until two years later that I had it all backward. The first step to learning that was hitting rock bottom.

My journey to the bottom started off one Saturday afternoon in November, when we had just gotten home from an Alabama football game. The whole family had been together and had what I would call, 'a good day.' Good days typically meant there was not a lot of fighting, everyone got along, and there was more laughter than crying. That night, as we were all getting ready for bed, Morgan came to me, trembling and in tears. She had scratches all over her body where she had been 'picking' and told me that she was consumed with the thought of killing herself. The only thing she said was that picking at her skin and eating excessively were the only things that took the pain away and she was pleading for my help. Hearing those words coming from my child brought me to my knees. We rushed her to the ER, and after several hours of observation, were sent home. As I climbed into bed with her that night, I laid there watching her breathe. I was too afraid to leave her, too afraid that she would harm herself. I didn't sleep at all that night. It was in those hours that I felt as though something 'awakened' me. A little voice inside me said something has to change and that something is *you*. For the first time, I recognized that Morgan was drowning, and I was allowing her to take me down with her. I had become her emotional lifeline. I could barely take a breath of my own because she was sucking all the air out of my lungs.

I had to stop. I had to step off the merry-go-round. The cycle of mental illness that had invaded my family for years had to be broken. I was lost in feelings of fear, sadness, anger, confusion, and helplessness. My 'go to' had been to push those feelings down and martyr my way through, but I knew that doing something different was the first step to change. I lay there weeping... longing for connection... desperate for a lifeline from someone who had gone through what I was experiencing. But who? Where could I find them? How do I find that person who won't judge me... who would hold me and allow me to share this secret and cry? I needed to hear that someone understood and to watch their head nod up and down, giving me the comfort that I was not alone anymore. My happiness was gone, and I so desperately wanted it back. But, then I began to question myself. Had I really ever been happy, or truly safe or authentic in being the mom I wanted to be? At that moment, all that I knew was that I could not help my daughter if I couldn't help myself.

Finding that 'someone' was hard for me. I was ashamed, scared, and so afraid that the mom I had become would be judged. The easiest thing for me to do in the beginning was to go to 12-step meetings. I found the courage and strength to attend my first Al-Anon™ meeting. I was petrified, but I was desperate. As I walked in the door, I was immediately welcomed. Those faces in the circle nodded their heads up and down as I slowly began to share parts of my story. They understood. They didn't judge me. They gave me hugs after every meeting and told me that I wasn't alone. From those meetings, I began to find other ways to generate feelings of happiness again. I found like-minded people who shared parts of my journey. I began to meditate, exercise, eat more greens and fruits in my diet. I got out in nature. I listened to music and played with my kids. I found ways that made me happy. Once I could connect with my own magical and mystical self, I could connect with my daughter.

As the months progressed, we both set off on our own paths to healing. I felt alone on this path. But through grace, the Universe, God, or whatever you want to call it, I finally got to the place where I let my sword down and put my armor away. I slowly began to take off the masks that I had been wearing. I stopped being the person that others wanted me to be and started to uncover the person who I knew I could be. I was beginning to see the glimmering of lights shine through. Days of feeling happy were peeking their way through into my previously shadow-filled life. I dug deep into my soul and started to heal the child within me who was so desperately wounded. I finally freed myself from the shackles that bound me to my childhood.

Emerging from the immense pain in my life was a mountain of growth and healing. But climbing that mountain is a choice that we ultimately have to make for ourselves. Pain is inevitable, but misery is optional. I kept asking myself, "Do I want to stay stuck in my misery, or do I want to go deep inside, find just a tiny bit of courage, and start to look for the key to unlock the happiness that is already within me?" Staying in my misery was, in some ways, easier. It was comfortable because it was all I ever knew. Jumping off that cliff and making the decision to go back to my past, dredge up the memories and relive that pain was scary. It was both messy and emotional but I had to go through the muck to clear the waters. It was the only way.

Morgan and I are on now a path to recovery separately, and we are on one together. She works on herself, and I work on myself and we come together to work on our relationship. The most important thing that I have learned is that my own happiness comes from within me. It doesn't come from the outside. It doesn't come from waiting on my mom or child to find their happiness. It certainly doesn't come from waiting on any other person to change.

Trust me, I have tried it all. If only my husband would make more money. If only I was skinny enough. If only I drove a fancier car. If only I was smarter and had a career. If only I had more friends, money, a bigger house… then I would be happy. It just doesn't work that way. I searched for years for that 'thing' to bring me joy and make all of my pain go away. None of it worked. I had to dig and I had to dig deep. I have learned that no one can make me happy and really no one can make me feel anything, unless I let them. I am in charge of myself and how I allow others to have power over me. I still struggle with it, but most days, I am content… with just being me!

Today, I can be happy if my husband or children aren't happy. My kids have been my most excellent teachers. They have helped awaken me to my true self. At the essence of each of our 'true selves' is a child who is ready to be awakened. When we make the decision to change and look for the light within us, that is already shining brightly, we will feel a true sense of happiness from within.

No matter the amount of treacherous waters that you have had to navigate in your life, the choice is yours to get out of the boat. Find that life preserver and step onto land. Feel the ground beneath your feet. Find that person who will help hold you steady until you can start taking those tiny steps forward on your own. Then begin to share your story, even if it's little bits at a time. Lean on them, let them hold you up, and then find your inner strength to rise up and define your own sacred happiness.

IGNITE ACTION STEPS

Sit back and take three big belly breaths. In from the nose and out through the mouth. Feel your belly rise and fall as you breathe. This was one of the very first exercises I started to do as I approached my healing and recovery. When that feels comfortable, ease your way into meditation. There is no 'right or wrong' way to meditate, just find a quiet space, close your eyes, feel your body, and go within. Observe your thoughts and release them without any judgment. See them as just thoughts not as a part of your belief system. Stay in the moment and focus on your breath. Be thankful for *everything* that comes up.

Go out and buy the most beautiful journal that you can find. Look at all the colors and patterns. Does one of them speak to you? Hold it, touch it, feel it. Open it and look at the pages... can you see yourself writing in it? It's such a wonderful place to release your thoughts... especially after meditating. There are times that I just write. I write and write and I don't even worry about capitalization or punctuation. This process is so helpful when you are having some anger arise.

Move your body! Moving your body releases anxiety. Feel your feet moving on the ground. Walk, run, or dance. What feels good to you? Throw your headphones on and play some music. Sing out loud!

Joye Madden – United States of America
Parent Coach and Consultant
joyemadden.com
☺ *@jmmadden*
🅕 *Joye Coons Madden*

Gabriela Trauttmansdorff -Weinsberg

"The key to self-acceptance is to stop trying to be who you think you should be and embrace who you are."

I want my experiences to help you realize that you *are* enough and there is nothing that you lack, no matter what anyone tells you. In my story, I'll share some examples of situations in my life when I felt confused about whether I belonged and I questioned my worth. As I explain the difficult things that I have gone through, I talk about how it is that I was able to combat those negative feelings and discover more about myself.

No One Knows You Better Than You Know Yourself!

If you've ever moved cities before, you know just how difficult it is. Between packing all of your belongings, to adjusting to life in a completely different place, the transition is never really easy. I'm definitely no stranger to the process because at 16 I've lived in three different states and three different countries. Although my experiences so far have been really challenging, they forced me to become my own best friend and taught me so much about how to deal with certain situations.

I didn't grow up with a strong sense of belonging. I am Colombian, Austrian, German, and Spanish. There are a lot of perks that come with being multicultural, but it is also frustrating because I've never identified with a specific culture.

I felt like I was floating between being Caucasian and Hispanic. I also didn't have a city that I belonged to, much less a house that really felt like a home to which I could attach all of my childhood memories. You can imagine the thoughts running through my head when someone asks me where I'm from. Do I say where I live? Do I say where I was born? My ethnicity? Or do I have to explain my whole life story so that they understand that I'm from so many places but don't solely belong in any of them?

Between the ages of two and 15, my family moved many times and during a lot of those transitions, I was still discovering myself, which meant that it was easy for me to be influenced by the people I wanted to be friends with. I desperately yearned to have friends, so I started to act like everyone else and pretended to have interest in topics that I didn't truly care about. At the time, I seriously thought that acting like what I thought others wanted from me would make everyone like me. However, my classmates could (unsurprisingly) sense that I was being inauthentic and even a little bit pushy because I was so determined to practically force people to be my friend.

In fifth grade, I began to discover that if people obviously didn't want to be friends with me, I should just leave them alone and find people who did. But that is way easier said than done. It's been incredibly hard for me to find the right friends and I've repeatedly felt like I'm not enough. I questioned everything about myself because the only explanation I could find for why I didn't have friends is that there was something wrong with me, some repelling quality that I just couldn't figure out.

I will always remember the moment in 5th grade when I was in the cafeteria looking for a place to sit and spotted the table of girls that I wanted to be friends with. They were all pretty and well-known around the school, so naturally I wanted to be a part of their group. I asked if I could sit with them and they replied with slight disdain, muttering the words "Yeah sure," under gritted teeth. I felt completely out of place and knew that they didn't want me to be there, but my desire for their acceptance was stronger than my sense of reason.

I put my tray on the table, along with the can of soda that I had purchased at the vending machine. The girls were giggling and chatting with their 'boy-friends' and I tried my best to join in. Suddenly, one of the girls jokingly took my soda and waved it above the nearest trash can, pretending like she was going to throw it in. I smiled, attempting to play along with the joke, but my heart sank when she actually dropped the soda can into the trash. Everyone at the table laughed as I stared at the girl, shocked that she would so blatantly make fun of me. I quickly got up and ran out of the cafeteria, not necessarily sad, but just plain angry at her. I was even angrier at myself for giving her the power to make me feel inferior.

Since I had such a hard time making friends every time I moved, I spent a lot of time alone, which was really a blessing in disguise. Although being alone can be kind of boring, it allows you to think without interruption, which can be good or bad, but for me, who had a lot of self-discovery to do, it was really helpful. When you don't have many friends to hang out with, you start figuring out other things that make you happy. I started baking, cooking, playing tennis, pampering myself (which I highly recommend), and reading A LOT. I figured out what I loved, without trying to change myself to be accepted by someone else.

Those times alone, being myself, enabled me to develop a strong sense of who I am since I didn't have that feeling of belonging that other people grew up with. Being alone and becoming your own best friend is incredibly important because you are the one person who you are going to spend your entire life with, so you might as well enjoy it. I realized that self-love should be my main priority because no one else's opinion should matter more than my own and I needed to take care of the body that I've been given because it's the only one I'm ever going to get.

When I began high school, I was so excited to have a fresh start. I attended a boarding school in California and was finally not the only 'new kid' in school. Being at boarding school meant that I was now responsible for my own health and mental well-being. It wasn't an easy adjustment at first, and the next two years involved a series of emotional highs and lows as I made amazing friends but continued to struggle with the insecurities I had been trying to supress.

I constantly felt underappreciated and terrified to show anyone that what people said actually did affect me. My sophomore year was by far the hardest. When I was excluded from something, it felt like I was in fifth grade again, unwanted and rejected by those I admired.

I felt like I was losing touch with myself and I was extremely unhappy with my life at school. I was forced to rethink how I was approaching social situations and just how miserable I was feeling. I felt alone, and not in the good way. Soon into the year however, I began to realize that being alone wasn't that bad. I actually quite enjoyed the feeling of liberation that I got when I could fully be myself, away from the rest of the world. When I was alone, I could think freely, and in that space, I started to process why I was feeling so dejected and what I could do about it. I realized that who I was and who I wanted to be were two completely different people. Once I discovered who I was without trying to become someone else, my self-assurance grew.

Since I already knew what it was like to feel unfulfilled and out of place,

I no longer tried to sacrifice who I really was for the version of myself that other people wanted me to be. Frankly, it's not their life and I don't want to give others the power to make me feel like I'm not enough. I learned to focus all the effort I was putting into making other people like me, into investing in my own well-being. No one knows you better than you know yourself, so I refused to let other people sabotage my journey of self-discovery.

Often we are influenced by people who don't intend to actually hurt us, but instead want to see us succeed. However, they want us to succeed in their way. Humans always want to be right, and they subconsciously look for assurance from everyone else, so when someone copies their methods, they feel important and valuable (which is all anyone really wants). In order to really find out what made me happy in life, I had to discover what didn't make me happy and what factors had been causing me to continue down a path that was lowering my self-esteem and causing me to question my worth.

I would totally be lying if I said that the opinions of other people were the only thing that caused me to look at myself and feel inferior. As much as we try to resist it, the media plays a huge role in shaping what we want ourselves to be. I can't count the amount of times I've looked at an advertisement and compared myself to the woman in the photograph. Even though my conscious mind knows her legs and face have been airbrushed and her figure was probably altered with photoshop, I can't help but think, "Why can't I look like that?"

As a teenager, it's even worse because with social media, everyone's posts are really just their 'highlight reel,' giving the appearance that their life is perfect, when no one really sees what they struggle with behind the scenes. Although I know that no one is actually perfect, I can't help but wish that I was. Especially, because as a female, there are so many things that society *expects* us to be. We are expected to be pretty but not try too hard, be smart but not bossy, be social but not too talkative — the list could go on and on. These expectations are so powerful that they cause me to constantly compare myself to other women. *Why can't I be as pretty as her? Wow, I wish I was that smart or athletic!* When I had these thoughts, I felt so much worse about myself but also frustrated that most women also feel this way and that as much as we try to fight against it, it always impacts us more than we care to admit.

Something that I've tried to do is acknowledge the features that I like about myself and that make me unique instead of looking at myself in the mirror and criticizing my face and body, like the iconic scene from *Mean Girls* (if you know, you know). As someone who hates standing out in a crowd, I know it's hard to feel different. I hate being tall and feeling like people are looking at me when I don't think there's anything particularly pleasant to look at. Yet, one thing that I realized is we all have at least one feature that someone else wants. Maybe it's your build, or your face, or your clothing style, but always remember that there is something about you that you could appreciate, rather than searching for things to judge.

As a teenager today, sadly, a lot of our humor revolves around self-deprecation. I hear people do it and I do it myself all the time. These jokes normalize self-hate and although they can be funny, they only end up making us feel worse about ourselves. Teens feel pressured to use this humor because they think it will make them fit in and therefore, not many of us have the courage to speak out against it. When I became more mindful about making these jokes, my self-esteem increased as I had stopped putting myself down without even realizing it.

Mindfulness has been an incredibly useful tool for self-reflection. It helps me visualize what I want to manifest in the future and start planning how I am going to get there. Practicing mindfulness is also hugely helpful with improving mental health and calming stress. At first, I doubted the effects it would have, but it gave me so much clarity and allowed me to find peace within my daily life.

I still make plenty of mistakes and let other people's opinions influence me. I do have days where I question my worth, but my power lies within the fact that I'm aware of these feelings. Even though I know what I *should* be doing, sometimes I just can't do it all, and that's also okay. I need to give myself permission to make mistakes and know that I'm going to survive. I'm still learning more and more about myself everyday and continuing to push myself to grow.

Fortunately, I've been able to figure out a lot about what I want out of life and which things have affected me negatively, but I am in no way an expert at dealing with social situations. The truth is, most of us have felt like we are not enough at some point in our lives. We feel confused about where we belong in this crazy world and why we were chosen for the life we are currently living. We feel like we are disappointing others or won't be accepted by society unless we conform ourselves to what everyone else expects from us.

I'm here to tell you that you aren't the only one! Once you start living *your* truth, you will feel a million times better and more satisfied with your life. Everyone goes through experiences that shape who they are. Overcoming your challenges helps you learn more about yourself.

You have the power to take control of your life and live it to the fullest, so go do it!

Gabriela Trauttmansdorff – United States of America

Ignite Action Steps

- SPEND SOME TIME ALONE! I can't stress how much this can help you. It's so important to distance yourself from social situations in order to focus on taking care of yourself. Alone time allows you to better process certain things in your life and really reflect on what makes you happy and what doesn't. As much as it can be hard to find some down time if you have a busy schedule, do your best to set aside time to take care of yourself! Your alone time doesn't have to be filled with deep internal reflections either. Try to find an activity that really makes you happy, an activity that you do for yourself and for yourself only (not something on your to-do list). Don't focus on being productive, just try to unwind in a way that improves your state of mind!

- Invest more time into getting to know yourself. It seems kind of odd to do this when we already feel like we do, but you would be surprised to discover how many of your opinions about yourself have been influenced by others. Try to uncover what you love about life, and make sure you're incorporating it into your daily schedule!

- Practice self-love and appreciation. It's really difficult to get to a place of complete self-love where you accept yourself no matter what. Start by acknowledging the physical features that make you unique and parts of your personality that you appreciate.

- Be aware of when someone says something to you that causes you to question or devalue yourself. It's very important to realize who makes you feel that way and why that comment affected you. If their comment has come from a place of love, appreciate the intent but acknowledge that their approach was flawed and let them know. If it's said with malicious intent, ignore them! There's a reason that person is trying to make you feel worse about yourself (Hint: it's their own insecurities).

- Notice how the media makes you feel about yourself. What advertisements make you less confident and what does that show about your own insecurities? Also remember that normal people all have flaws! Advertisements are created specifically to make you feel like there is something that you lack (whether it be material or physical) so that you want to buy the product they are selling.

- Lastly, practice mindfulness! If you don't already practice mindfulness, start with a basic meditation or simply spend time thinking about what you are grateful for. Mindfulness is a great tool to help center yourself and appreciate the present moment.

Draw a picture of yourself highlighting the things you like. Full body or just your face, or both. Have fun with it… remember, it has to show the things that make you unique.

ADONIE S.

*"Never give up or give in because no matter what,
there is always a light at the end of the tunnel."*

**Never give up. Never give in. Things will always work out. Nothing is going
to be the same. Stuff will change and things will get better.**

THE LOST BOY

Where do I start? A young boy with no knowledge. A free spirit in need of
guidance. An empty notebook waiting to be written in. Many say I was a cute
baby, but I can't remember back then. Fortunately, I grew up in a very loving
family with a wealthy mom and dad, and I lived in a beautiful neighborhood
and city. I was born with many gifts, to say the least, but this never affected
me. I was too busy playing with toy cars and learning my ABCs.

One day, when I was about 6 years old, I asked my dad what his favorite
sport was, and he said hockey. He told me that that was his favorite sport at
the time and his number one team was the Calgary Flames™. Just like any
son, I wanted to follow in my father's footsteps. At the time, I was fed this
idea that 'we are the best,' and as a result, my young mind believed my dad
must have played in the NHL™. All I wanted to do was be just like him, so
I watched every hockey game on TV with my dad and played mini sticks as
often as possible.

But then one day, everything changed. One day, he was gone. Then he
was gone the next day. Then gone for the week. My parents had divorced and,

back then, the 6-year-old me had no clue what that meant. All I knew was that my dad wasn't there anymore and it would be a while before I saw him again. My sister, mom, and I moved to a small city in the Canadian prairies where my grandma lived. She provided us with a house to stay in while my parents sorted out their problems.

Our life in that small town was very different. We were very close to the edge financially and I wasn't used to a struggling lifestyle where we needed to be careful with groceries and very conservative with our spending. We lived very low-key and cautiously, but then a man appeared. A man who was bound to be a role model and leader for me. A second dad. Of course nothing could ever replace my father, but at 8 years old, I looked up to this second father figure. Not longer afterward, we left my grandma's and moved to a town of his liking.

At the time, he was our savior, rescuing our lost little family and carrying us off to a beautiful town in the valley surrounded by 90 kilometers of lake. Little did I know of his true colors: this man was a wife beater and a drug addict. Although he had a very rough childhood, it's no excuse for what he did and I don't condone his actions. This man assaulted my mother and stole from her. But what could I do? I was still a child.

One day, just like with my dad, he was just gone. It was as if I already knew the procedure of what was going to happen. Once again, I was alone, this time with my second dad in jail. My family was in discord to the point where we couldn't even trust each other. I felt so alone. This was when I made the biggest mistake of my life: for comfort and happiness, I turned to food.

I just kept eating and eating as food became happiness for me. I didn't know what dangers eating this way would create. It was like an addiction. I just couldn't stop eating the sweet flavors and salty tastes I was always craving.

My mother was still in a super dark place after her past experiences, staying locked in her room working to the point where she literally couldn't even walk from a sore back and pinched sciatica nerve. I was pretty upset. I had to help her to her bed and out of bed; she could barely move. Every Sunday, we were supposed to clean, but she could only sit in her chair while we did the cleaning for her. To me, this became our new ordinary. From that point on, that was what I thought life was: struggle and food.

I was never good at school. I always got into fights and had problems with teachers. And the biggest problem was that we couldn't afford to have a healthy diet. My performance slowed in sports. My craving to just eat and watch YouTube grew stronger and, with it, so did my weight.

The first day I really noticed something was wrong was when my mom was taking a picture with me and my sister, and she said, "Suck your stomach in." That's when I realized I had a problem, but I never cared to fix it.

I always thought to myself, "Oh, I'll worry about it when I get older," which was a terrible idea. I just kept getting bigger and more unhealthy. It was the worst thing that could happen to me.

Not long afterward, when I was 13, we moved back to that small town to be with my grandma again. I didn't know anyone. I was alone and felt depressed because of my weight. I had trouble making friends, except for with one person, Jake, who saw me for me and not just for my weight. He was bullied lots due to the fact that he had a medical condition known as Tourette's, but he and I just seemed to click. He really helped my depression. We were so close, but then he made a big mistake. He started getting into vaping. He claimed it helped his Tourette's, but I never believed him. I would always say, "Stop," and "That's bad for you," but he wouldn't listen. Later, I would meet a very good friend named Kyle. For all of grade eight, those were my two friends.

After the summer, when I came back to school in grade nine, Kyle and Jake were still my only friends, but my new high school was the hot spot for lots of middle school students to go to. The first month went well, but everything after that went super poorly. Jake started leaning way more toward alcohol and weed. My best friends began to make fun of me, calling me out for stuff I would never do and making me look bad in front of others to make themselves look better.

One day, we were taking the bus and Jake said, "Oh my God, you're so fat," when I sat down on the bus seat. This would happen for months, but they were my only two friends, so I thought this stuff was normal. Although it may sound like I was under the radar of everyone else in high school, I was actually pretty well-known, but not in a good way at all. As a matter of fact, I would much rather be hiding under the radar than receive the treatment I did. Basically, by now, Jake was very associated with people that did drugs and made friends through getting high and drunk, and he would always make fun of me in front of those people, which instantly gave me a bad reputation at school. I felt that I would have to associate myself with bad people just to be happy. This led me to a massive depression that I bottled up and never showed. I would come home and play video games and eat unhealthy amounts of food just to get away from the stuff that was going on at school. Eating and gaming felt like the only happiness there was.

My mom had found a new happiness of her own with her new partner, Peter, but they were never able to spend much time with us because of how much they worked. The only person who I ever told any of my problems to and who

I actually felt comfortable talking to was my stepbrother. At times he got fed up with me, plus he was all the way in the United States while I was in Canada. I was very lonely and my only comfort came from people I met online while playing video games.

It's safe to say that video games were my drug, my escape from my real-life problems, and a gateway into a great experience. I never paid attention to school work. I would lie to my mom and say I was done with all my work when I wasn't. I had no intention of getting a girlfriend. I had no intention of going out with friends. I just wanted to stay home and play video games.

One day, I just had enough. Off campus away from people, my friend Jake and I got into a fight that left me never intending to talk to him again. Kyle sided with Jake and, just that fast, I was officially alone.

Summer finally arrived and though I barely passed all my grade nine classes, I was finally free from the stress of school and the bullying. I didn't intend to make friends or socialize with anyone that summer; I just wanted to go to my grandmas and play video games to my heart's content. Of course, this led to a super unhealthy lifestyle. I became paler, fatter, and more socially awkward when face-to-face with people.

When September came around, the thought of returning to school had me in tears. I didn't think I was going to survive another year there. I got anxiety from school and I didn't want to go back, but I knew I had to.

On the first day of my sophomore year, I had science class with this one guy who was friends with Jake, so I kind of knew him. He was very friendly and nice and offered to sit with me, so I agreed. Unfortunately, our second class together had a seating plan so I could no longer sit near my new friend. But I was paired with this person, a girl, and immediately I wanted to know her name.

She was friendly and had a nice smile. That class was my last class of the day and on the bus ride home, all I would think about was her. I became really confused. I had never felt like this before. Days would go by and every day, I was more and more interested in her. All I wanted to do was hang out with her and spend time talking to her.

One day, she sparked a conversation with me, something about an assignment. We talked a little bit. After that, I learned her name and began searching for her social media accounts, as any teenager would. I tried to spark a conversation with her online, but it ended awkwardly. This left me puzzled. Up until then, all of my successful friendships were online and I was awkward in person. With her, it was the opposite. I was up all night trying to figure out exactly what I was feeling, why I cared, and why I was so interested in her. Then it hit me. I had feelings for this person! This left me even more puzzled because social interaction was something I'd been avoiding.

A week of school went by and she and I had a long conversation. I discovered she was super caring. She asked me what was going on with me and when I told her my problems, she was interested and wanted to help. After that day, I knew I liked her a lot. And in my head, I came to the conclusion that she wouldn't like me back if I was fat. That's what I thought everyone avoided me for — being fat — and not because *I* avoided people. That night, all I wanted was to be popular and have her like me. The question was, how?

School lunch was one and a half hours long and we were allowed to go off campus and do whatever we liked. Me and my buddy from science class would usually go to lunch at Dairy Queen™, the closest place to eat, only a three-minute walk from my school.

But then one particular day was different. Another student told me something was taking place at the nearby community center and I should check it out. The center was not even a minute's walk away, so I decided to go and see. Coincidentally, as I stepped through the doors of the center, I stumbled upon my phys ed partner, a little yet muscular kid I had been randomly paired up with in class but was not really friends with. At the same time, I noticed above the front desk a sign describing the cost of memberships and gym passes. I asked my gym partner why he was there at the center, and he said he played basketball there.

That was it! A sudden thought popped into my mind and I knew I was going to play basketball too, lose weight, make my varsity basketball team, and be popular. Later that day, I begged my mom to buy me a pass for the month of November, convinced that this would work. I just *knew* that it would fix everything and all my problems of being at home, not being popular, and having no friends would all just go away.

The next day, I went back to the community center at lunch and picked up a basketball. I started bouncing it and started shooting hoops. I was, of course, very bad at it, but I was so dedicated. My phys ed partner didn't really want much to do with me, so I sort of minded my own business and played on an empty hoop. At first, I would only play at lunch; but then, I started to go to the gym after school. I loved it so much that I started to play in the mornings as well. I would take the 5 AM bus to school and walk to the center even in the middle of winter on snowy mornings. Each day I spent about three hours just playing basketball and working out.

Christmas was coming up and I went to visit my dad in the Bahamas where he worked. It was a really enjoyable experience because I got to spend time with my dad and my sister, all while lying in sun chairs around the pool. I didn't really talk about it with my dad, but I did think over my basketball experiences and how it had impacted my weight-loss progress. I realized then that I felt *happy* — something I hadn't felt for a while. I wanted more of this happiness feeling and I knew it came from the beautiful atmosphere and how confident I felt in my body.

During my time in the Bahamas, I realized I was just done with everything negative that had come before. I was focused on trying to better myself and surround myself with people who would support me, like my family, not people who wanted to criticize me or put me down. When I was surrounded by those who were there for me and cared about me, my first real-life friends, I felt very, very happy. They were there for me. They were actually concerned about my well-being and wanted better things for me. I knew that from online friends, but when it came to real-life friends, it felt different. It was *real life*, not a game. It was people who I knew and who knew me, not strangers. And it made me happy.

It took me a while to understand where happiness really comes from and how to find it when it feels like it is unobtainable. I searched for it at first in other things and other people, but soon found out that my greatest happiness came when I made myself more important than anyone or anything else.

It isn't easy being a teeneager or dealing with divorce or the letdowns life sometimes delivers. Food is not a substitute for happiness, nor is wanting the acceptance of others. Real happiness came when I took charge of my life and got focused on my health and what made *me* happy. I'm still growing up, but what I do know is that when you trust yourself, you find what makes you happy, and *that* feeling is worth the time and effort it takes to find it. So go find *your* happiness. Move beyond the bad stuff and focus on what you want. Ask yourself what really matters to you and then do that. Find the friends who are there for you and care about you. See yourself as capable of being happy and then just be that. Happiness is always there. Never give up or give in, no matter what.

IGNITE ACTION STEPS

Get active. Get out of your comfort zone. When I slowly started building a new life brick by brick, I found I was able to build a strong, solid wall that holds me up and that I am happy with. Make just one small change and keep doing it. Just start today.

Whether it's basketball, hockey, running, biking, or just playing with friends outdoors, find ways to be active in a fun way. Exercise feels so much better when it is something you love doing and you fill it with happiness and fun.

Adonie S. – Canada
Athlete, Supportive Friend, Great Son

Bela Fayth

"Speak up even if your voice shakes."

My wish for you is to understand how loved and important you are. You have a power that no one can take from you: your voice. Sometimes the steps forward are hard and painful, but with those steps comes unimaginable joy and freedom. You are not alone in the daily desire to be joyful. It is a choice. Let's use our voices to create space for happiness together.

Joy is Found Where Healing Begins

Have you ever felt heavy? Like there are bricks on top of your shoulders that you carry everywhere? Me too.

Have you ever wanted to speak but felt that lump in your throat that makes you want to scream? Me too.

Not too long ago, I was the girl who held her tongue. I would shrink and keep quiet so that people would like me and I wouldn't hurt anyone's feelings. I still struggle with this. I felt like I was not allowed to speak up or have emotions, and that what I had to say or what I felt did not matter. Speaking up wouldn't change anything. It wouldn't alter the circumstances of my life, make people change, choose me, take back harsh words that crushed me, or undo the things that broke my heart. Why would I ever speak up?

Every single person on this earth has a conversation they need to have.

One that makes you sick thinking about it. One that triggers the lump in your throat and tears in your eyes. The one that keeps those heavy bricks on top of your shoulders.

It took me a long time to realize that those bricks were the words I had left unsaid. The lump in my throat that causes me to feel like screaming shows me that I'm suffocating myself by not speaking up.

To be completely honest, I would never have chosen any of the hard stuff that has happened in my life, but I would not change it either. The things that have broken my heart and brought me to my knees have made me who I am. Without them, I would not be able to relate to other people's heartbreak, hardships, betrayal, abandonment issues, and struggles in life. I would not begin to understand how it feels when your heart drops and makes you sick to your stomach, or grasp the feeling of hurting so badly that you can barely eat or breathe. I would not fathom feeling so angry that you want to run through a wall and I would not know how suffocating it is when you feel like you do not matter or are not noticed. But I do know, and I understand it all too well.

These are the things that have taught me to get up after being knocked down. They lit a fire under my butt to take care of my heart and take steps to heal it. I want a heart that is full of gratitude, love, joy, and all of the good stuff. I do not want to keep the bitterness, hate, and unforgiveness in my heart. I do not want to stay buried under the things that have made me feel helpless. I want to speak up. I want to face them head-on. Sometimes the only way out of pain is through it.

I have learned that there will never be a day where I just wake up and joy appears. The truth is, life sucks sometimes. It's hard, people are mean, and a lot of times things straight up do not go our way. I have learned that I do not have to be joyful *about* my circumstances, but I can have joy *in* my circumstances. You can have joy even when you're hurting. In the middle of heartbreak. In the middle of crying on the floor. In the middle of anxiety and fear. In the midst of dealing with the mess that comes with being a human. You can have joy right smack dab in the middle of all the chaos. Joy is a choice.

Joy does not take away the hurt. You get to choose what you focus on. If you look for the bad, crappy, and negative, you will always find it, even in the best circumstances. If you look for the good, positive, and uplifting, you will always find it even in the hardest situations. You get to control how you deal with the crap that hurts you. When you take time to heal those wounds, you make room for so much goodness in your life. I do this by speaking up.

It wasn't always that way. I remember sitting in my parent's closet when I was 12 surrounded by my mom's shoes. I was shaking and could barely speak. I was like a combination of soda pop and Mentos™, waiting to explode, fueled with unsaid words built up inside of me. I silenced myself to protect my biological dad. He left when I was five years old. He was never part of my life and my heart grieved the relationship I desperately wanted with him. He had never watched me play sports or sat in the audience of my school programs. He wasn't at my birthdays, graduation, proms, or any special moments. He was missing from all of the memories I cherish in my heart. There were days that I thought it was my fault that he left and I would try to think of ways that I could fix it. I thought maybe if I could be better, he would come back. He never knew exactly how I felt because I kept it from him. I hoped that maybe if I just stayed quiet and pretended like everything was okay that he would want to be in my life. I felt so unlovable. If I wasn't good enough for my own father, who would I be good enough for?

As he said goodbye after a short unfulfilling visit one Christmas, the pop and Mentos exploded and I had a meltdown. All of the hurt, feelings, and words that I had not said burst out of me. I sat on the floor in the closet with my knees pulled tight to my chest shaking uncontrollably. My mom was sitting outside of the closet listening while I talked it out with her. I was terrified to tell my biological dad how rejected I was feeling and how distraught I was. It was so difficult to gather the courage to speak what I had left unsaid for so long. But I knew it was a conversation I had to have with him in order to heal the 'dad-shaped' hole in my heart.

My mother encouraged me to write down what I would say and I trusted her advice. Later that night, she insisted that I call him and tell him how I felt. That was the *last* thing I wanted to do. I was shaking, sick to my stomach, and the lump in my throat was back.

While sitting in the closet, I finally got the courage to call him; I asked him to let me talk so I could tell him how I was feeling. I told him how hurt I was, how much I wished he was him in my life, and that I wanted our relationship to be different. I told him everything I had written down about how upset I was. After I got everything off of my chest I gave him a chance to respond. His response was nowhere near what I had hoped for and absolutely nothing about my situation changed after having that conversation. Except something changed in ME. Those bricks on my shoulders were lighter. I felt free. I healed a piece of my heart that day, and I felt joyful about it.

This was the first time that I realized that these conversations that make me so sick and scared are not about changing the outcome *or* changing the other person. When I finally wrapped my head around the fact that these conversations were *for* me, everything changed. Speaking up has nothing to do with the *other* person, and everything to do with valuing *yourself*.

It was the first time I felt that knowledge so profoundly, but it was not the last. Someone who has been my best friend since birth hurt me immensely. Our families grew up together and we have always been in each other's lives. We shared deep dark secrets, helped each other through hard times, and told the truth even when it hurt. As we grew up, we were still close but had different aspirations in life. One day, he used one of my secrets against me in front of other people.

I could feel the lump in my throat rise and tears starting to form. I felt betrayed and angry. The rage made me feel like I wanted to run through a wall. I wanted to disappear. How could a person so close to me use something so hurtful against me? I told him how angry I was. He brushed me off, telling me to get over it and that I was overreacting. Heat flushed through my body. I could feel my blood boiling. I did not like how someone important to me was treating me so poorly. I told him I loved him and I valued him, but he had no right to treat me like that, and for right now I couldn't have him in my life and I needed time to process the words that he had spoken.

We had built our friendship and trust for years and I felt at that moment all the trust was gone. The thought of seeing him made me nauseous. I felt it eating me up inside. I knew I was becoming bitter and full of hate and anger. The last thing I wanted to do was talk to him and about seven months went by without us speaking to each other. When his family decided to book a trip to stay with my family in California, I was anxious about seeing him. It made me question my resentment toward him and I felt heavy. My heart was hard. I was changing as a person and I could feel it. I knew I needed to talk to him.

One day after they arrived, I pulled him aside. I felt sick, nervous, and scared. I was shaking, but I knew in order to heal and be happy, this was what I needed to do. We sat outside on our patio and I was finally able to tell him how badly he hurt me. I told him that it stung even more when he did not own up to it or take the time to understand why I was upset. It sucked not having him in my life. I loved him and forgave him, but I didn't think things would ever be the same between us. I told him it would take time to build our friendship back. As soon as the words left my mouth, I felt lighter. I felt stronger. I knew I wanted to heal our friendship and work on it, and now it was a possibility. I was truly happy I chose to speak from my heart.

Those conversations freed up space within me. The point wasn't to change the person or situation. Speaking up and dealing with what is in my heart is what makes me happy, not the conversation. Talking to the person who hurt you will not magically fix everything. The hurt will not automatically go away. You will not forget. Forgiveness does not always mean restoration. You can speak up, forgive, and still keep a healthy distance until you feel your heart is ready. It is okay and healthy to have boundaries. What is not healthy or okay is to let hurt, hate, anger, and bitterness fester in your heart. It is like drinking poison and hoping someone else dies. By holding on to this hurt and those unspoken words, you are only hurting yourself.

You cannot outrun the pain that lives in your heart. Trust me, I have tried. When we run from the pain, it is simply running with us, because it is inside of us. The moment you stop running and face it is the moment you are the closest to joy.

No one knows exactly how you feel or what bothers you unless you tell them. Feelings are okay, living in them is not. Voicing your feelings does not mean that everything goes back to normal. But, when we take the time to speak our hearts, face our wounds, and do what we need to do to heal, joy is not too far behind.

Speaking up can be scary. Sometimes the truth is harsh and we feel ashamed or embarrassed about our feelings. Maybe we tell ourselves that it is not a big deal and we should just suck it up. I get it and have felt that too. We are often our own worst enemies. I know I can be.

Imagine that you are in a grocery store and you see a mom with her baby girl sitting in the cart. The baby has an adorable pink bow on her head. She is content and happy as can be. In the baby's hands, she is holding her favorite stuffed animal, a rainbow unicorn. The baby drops the unicorn and starts to cry. The mother looks at the baby and tells her to stop crying. It is just a stuffed animal. You're fine. Knock it off. It is not a big deal. You are being dramatic and embarrassing. You sit there astonished at what you just witnessed. Did that mom really say those things to her baby? How insensitive and belittling. I would never say that to my kid.

Let's try reframing that.

That same baby girl is sitting in the cart crying over her stuffed unicorn. Her mother immediately picks it up and gives it to her, comforting her by saying, "It's okay honey. Everything is okay." The baby calms down and is content again. The second scenario is way more socially accepted and healthy right? So then, why do we talk to ourselves like the first mother speaks to her baby?

Why do we shame ourselves for our feelings? If something bothers you, it matters. If something hurts you, it should be addressed. If something makes you feel like running into the wall, you need to have the important conversation. When you stub your toe, it hurts horribly for a tiny toe. Just because someone has a broken leg does not mean that your stubbed toe does not hurt.

Whatever you are feeling right now is okay. There are no good or bad feelings. Whatever you are struggling with right now is valid; struggle is normal. You will always have to face hardships. You get the choice if you are going to struggle while healing and trying to be better, or struggle staying stuck where you are. Either way, there will be a struggle, so why not struggle while taking steps toward discovering your internal joy?

The more you speak up and communicate your feelings, the easier it will become. This starts with the little things such as: saying no, telling someone you don't like the way they speak to you, talking to someone about what they said that struck you the wrong way, taking a step back from a hurtful relationship, and listening to the small still voice in your heart and trusting it. If something feels off, it probably is.

To be able to have a hard conversation with someone else, you have to be willing to first have one with yourself. If you do not know what hurts you or why something hurts you, you will not be able to voice it to someone else. If you do not take the time to sit with your own heart, let it speak to you, and validate what it says, your heart will never feel the freedom to speak to anyone else. The freeing conversation starts with you.

Here are some questions to ponder:
- What am I afraid of?
- What are some things that get on my nerves?
- What has hurt me in my life?
- What situations do I feel shameful about?
- How do I want to be treated?
- What are my boundaries?

The hardest thing to remember when stepping out of your comfort zone to have these conversations is that they are FOR YOU! You cannot control someone's words, actions, thoughts, choices, or anything about them. This conversation is not to change the situation, it is to free space within you. It is to honor yourself by using your voice to say how you feel and what you want. Other people's words and actions have more to do with them than they have to do with you.

This is for you to step out into your power and own the things you can control. You can control your thoughts, words, actions, choices, and what you are going to allow to hold you back. The more you are willing to face and deal with, the more you will heal. The more you heal, the more joyful you will be. Who doesn't want joy in their life? Are you ready for those bricks on your shoulders to be lighter? Are you ready to get rid of that lump in your throat? Let's do it together. I cannot wait for you to feel the empowerment, freedom, and unimaginable joy that comes with healing through honest, heartfelt conversations. Be willing to step out and *own* your truth. Speak up even if your voice shakes. Use your voice; it is your power and cannot be taken from you.

IGNITE ACTION STEPS

- Start by having a conversation with yourself. Where are you hurting? What do you need to heal? Have you let your voice go silent? How could you use your voice to heal a situation?

- Write a letter to someone you need to have a conversation with. Be sure to write out everything you want to say. Prepare yourself by also writing to yourself reminding yourself that your feelings are valid and that you are doing this for your heart, healing, and happiness.

- If there are circumstances where having a conversation is not physically possible or if the person is no longer with you, it is still very important to get those words out. I do this by writing a letter with what I would say. In this way, I stop carrying around the words I wish I would have said and free up space in my heart.

- Now go do it, and then celebrate yourself for stepping out and using your voice!!

Bela Fayth – United States of America
Author and Empowerment Speaker
http://www.belafayth.com/
@ @belafayth

IGNITE HAPPINESS ACTIVITY

These are the words I have left unsaid and feel the need to share...

_____

_____

_____

_____

_____

_____

_____

_____

_____

_____

_____

_____

_____

_____

_____

_____

_____

_____

_____

_____

_____

_____

_____

Dear my beautiful self,

SARAH CROSS

"Happiness is seeing life through the eyes of a child."

Through my story, I hope to bring clarity to the many blessings you already possess. I wish for you to rediscover how happiness is living like a child: seizing the wonder of life, throwing fears to the wind, and getting lost in the moment. I would love to inspire you to embrace new challenges and step outside your comfort zone — to ride the wave of deep fulfillment.

OUR CRAZY BOAT TRIP

"No!" I said firmly to my husband, "I'm not taking our two young girls on a small open boat with no cabins, no galley, or even a toilet, across the English Channel to France next week." The idea was preposterous!

I paced up and down the hard Spanish tiles in our Mallorcian living room. My heart was racing; 1001 motherly protective 'what ifs' were swimming around my head. What if it rained? What if one of the kids fell overboard? Was it safe? Where would we stay? What about food?

"We will figure it out," was my Kiwi husband's laid back approach. I felt the immense weight of responsibility to make a wise, maternal decision. Suddenly my elder daughter woke me from my inner world of worry. "Are we going?" she asked excitedly, clearly oblivious to all my concerns. I told her that my racing mind meant I was struggling to decide. She fearlessly responded that she would happily go with Daddy and WITHOUT me! I knew in that moment that I needed to harness my inner warrior. I was not to be out-challenged by my intrepid, adventure-seeking five-year-old daughter!

I had traveled extensively before children, but since becoming a mother, my life had become routine, caught in a web of safety first. I had created a life of certainty and could not remember the last time I embraced anything that laid outside my comfort zone. Having children means your life is suddenly not just about you. I had lost the carefree attitude I possessed in my youth and replaced it with a heavy obligation to protect my daughters. I had pushed aside my desire to learn, grow, and challenge myself. My life was void of the thrills that make life explode in your face!

Despite my reservations, in the back of my head I knew it was an amazing opportunity. I reluctantly agreed with my husband and daughters that this was indeed a unique experience that we, as a family, needed to seize. That summer, our girls were four and five years old, growing independent, more capable, and able to carry their own backpacks during the adventure. Still feeling a lot of trepidation we found ourselves embarking on a spontaneous, crazy, seafaring voyage of a lifetime.

The moment the decision landed, I rapidly dove into organization overdrive and arranged all the permits, logistics, and flights, so we could arrive in London within a matter of days. Yet still upon departure, we had no guide books, no real plan, no idea what lay ahead of us, just driven by a keen spirit of adventure.

Standing on the banks of the Thames, with Hampton Court Palace in the backdrop, we first sighted the 30-foot white, open-top motor boat we were soon to board. Beige cushions tightly covered the forward seating area and a raised bench supported the console for driving. It looked comfortable enough, as long as we had a cover.

Gray clouds loomed overhead. The rain cover was missing! All my fears rose to the surface. I smiled, unconvincingly, while wallowing in worry and drowning in uncertainties — we had come this far; there was no return. My girls needed me to be strong. We meticulously studied the tide timetable so as not to get beached downstream at low tide. Our challenges were starting to mount up: the onboard water tap was not working, we had no maps, and the rain seemed imminent. But we were committed. Safety equipment aboard. The engines purred to life. Lines released. Our journey began.

Yet that first night it was as if the Universe sent us a rainbow assurance to trust in the unknown, as everything just fell into place. We found a perfect berth on Cheswick Pier to tie up and a nearby hotel with vacancies. On route to the hotel, we passed along a delightful cobbled lane, adorned with charming cottages reflecting yesteryear, like a free pass through a magnificent historic museum. We watched our girls and felt pride in their tenacity, loaded with their overnight essentials, walking, what was for them, a considerable distance without a single whinge! Our first miracle! Ignorant bliss of the plethora of roadblocks that lay ahead!

Passing beside Big Ben, underneath Tower Bridge, and alongside numerous famous monuments, it was a brief but deeply memorable London tour from the eyes of a fish. Onward to the beautifully set Port of Ramsgate. I gazed across the Channel and felt a sea of stress arise within. Huge container ships, back to back in line. I struggled to picture crossing these busy shipping lanes safely in our comparatively miniscule boat. White horses danced on the waves in the distance; surely we would be tossed about like glitter in a snow globe?

Crossing the English Channel was an unforgettable experience. The morning haze had just lifted. Life jackets were harnessed. My two girls huddled up close to me — spray tinged our faces; salt hung on our tongues. As we hit the open sea, we rocked and bounced in a helter-skelter of directions. As I gazed upward, the contrasted stillness and serenity of the infinite blue offered me a real sense of peace; it felt like time froze.

A mere couple of hours later, we were hugging the French coastline and I felt much of my apprehension drain away. The Port of Dunkirk lay just a short distance ahead, almost safe. Then, without warning, the wind picked up, the sea state quickly escalated and waves reared up around us. Suddenly the boat crashed down. THWACK! A wall of water arose in front of us as a monstrous fear sprung up within and I let out a silent scream. The inevitable flood fell upon us. Instinctively, I threw my body upon my little one, beside me, to protect her. I came up spluttering, shivering, and unable to catch my breath. I scooped her up in my arms and rushed to the relative shelter of the console where my husband and elder daughter stood. What were we doing? Had we misjudged the balance of excitement and recklessness? I continued to shake uncontrollably until, finally, we arrived in Dunkirk, wet and shaken, but relieved and safe.

As it turned out, crossing the Channel was not actually the event that proved to be my greatest challenge and awoke me from the hamster wheel life I had been leading.

Early the next morning we were set to enter the canal system of France, constructed to allow immense commercial vessels to navigate on a daily basis. I was totally unaware of the scale of these gigantic locks, a true engineering masterpiece, that left me feeling like our boat was a fly on the elephant's back.

I had woken up fresh and relieved that we had crossed the English Channel and happily awaited the calm waters of the canals. At 10 AM sharp, we pulled up outside the biggest set of doors my eyes have ever beheld. The gateway towered above us 45 feet across and 25 feet high. Now all I had to do was the *simple* task of calling the authorities on the radio. I was the only person in our little family who could speak French and so the responsibility to request permission to enter the lock fell entirely on my lips. Navigating the Channel had been my husband's role, but this was mine.

My husband passed me the radio and suddenly a huge fear overwhelmed me. Still, to this day, I cannot logically describe where it came from. I had been at sea many times before and I had previously called up large ships on the radio to confirm their course, but at this moment, dread almost paralyzed me. My heart pounded furiously; I must have repeated the same sentence four or five times and still I momentarily lost the ability to retain any information. "What do I have to say again?" I asked over and over to my husband, his words echoing, but not sticking.

My husband's firm perseverance shook me out of my paralyzed state and finally my shaking hand sparked the radio into life. "Dunkirk Port Authority," I repeated three times in French, followed by the name of our vessel. "Permission to enter the Trystram lock." Something so uncomplicated, so why had it been so hard? What exactly had I feared? The radio crackled back in a strong french accent. *"Autorisation d'entrer "* (permission to enter granted). A huge smile of accomplishment spread across my face. Having climbed the mountain of fear, I embodied a renewed sense of gratitude for my true capabilities. A blanket of peace floated upon me and I knew that whatever challenge arose, I would find a solution.

I realized that safety is something our prehistoric brain loves. Not stepping out of my comfort zone in such a long time had made me forget about the sense of satisfaction of achieving a new goal, of pushing aside my fears and acting despite them. I felt a resurgence of my former self. A return to the courageous woman that I had neglected.

The colossal doors slowly hinged open and we passed into the lock, clueless as to how we were to secure the boat. Locks are nothing like berths and marinas, of which we had plenty of experience. Yet, we figured it out together and I awoke to the realization that my adventurous desire and protective need could playfully dance with one another.

Dunkirk and the city noise fell away as the serenity of the French countryside opened up. Like the ferocity of the sea now behind us, my inner stresses melted away and a new joyous sense of gratitude took hold.

Looking back, I am struck by the amazing adaptability of my children.

Despite all that we went through, not once did my girls say they were scared, homesick, or bored. Sometimes they were cold, sometimes they were hungry… well most of the time they were hungry! But always accepting of what was. In fact, they were almost always happy and found joy in the smallest of things.

As we motored along the tree-lined watery avenues, relieved of my fear, my husband and I watched as our girls spent hours playing with the fenders and lines in an area about fifteen foot squared. They invented games, created knots and obstacle courses, chatted and laughed.

Those moments watching my girls gleefully play with so little were remarkably revealing. Laughing stress-free, like the flowers in the wild, both were intent on enjoying the magic of the present moment. It took a crazy boat trip to reignite a genuine knowingness of happiness in me. It was a lightning moment to fully treasure that when I am absorbed in the creative wonder of the moment, the many worries of the future, as well as the stresses and regrets of the past, just fade away. I realized that my life is made up of a series of breaths and, to quote Roy Bennett, "If you aren't grateful for what you already have, what makes you think you would be happy with more?"

Before children, I thought parents were always the teachers. What a fallacy! Actually we need to look more to our children to remind ourselves what we have forgotten as adults — the adventure, the joy, the bliss, is in loving what we have. Their curiosity and way they look at life with awe and wonder is something we, in our busy lives, caught up in fear of what might happen, can forget to do. For children, life is one big adventure; they see excitement in the mundane and their curiosity and ability to reframe their world is truly inspirational.

As the days went on and we traveled further into France I found my daughters' outlook on life infectious. I had overcome my fears and was now appreciating and even *loving* how little we had and how happy I was. My daily thoughts revolved around having enough to eat, plenty of water to drink, and a safe place to rest our heads. When our life was stripped back to the basics, I realized that so many of the thoughts that clutter our minds are nothing more than pointless, wasted energy.

Passing through Paris, we were so privileged to witness the magnificence of the Eiffel Tower claw skyward above us and pass in a time when Notre Dame stood majestically in untouched splendor. These are memories that will last a lifetime.

This trip was a perfect lesson in how making up negative stories in my mind about what *might* happen in the future is a futile process. NOT ONE of the 1001 'what ifs' I had envisioned EVER came true.

Does this mean everything went perfectly? No! Our radio did not work in the French canal system. It took fourteen cans and a full day to refuel. One night, we could not find a safe place to leave the boat and had to say onboard in a tent. Another night, we found ourselves trapped between a lock and a tunnel because we did not know the locks shut earlier on a Sunday. We could not access riverside drinking water because we were unaware of the need to purchase a water key in Dunkirk. One unmarked canal was permanently closed and we had to backtrack.

Although our challenges were substantial, we overcame them all! Miraculously, it never rained heavily. Every night we were able to find somewhere to stay. We always had sufficient food. The boat never sank. The girls never fell overboard. We did not get lost. Even the night we nearly ran out of water, an old fashioned hydrant pump miraculously appeared on the bank providing fresh drinking water.

I rediscovered how our life was already awash with blessings and an abundance far beyond the necessities for survival. I learned that when we step into challenges, regardless of our fears, and become absorbed in the process, we can truly experience the exhilarating ride that life has to offer. We had an amazingly unique, life-changing experience for which I am eternally grateful.

Upon returning from France I made certain uplifting changes in my life. I committed to seeing life more through the eyes of my children, taking pleasure in the small things, laughing as much as I can, appreciating our many blessings, and reminding myself of the magical gift of the present moment.

I am a planner, an organizer, and this trip taught me that you do not have to know all the answers before saying 'yes' to something new. If not for my husband, who counteracted all my negative projections of what might go wrong, I would never have embarked upon this life-changing adventure. Sometimes we need to just say 'yes' and figure out all the *hows* after. Often if we wait until all our ducks are in a line, the opportunity has sailed out of the port!

It is time to become resourceful and disperse with the negative mental chatter. Release the chains, take one small step forward. You never know what is waiting for you on the other side of 'yes'! Bon voyage to a happy life!

IGNITE ACTION STEPS

Look at the map and color in all the countries you have always dreamed of exploring.

- Pick one of those locations that you could commit to visiting within the next three years.

- Do some research. Do you know someone who lives there? Talk to friends and family and find out who has already been. Join a local online group to find out more about the local area.

- How could you be more resourceful? Could you do a home swap, house sit, or work in exchange for food and board? What could you cut back on to put aside 20/50 dollars a week to save over two years?

- Now tell someone about your plans so that you hold yourself accountable. Put that dream trip into action and create memories that will last a lifetime.

Sarah Cross – United Kingdom
Lover of life, mother, world explorer.
sarahworldtravel@yahoo.com

JORJA GIESIN

"Happiness comes with change, even when you're not expecting it."

My intention is to reassure you that even though you might not be in control of every aspect of your life, the changes in your life that you fear may turn out to be way better than what you were expecting. And, in the end, they may make you happier.

SAVE 'NORMAL' FOR ANOTHER DAY

I was in sixth grade and the summer was approaching fast. I was living in New Jersey, USA at that time. My life was just like any normal 12-year-old girl. I would go to school every morning, come home, wait for my dad to get back from his work in the city, go to soccer practice most nights, and hang out with my friends on the weekends. Just like other kids, I did everything to fit in with the crowd both in and out of school. I made sure I was one of the 'cool' kids and had lots of friends to cover that. When I wasn't with my friends, I was with my dad. He was everything to me; we were our own little team and we still are. My brother Jackson, five years older than me, was rarely home and wanted nothing to do with me or my dad 100 percent of the time. He spent most of his days in his room on his Xbox like most 17-year-old boys.

My dad and I had so many great adventures together. On the weekends, we would take the train into New York City, leaving my brother behind. We would have the greatest times making fancy dinners and pretending we were on a cooking show. He would be the one driving me down the coast to Virginia for a soccer tournament. Great talks emerged from those car rides. Dad and I were basically inseparable, but he was getting a little lonesome.

My dad had been trying to find a way to connect with new and exciting people for a while. He wanted something fun in our lives that we could do as a family. One day, he came across an event called Mindvalley and thought that it would be an incredible experience for the three of us. We made some arrangements and, sure enough, that May, my dad, brother, and I were off to Barcelona, Spain to take on the new challenge of Mindvalley University — a month-long event filled with inspiration and new beginnings. A lot unfolded that summer, including the beginnings of a whole new family and a life that I did not know of yet. Living in a small flat in Barcelona with five other people can bring the most unexpected people closer together.

When we got back to the United States after an amazing summer, I spent the last couple of weeks before school started with my mom and my friends. They were all happy to see me and the feeling was mutual. They didn't have much interest in hearing about the places I went or the experiences I had while away that summer. Thankfully they didn't ask lots of questions because it's hard for me to explain what happens at Mindvalley. They saw it as my Dad wanting to go to this thing in Spain and me having to go with him because that's just how it goes.

I hadn't wanted to go in the beginning, but I loved it in the end. It was a new environment — new country, new friends, and new opportunities. I felt adventurous and loved going out and exploring places that I hadn't known of before. I got to experience cool stuff most kids my age will never get to do. I went to two different countries in the span of a month. I walked the halls of the Vatican and ate way too many empanadas from the bakery down the street from *La Sagrada Familia*. I made countless memories in that month, the kind you tell over Thanksgiving dinner for years, yet I was still somewhat ungrateful. Coming home and hearing all the 'normal' things that my friends had been doing all summer made me feel like I had been missing out.

I knew that the opportunity I had just been given was amazing. Most of me was happy and proud of all the things I did and accomplished that summer, but part of me still wished I could have stayed in New Jersey. Even though I had the time of my life, created deeper connections with my brother, and new connections with people at Mindvalley, my thoughts were that I had been robbed of my summer. My friends were partially the reason I felt that way because they were telling me things like, "Oh you missed out on such a good summer here; you shouldn't have gone with your Dad." They were sending me pictures of them at the amusement park and I was jealous. That made me feel that I had made the wrong decision, even though I didn't really have a choice — my dad had decided we would go. All of the good thoughts about that summer went catapulting out the window onto the concrete floor below, shattering like glass.

School was about a week away from kicking off when my dad got back from seeing the woman who had shared a flat with us in Barcelona along with her two kids. His trip to see her felt like an undercover mission to me. I was not expecting to see JB or her kids after we all said goodbye to one another in Rome, but that changed quickly. Days later, JB herself came to visit us in New Jersey. She and my dad sat me down and told me that things were going to change really soon. They did not mean small changes; they meant BIG changes and I didn't know how to process it.

We had a week to pack our bags and then we were combining families and moving to Alberta, Canada. Moving from the United States to Canada wasn't on my agenda. The second I was told by my dad that we were moving, I was absolutely devastated. My initial reaction to this plan was "NO." It didn't help that my brother Jackson was excited to move. I felt singled out and I simply did not want to go. I was scared that I wouldn't be able to start a whole new life. Everything was in New Jersey: my friends, my mother, and my school. I tried to put up a fight. Even though I knew I had no chance of winning, I insisted.

I knew that there was love attached to their situation and I couldn't break it no matter how hard I tried. No matter how bad I made my dad feel, he was not going to give up. Tantrum after tantrum, the only thing changing about how my dad felt was how annoying I was — and I, too, was getting tired of myself. Every day ended with tears and I would not listen to what my father was saying even if it was for my best interest. I didn't care what he or JB had to say; I was on a mission to hold on to my life and flying full speed ahead. I didn't want anyone to stop me.

I asked myself things like, "Why me?" Why did my dad have to be the one to go on vacation for a month with his two children and then come back and say that we are picking up a whole new life plan? Why couldn't I just have a normal life? Why did I have to move so far away? Why did I have to be the one to drop everything just to make him happy? I didn't want to start a new life. I liked the one I had already — a lot. I would rather give up everything I enjoyed like school, soccer, and meeting new people than to give the move a chance and see how it went. I didn't want to be the new kid in this new school, let alone this new country.

I was told by my parents to see this as a new beginning, to keep an open mind, but that still didn't shake me from my resistance. All the way up until the day we stepped foot in Canada, I was furious. I had lost the battle I was determined to win. I refused to go to school no matter how many times my family told me it would be better than learning online and being home all day, every day. Before moving, school was my life. I woke up every morning more excited than ever to go to school. My parents knew how social I was and how much I liked hanging with my friends. Being at school made me happy. I knew staying home all day still wasn't an option, but I didn't get to make the decision. Looking back, it was for the better.

The last big argument we had about the move was to get me into the car to go to school. They essentially forced me to go. I sat through meetings with my new principal who was way too enthusiastic for my liking at the time. Despite that, his words reassured me. He told me I would fit in. He said that all the teachers were excited to meet me and that everyone would love me. It took all of my strength to keep looking as miserable as possible, but my brain wouldn't let me stay miserable. I started thinking, "I guess this isn't the worst thing after all." I began to loosen up, go with the flow, and see where I ended up. It was time to pick my elective classes for the new school year. These are the best hours of the school day for most students; the thing we look forward to on a daily basis. I saw that there were so many new things that I could choose from that my school in New Jersey would never think to offer to middle school students.

A couple of days after I met with the principal, I started school. My stomach was doing backflips when I walked through the door of the building. I was nervous about starting my school year after everyone else. Then, everything got easier. During my first period class, which was Band, I made friends with a trombone player named Mary in the section over from my left. I wasn't even 30 minutes into my day and it had already started to be better than I was expecting. That was when I realized that this new life of mine might turn out okay. My band teacher made sure to introduce me to everyone and let me toot my own horn about the two extra years of playing experience I had over everyone.

The students in every class I went to were fascinated by the fact that I moved from the United States, but I felt like I fit in. Some of my friends would later give me the nickname 'Jersey.' It was just like being back home. Just like my life prior to moving. I met people those first couple days that are still my really good friends now, three years later. These are people I've ended up caring about more than anyone I'd ever been friends with before. They ended up making me the happiest kid ever and it all happened because I didn't get to make my own decision about moving to Canada when I was 12.

If my parents would have let me decide my future, I would not be in the place I am now. The friends that I've made here in the past three years surpass most of the people who I thought had my back in New Jersey. They care about me more, they include me in more things, and they just have that sense of true friendship when I'm with them. I thought the way my friends in the States were treating me was right. That belittling and making fun of your friends was how it was supposed to be. My attitude toward others was influenced by those friends; so, to most people, I was harsh and mean. I used to be quick to judge and found myself snapping at others for no reason. My mind was wired like that from being treated that way for so many years.

I quickly adjusted my ways and became compassionate and understanding of others — I became a friend who was there for others in a way I wanted them to be there for me. I adopted qualities that I had never embraced in my life before, and this brought true happiness to me and to everyone around me. I can see now that moving might have been just the thing I needed to make me the best version of myself in the long run.

Moving to Canada has not only given me better friendships with the people around me but so many amazing opportunities to have with my family and create bonds with them. It has shown me that having a 'normal life' is just a bit boring. My step siblings and I still joke about how we didn't want to meet each other and share an apartment that first summer at Mindvalley. Now, we love to spend time together, travel, laugh, and make unforgettable memories. The family that I have grown into is built from the most amazing, smart, funny, and loving people I've come across and I am so grateful now that I have the opportunity to grow and expand as a family with them.

If you had told me four years ago that I would be a part of this family and living in Canada with them having the best times of my life, I wouldn't have believed you in the slightest. The things we've done together since the minute we met are incredible, and more keep coming day after day. From driving a van that was way too big for the roads across Turkey to doing five-man stacks in the pool in Spain. Or whitewater rafting in Europe with a bunch of foreign-speaking people and not having a clue what they were saying (nonetheless, that didn't stop them from playfully throwing us overboard).

I've grown to love Canada. I've enjoyed swimming in the hot springs in the Rockies, seeing a grizzly bear at the National Park, and riding the bike paths right outside my house during an unseasonably warm autumn. We have connected tremendously through experiences that I would not have had if it weren't for the move across the country and into Canada.

I have learned that it is okay to not have both hands on the wheel of your life and to let the people you trust take control once in a while. The changes made to your life may just be the best things that have ever happened to you. You're not alone. People have your back; trust them. Have an open mind and believe that happiness is waiting for you no matter what.

Ignite Action Steps

Separate Happiness and Unhappiness

- Start by grabbing two pieces of paper. On one of those pieces, write down all the things in your life that could be making you unhappy or make you feel not true to you or who you want to be. This could be a little difficult, so dig deep! You can draw pictures, write words, jot down a simple list, or be over-the-top creative.

- After you finish, take a good long look at what you've created.

- Now, work on getting rid of those unwanted feelings. Take a deeper look into what caused them to be there. Start by letting go of the things on your list that make you feel bad, unhappy, or deflated. Get the factors that make you unhappy out of your head and start the next step of the process.

- Take the second piece of paper and fill this page with all the things that make you happy: family, traveling, or anything it might be to you.

- Paste pictures onto your page, decorate it with colorful markers — whatever makes you happy — do it. Keep this page near you; look at it when you need to be reminded of all the things that bring you true happiness.

"The greatest happiness arrives with unexpected change, especially when you embrace it."

Jorja Giesin – Canada
Great cook and saxophone player

HAPPINESS
to me is-

HEATHER DALTON

"Stop pushing so you can be pulled by the Universe."

My intention is to inspire you to tap into your inner Wild Wanderer. This is the rebel in you, a spirit of the earth; a soul looking for adventure and new experiences, places, and people; a free-spirited being getting lost to find themselves; the most magical kind of creature. It's time to remove any blinders you've been wearing so you can see new possibilities waiting to rush in.

WANDERLUSTING MY WAY TO HAPPINESS

I am writing this from a tiny cabin floating on a lake that is nestled deep in the heart of the North Cascade Mountains in Washington State where I have manifested my dream job. I am working and living at a remote floating-cabin resort surrounded by the most majestic forest whose trees reach for the clouds against a backdrop of rocky mountain cliffs and snow-capped peaks. It took me over two hours of driving and two boats to get here, but the magnificence of my surroundings was worth the journey. The experience of being here nourishes the three core values that I have determined bring me the most happiness: freedom, nature, and wanderlust.

My life hasn't always been this amazing. In fact, there was a period when it looked much different. There was a time I was working in a highly stressful management career. It was not uncommon for me to work 80+ hours per week, as it was just the owner and I running the entire company. I didn't take good care of myself at all. I was an overweight smoker who didn't eat well and never exercised. To top it off, I was a complete control freak! Not only did I try and control every aspect of my life, I tried to control everyone in it as well. Having a self-care plan was nowhere near my radar until suddenly one day I dropped to my knees in unbearable stomach pain.

After a series of tests, the doctor told me stress was causing my pain. I laughed at him. I knew I had stress, but I also thought I was handling it. Obviously I had it wrong. My body was doing what it was designed to do during times of stress: producing excess stomach acid. I was a 32-year-old woman propping herself up with pillows to sleep and vomiting most mornings. The Universe was talking to me, but I wasn't ready to listen. I knew something had to change, but I had no idea what.

The Universe tried to get my attention again, this time presenting me with two significant losses in my life. The first was my grandfather. He was my mentor, the stable male figure in my life. He taught me my work ethic and his approval was important to me. I loved him so much and his passing was devastating. Coming from a big Italian family, this was a loss that we all felt deeply. On the same day that my grandfather passed away, I received a call that my first love, whom I had dated for six years, had taken his own life. I had just spent the last 24 hours with my grandfather, waiting for him to take his last breath, and I was delirious with exhaustion when the phone rang. Upon hearing the news, I dropped the phone. In that moment, I felt something inside of me snap.

Mentally and physically, I was in a bad place. Emotions I had been suppressing for a long time were coming to the surface. I was angry, hurt, overwhelmed, really uncomfortable, and achingly unhappy. I remember my partner at the time sitting me down and saying, "I really think you need to talk to someone."

Not wanting to ignore these loud signs any longer, I nervously made an appointment with a therapist and joined an online fitness community. I fully expected this to be just another 'diet,' but for the first time, I was introduced to personal development. This, paired with the work I was doing with my therapist, opened up a whole new world for me. My self-care became my priority and I started incorporating mind and body practices into my routine.

My life started to shift in powerful ways. As my physical health improved, my painful symptoms disappeared, but more important were the shifts I was experiencing in my mind. I was shocked to discover I no longer wanted to work in the management field. Despite earning a good living, it was soul-sucking and dangerous to my mental and physical well-being. I was able to see how unhappy I truly was and I wanted to believe there was more to life. I knew this would take drastic life changes.

I boldly made the decision to leave my job and pursue a future that would make me happy. The changes in me were drastic and immediately visible to others. A number of people asked me how they could have the happiness they saw in me, so I became an online health and fitness mentor to share my journey with them. While I supported others in improving their health, I continued to make my own personal development and self-care a priority. Not only did I read books and watch videos, I also worked with a number of therapists, coaches, and healers. I loved attending any kind of event that would inspire me to live my best life!

Unexpectedly, I discovered I was going much deeper with my clients to determine what was *really* driving their unhealthy habits. I was feeling a disconnect between the outward goals of my business and the work I longed to be doing with my clients. It wasn't until a Reiki healer I was working with said, "Heather, you're not a health coach, you're a life coach. Go be one!" that it all started making sense. It was an aha moment and I eagerly enrolled to obtain my Life Coach Certification.

I knew that I would be receiving tools to help me better support my clients. What I didn't bargain for was the spiritual awakening I was about to enter. The missing piece was *spirituality*. I grew up with a skewed view of God, so religion didn't resonate with me. I never realized that I got to decide what that looked like for ME. I didn't have to call it God, I could call it Source or the Universe. All that matters is that I believe there is something out there much bigger guiding and supporting me. For a recovering control freak, letting go of the reins was a hard process!

I went on to specialize in supporting women to empower their minds, celebrate their bodies, and awaken their spirits. I published a workbook and supported women all over the world through one-on-one coaching sessions, online group programs, and "Unplug for Self-Love" retreats. Speaking at various events, workshops, and retreats was exhilarating, but I still wasn't completely happy and I couldn't understand why.

I felt extremely lost and almost ready to walk away from my business. It was that same familiar feeling and I was desperate to not feel this way anymore. Thankfully my business coach sensed this and said, "Heather, there is something holding you back." That same day, she introduced me to a special healer who would change my life.

The idea of enrolling in this healer's 12-week program of weekly calls and soul work sent me into a spiral of overthinking. Signing up sparked nervous butterflies and excitement to delve into the unknown. During the first two days of the course, she intuitively felt that I needed to uncover the beliefs I've been carrying since childhood. We explored my subconscious mind and the imprints created by my parents. This was deep work that I had never done before and it completely rocked my world! I learned how my childhood experiences contributed to the stories I had been carrying my whole life and how they were the root of what was holding me back. I realized I could stop repeating the patterns that were no longer serving me and I have never felt so empowered.

My progress was unbelievable! I didn't hesitate to continue working with her. Once you have identified your childhood imprints, acknowledged your stories, and released what's no longer serving you, the sky's the limit!

This work was the hardest I've ever done. There were times it triggered raw, painful emotions; and other times I felt like I might never get to the other side of it! However, my motivation was knowing the end goal was the ability to manifest my deepest happiness.

My healer convinced me to do something I was very resistant to at first. She suggested I take a break from my business and focus on what brings me joy. This completely terrified me and I was instantly triggered, trying to determine how I would make enough money. I'll never forget when she said to me: "Your passions don't have to be your source of income and your income doesn't have to be tied to your passions!" She also presented the idea of manifesting multiple streams of income, which sounded ideal to me. I have always loved to engage in different projects and it's in alignment with the vision I have for my life of freedom.

I'm not gonna lie, I remember thinking, "Ummmm, OK, so how do I pay my bills then?" The thought of not working a business I had busted my ass for years to build felt slightly crazy to me! But that thinking was still coming from a place of control and scarcity, because it was comfortable.

It was at this time that the Universe really started to test my faith and willingness to surrender. My 13-year partnership ended. I had a falling out with someone I considered a sacred friend. I moved in with a friend and her family because I could no longer afford my rent. I was swimming in debt, my business was failing, and I had no idea how I was going to make money to pay my bills.

I realized I had two choices: I could do what I've always done in the past, which was lean into fear, make decisions from a scarcity mindset, and replay all the old stories from my childhood. Or, I could embrace the unknown, fully surrender to the Universe, tap into my inner Wild Wandress, and trust with every ounce of my being that I will be supported every step of the way. Something was Ignited in me and I chose option number two! As soon as I did, major shifts started happening.

Out of the blue, the pet-sitting business I had begun as a hobby started to pick up momentum. It quickly turned into my main source of income and it brought me immense joy! I adored all of my clients and fur babies, and there were months I was booked out three weeks or more. I realized that once I took a step back from my business and removed the blinders I had been wearing, there were new possibilities waiting to rush in.

In January of that year, I put my 'stuff' in storage, moved out of my friend's house, and fully committed to letting the Universe guide me on my path as I set out to live a nomadic lifestyle based more on *experiences* and less on *stuff!* I had no place to live and no plan. Just hope. It was the ultimate leap of faith.

A long-time curiosity helped me manifest a tiny home for two months, right on the Puget Sound in the Pacific Northwest and within walking distance to a state park. It was a dream come true, but it was also hard. I was in this tiny house, alone. I didn't know anyone. I was heavily grieving the loss of my two best friends and I had no idea where my next paycheck was coming from. So what did I do? I cried a lot, meditated, connected with nature, drank champagne, and processed my emotions. I had decades of processing to do and this tiny house created the perfect sanctuary for me to do so. Even through some of the deepest pain I had ever experienced, I felt divinely guided and knew this was all happening to serve my highest good.

My intention is to honor the flow and acknowledge resistance. To me, living a nomadic lifestyle is the ultimate form of surrender. It forces me to live in the present and trust in something bigger than myself. I also have to embrace that everything is happening *for* me, not *to* me.

In March of that year, my schedule cleared overnight. I had no booked clients, nowhere to stay, and a 100 percent loss of income, but I didn't panic! Even with being thrown this curveball, I knew I was being divinely guided and supported.

I accepted an invitation to stay at my friend's house with her and her five boys, which would push this solo nomad way outside of her comfort zone! My space was an area in her living room with a mattress and a small privacy screen. I knew the Universe was testing my progress. Over the course of the next three months, I would face each of my triggers head on. I was being called to go inward and I devoted more time to personal development and self-care. I meditated more often, engaged in enlightenment programs, read books, exercised, completed a 60-day detox cleanse, journaled, tapped into my creativity, worked closely with my healer, and got intentional on what I wanted to manifest.

Despite all of the chaos, I continued to see the blessings and opportunities around me. I didn't worry about losing my clients temporarily, instead embracing it as a sign that it was time to explore something else. I was really clear about wanting this opportunity to include my three components of happiness. And just like that, the opportunity fell into my lap. One storage unit, multiple cities, an abundance of couches, and hundreds of miles later, I'm writing this chapter from my dream job in the heart of the world-renowned North Cascade Mountains.

If someone would have told that young, stressed-out management professional that she would be a zen nomad working at a floating-cabin resort in the heart of the mountains, she would not have believed it was possible! I made the decision to fully surrender and focus on what Ignites happiness in my life. I don't know where my wanderlust will take me after this adventure, but I don't need to know that today. What I do know is that I'm really happy! And I am divinely guided and provided for every step of the way.

IGNITE ACTION STEPS

I want to leave you with a few action steps you can take today to open the door to igniting YOUR happiness and tapping into YOUR Wild Wanderer or Wandress! May you be blessed to live a life you can't wait to wake up for, and remember… stop pushing so you can be pulled by The Universe.

- **Self-care:** Make your self-care your top priority. We can't give others our best if we are not giving ourselves our best. Make a conscious effort to track the things that bring you the most peace and joy. Also track the things that trigger stress and negativity, and note the time of day when you find yourself most easily triggered. Make a daily appointment with yourself during those times to engage in what brings you joy. Recognizing my patterns and deciding to choose gratitude and happiness helped me so much that I designed an eCourse around the idea, entitled *Thrive: Creating a Balanced, Connected, Healthy Life You Adore!* that can guide you in creating an exceptional self-care plan with mind, body, and spirit elements.

- **Personal development:** Making the commitment to myself to be a student of the Universe by reading, attending workshops, and continually learning has helped me thrive. Knowing where to begin focusing your energy can be a challenge. I invite you to sit down somewhere you find peaceful and calming. Take a few minutes to write down what habits and behaviors you want to incorporate in your life. Pick the top three that you're *farthest* from and start investing in your growth and learning in those areas. If you have no idea what that looks like, I offer an exercise in *Thrive* called *The Perfect 10 Exercise,* which helps you pinpoint where you should direct your energy first. Once you determine where you're focusing, start exploring what you want to engage in and make your personal development a non-negotiable part of your routine.

- **Dream team:** Working with professionals is taking your self-care and personal development to the next level. I like to call it 'establishing your dream team.' Over the years, I have worked with a number of therapists, coaches, and healers, all of whom have offered me a different perspective and given me tools that I didn't have, impacting my healing and growth in profound ways. I always say there is no better investment than in yourself!

- **Step into your wanderlust:** You've learned, you've healed, you've grown. Now that you're clear on what brings you happiness, live your life unapologetically. Let yourself be divinely guided and start living your authentic, joyful life today!

Heather Dalton – United State of America
Certified Life Coach and Wild Wandress
www.wildwandress.com

KRISTIN KURTH-KOELZER

"Happiness is knowing in your heart that all will be well."

I would love to inspire you to look at your own story with deeper compassion. My wish is that you feel connected to something larger than yourself, knowing you are never alone. I hope you feel understood, and can find the courage to allow what's meant to be, to find *you*. When I finally did this, the biggest and best gifts of life came to me. When I accepted the fact that I wasn't at all in charge, happiness found *me*. Let go, let life unfold, and enjoy the gifts.

WHEN I STOPPED CHASING HAPPINESS, HAPPINESS FOUND *ME*

Less than a year after I began fostering Isaac, I received a call from his birth mother. It was odd. She usually called at bedtime to say goodnight and put her imprint on his tiny heart. We were about to celebrate his first birthday and my 50th that summer, on August 7th. What a coincidence that Isaac and I were born on the same day. Or was it? I sat on the floor of my bedroom, resting against the stiff wooden frame of my bed. It was a quiet Sunday morning and I was the only one home — a rare occurrence in our frenetic family. The house around me exuded a happy stillness and the ringing of the phone cutting through the peacefulness was jarring.

I answered hesitantly due to the strange timing of her call. Her voice was relaxed and calm as she asked, "Kristin, if I lose parental rights and my mom or grandma can't qualify to keep Isaac, would you ever consider being his mom? Adopting him? I wouldn't want him to be with anyone else." I held my breath on hearing these words, giving my brain time to process what was being asked of me. I finally exhaled. To my surprise, I said, "I've thought about this. We all have. This is not exactly how I had planned to live the second half of my life, but yes, we'll seriously consider this." The words tumbled out of my heart before my head even realized what I was saying. Where had those words come from?

I tried to picture her reaction, the expression on her face, the pounding of her heart. How many times had she picked up the phone and put it down again before calling? I felt so deeply connected to this woman who had become a part of my daily life. We spoke nearly every night and Isaac and I visited with her weekly at Children and Family Services. We met in a brightly-lit playroom filled with tiny tables and chairs and lots of toys. It looked like a mini pre-school classroom. She never missed a visit. She was very pretty, with long dark hair and Mediterranean features, and perfectly applied makeup. She smiled and laughed a lot, just like Isaac. I came to look forward to our 'play dates.' We even traveled out to see her at the rehab center where she lived for a few weeks as she was trying to turn things around. After several months, I could tell she was starting to come to terms with the fact that her son might be taken from her like so much in life had already been. The privilege of being called Mother, Mama, Mom, Mommy was about to be denied. The malediction of addiction had prevented her from receiving the gift I've most treasured in my own life.

In light of so much uncertainty, I made a habit of walking out of my house into the fresh air and beautiful surroundings. I had a feeling that much more would soon be revealed and I often looked up at the sky pleading, "Please, just tell me what to do." For once, I didn't have an easy answer. I was clearly not in control of what would unfold.

The months of uncertainty were starting to wear on our family. My husband and I felt we all needed some time away from the emotional rollercoaster we'd been riding. We decided to vacation in Mexico during summer break. Unable to take our foster child out of the country, our friends offered to take Isaac for the week so we could enjoy our three older kids and focus on our big decision. (As if we were in charge.)

This lucky little boy with his great big smile had been scooped up and loved by our entire community. Most of my friends' children were now teenagers and Isaac was a happy reminder of the early days of raising our families. This became his extended family — people who, like us, made it their mission to love him unconditionally for as long as he would be in our care.

Isaac was the last of more than 20 kids we had fostered over the years — some for a week, a weekend, or even just a day. We had others for longer. I still remember the day I picked up our first placement, a sweet African American baby boy at Children's Hospital at birth. He fit into the palm of my hand. His mother was 18 years old and he was her fourth baby. Handing him over to his adoptive family was one of the most difficult things I'd ever done. In the months following his transition to his new family, I became deeply depressed, feeling as though we had lost 'our' child. We took a break from fostering before dipping our toes in again by doing more respite care for other foster families, relieving them for a short time, while they took a break. I thought if we weren't as highly invested in the children and their cases, we might not get too attached. (As if I were in charge.)

Our friends and community showed up for us in ways we'd never imagined. After placing many previous foster children back into the hands of birth parents, adoptive parents, and other foster parents, I became good at compartmentalizing my feelings, never allowing myself to fall headfirst in love with these kids because of the pain that was to come from relinquishing my role as their temporary mother. I tried to build a protective coating around myself so I wouldn't have to experience the heart-breaking sadness of letting go of someone I had mothered. Isaac was different right from the start, creeping under my skin and reaching my heart despite my best efforts to protect myself.

Off we went to Mexico with our family to determine our next steps. The week was going by quickly — lots of pool and beach time interspersed with many meals together. The kids were certified to scuba dive on this trip, something my husband Tim and I had enjoyed over the years. By day five of the vacation, nobody had yet mentioned the question of Isaac. We weren't debating the pros and cons of keeping him. We weren't imagining what would happen if we did or didn't.

We knew there were a few people vying for him, all relatives of his birth parents and, in our minds, all inadequate, if not potentially dangerous. At dinner on the fifth night, I broached the subject. We heard our kids talk about their fears, the same ones that had been rolling around in my mind for quite some time. If there was a vote, it would have been split.

On our last night before heading home, Tim and I went to dinner, just the two of us, at a little restaurant near where we were staying. We sat at an open-air table overlooking a beautiful beach and never-ending ocean. We enjoyed the quiet hospitality showered upon us, as we were the only guests in the entire restaurant. Deep conversation didn't come easily for us, especially around emotionally-charged topics. Instead, we watched the staff slowly wander around the room setting dishes, glasses, and napkins on empty tables while we soaked up the serenity, lost in our own thoughts. The air outside rippled with the day's heat, so we were surprised to hear what sounded like Christmas music playing from the dining room speakers. It was a recognizable smooth jazzy melody.

"Is that Kenny G?" I asked Tim, laughing. We listened until we could both name the familiar tune — *"Away in a Manger... no crib for his bed, the little Lord Jesus lay down His sweet head..."* We burst out laughing at the irony of that quirky scene.

As our laughter faded, our eyes caught and locked for a moment. My breath stopped moving in and out of my lungs. I could see it in his face, this man I knew so well. He wanted Isaac as much as I did. I could feel it in my own heart, this rush of warm *knowing*. I exhaled, my body melting into a sense that Isaac was just meant to be ours.

It wasn't a decision we controlled after all. Rather, it was something that was being asked of us. Something neither of us could deny. I don't remember what I had for dinner that evening, but I'll never forget how I felt — a calm sense, a deep knowing in my heart that all would be well.

For the next year, we fought to become Isaac's "forever family." The county wasn't enamored with the idea of handing an infinitely 'adoptable' baby over to a short-term emergency foster family. There were many families yearning for a 'concurrent placement,' one in which they foster a child while anxiously awaiting the court's decision to terminate parental rights, freeing the child for legal adoption. We had been approved for adoption many years before this, when we first became licensed as a foster family. My intent had never been to adopt. I felt so blessed to have the three treasures God had given us and I wasn't longing for more. My very pragmatic husband had wanted to make sure we were ready in the event that we fell in love with one of the children we fostered. And we had fallen in love with Isaac.

Dealing with life on life's terms is a concept I began to understand during that year. When Isaac's mom contested the adoption, I was shocked. It resulted in another year of waiting to adopt Isaac. It was a long and arduous year that catapulted me into another serious bout of depression. I was in total fear. Fear that we wouldn't win. Fear that we would win. Fear that I was too old to start over, too involved in my career and my teaching to make time for him. Fear of the impact on our marriage. Fear that our lives would be ruined one day if Isaac ended up on the same path as his birth family, ravaged by drugs and alcohol.

I started seeing the film of my future as one filled with sadness, pain, and disappointment. It was time to change the channel. But I couldn't. The anxious worrier in me had a new job — his name was Isaac, which in Hebrew means 'he laughs/will laugh.' In the Old Testament of the Bible, Isaac was the only son of Abraham and Sarah. Although, like me, Sarah was well past the age of childbearing, God promised they would have a son, and they did. They named him Isaac. It felt like a sign from God that I needed to keep putting one foot in front of the other.

If I had paused at the time, I may have connected the dots. My husband comes from a family of 12 children. After our first daughter was born, we couldn't get pregnant. We hadn't even considered the possibility of not being able to have more children. Once you've experienced the joy of having a child, you can't unfeel it. The love, pride, and happiness were so intense that I wanted more. And nobody was going to stand in my way.

Getting pregnant felt like a full-time job on top of an already busy career and parenting a toddler. After two frustrating years of unsuccessful interventions, including three rounds of in vitro fertilization, I sat exhausted, across from my doctor, having lost faith in him and asked, "Who's your competition? This isn't working." Unwilling to give up, I wanted to find the best doctor possible. Having recently quit my job as a senior partner in a large advertising agency in Chicago, I knew I now had a new job — I put myself in charge yet again (or so I thought).

I dragged Tim up to a highly recommended fertility doctor in the northern suburbs of Chicago. This fourth round of in vitro was our last shot. We told our doctor we wanted to be as aggressive as possible. And he supported us. We were pregnant with triplets, but devastatingly, we lost one of the triplets at the end of my first trimester. Life on life's terms? I wasn't a fan. And up to this point, I actually continued to believe I was in charge. I thought I could fight anyone or anything and *will* a happy ending into existence through sheer determination.

Years later, when we welcomed Isaac into our lives, I learned through many other challenges, including my own battle with anxiety, depression, menopause, and alcohol (the perfect storm and ironic in fact), that happiness was possible as soon as I was willing to part with a little control. We weren't driving the decision about Isaac's future. The courts and a higher power would decide his fate. We were just characters in his story.

Isaac is now 8 years old and a super high-energy, funny, athletic, and loving light in our lives. There are challenges — we expected as much. What I didn't expect was that I would find greater meaning in my life and a path to deeper internal happiness through this journey.

Adversity has been my growth hormone. I've experienced some of life's most amazing moments while rising from the ashes of its darkest. My life is far from perfect and there are times when things don't look at all like the life I had imagined. I used to view happiness as an end goal, something to be chased after and achieved. I lived like a rat in an endless maze looking so hard for the path to the golden cheese. In doing so, I robbed myself of true happiness, the kind that comes from just *being* rather than *doing*.

Through Isaac's presence in my life, my thoughts and associations around happiness have evolved. When I pause and live life on life's terms, surrendering to what's meant to be, I feel happier. (It's so much easier to let someone else be in charge.) I am delighted to start each day with this simple prayer: "Let *Your* will, not mine, be done." Without even pausing to hold my breath, I know in my heart that all will be well.

In looking at my life through the lens of compassion, I gained so much happiness. I invite you to take time to pause and look at the story of your own life with greater compassion. I hope you, too, will feel connected to something larger than yourself. Know that God is carrying you and you're never alone. Find the courage to let go of the need to feel in charge. Allow what's meant to be to find *you*.

IGNITE ACTION STEPS

Worry dolls (also called trouble dolls, in Spanish, *muñeca quitapena*) are small, handmade dolls that originate from Guatemala. According to legend, Guatemalan children tell their worries to these dolls, placing them under their pillows when they go to bed at night. By morning, the dolls have gifted them with the wisdom and knowledge to eliminate their worries. (I prefer not to sleep with my worries; I like to wait until morning to face them.)

When you first open your eyes in the morning, ask yourself, what does 'happy' look like for me today? Sometimes big, sometimes small, there are many different thoughts that can come up. Remember, the heart never lies.

I keep a little notebook on my nightstand and after imagining a happy day, I ask myself, "What worries are standing in my way right this minute?" I write them down on a piece of paper, things like: Am I doing enough for Isaac? Are we going to run out of money? Will my adult kids make the world a better place? Did I help them develop their own relationship with God or something bigger than themselves? Is my marriage going to survive? Are we out of milk? Is our world going to survive? Will I ever find my purpose in life… my why?

I think of these worries as 'happiness hindrances.' I write them down to acknowledge that they exist, then I get them out of the way. I fold the piece of paper and stick it in the back of a notebook or folder. I jot a note of surrender on each, asking God to take care of what I've written inside, sometimes as simple as "Please take care of this for me," or "I'm handing this over to You. Thanks." After collecting these worries over time, perhaps every week or month, I just toss them.

The key is this: Once you allow yourself to get out of your own way and ask for help, you'll be off to a happier state of mind and a better day.

Kristin Kurth-Koelzer – United States of America
Co-Founder of EquiBrand Consulting
MBA, Adjunct Professor of Marketing
www.equibrandconsulting.com
kristin@kristinkurth.com

IGNITE HAPPINESS ACTIVITY

Instructions:

1. Make several copies of this Worry Doll artwork (made by my daughter).

2. Cut the dolls out and keep them near your bedside with a pen or pencil.

3. On the back of each doll, write down the first worries that come to mind when you open your eyes in the morning.

4. Ask God, or your own Higher Power, to take care of these worries for you.

5. Tuck them away in a drawer, box, or at the back of your journal.

6. Have a much happier day without these worries; know that they are handled.

7. Toss them after a few days or a week with gratitude that you are being cared for.

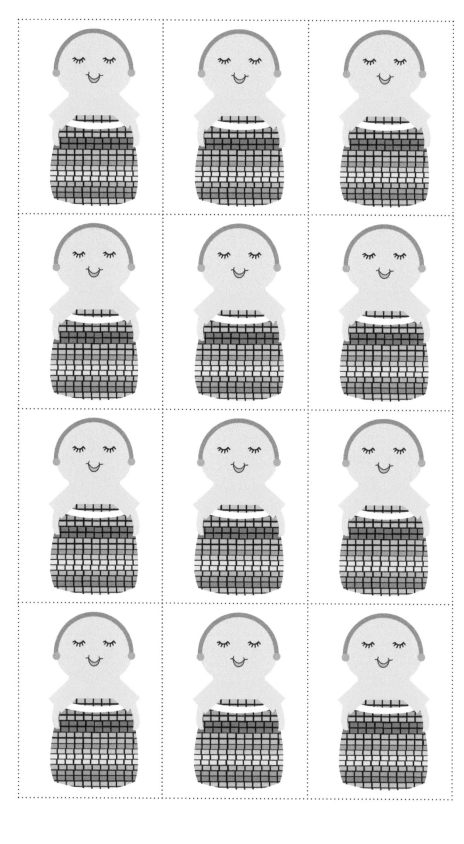

IGNITE
HAPPINESS

BEEJAL COULSON

*"Nature is the soul to the Universe, wings to the mind, and
flight to the imagination. It gives life to everything."*

**My deepest desire is for you to be in appreciation and awe of the beauty
of nature. It surrounds you every day. Through the power of your senses,
experience how nature connects you to the present moment, healing and
nurturing the depths of your soul.**

HAPPINESS IS CONNECTION TO NATURE

When I was six years old, living in England, I was deriving happiness
from nature every day and not even knowing it. A soft pink blossom tree, an
apple tree, and a sweet fragrant red rose bush took their pride and place in the
'garden of Eden' — my happy place. My grandfather had planted a variety of
vegetables and herbs along the verges of the garden. He would normally be
singing Bollywood film songs while mindfully tending and watering them.
There were juicy red tomatoes, white onions, potatoes, pink radishes, spicy thin
green chillies, coriander, rosemary, and chives. My grandmother would make
pickles from the chillies and Bramley apples. I would skip through the garden,
chasing the fluttering butterflies dancing in sequences of the infinity symbol.

An abundance of daisies and buttercups were sprawled on the rectangular
lawn. My best friend and I had fun making daisy chains. There were also
clusters of dandelions, which when transformed into white globes we would
puff on and make a wish, watching the seeds disperse in the air. We rejoiced

in collecting rose petals, squeezing them in water to make potions then gifting our homemade 'perfume' to neighbors. So many sweet delicious memories where happiness was endless, and where feelings of contentment and time seemed to stand still.

Two years later, my extended family moved out. Tears flowed from my eyes as a deep sadness engulfed my whole eight-year-old being. My heart felt hollow as I peeked out of the bedroom window and looked at the garden below. The wooden shed had been removed; the apple tree and plants had been dug up and cleared out. By early evening, the massacre was apparent. Grey concrete slabs covered the majority of the garden. The blossom tree remained along with a small central square patch of lawn; the rest was unrecognizable. I was devastated. My father was too busy earning a living to look after the garden; he went for a low maintenance option. This was an early and painful lesson for me in the challenge of prioritizing the benefits of nature over the distractions of everyday living.

When I look back on my early years, the essence of nature was central to my experience. There is a photo of me as a baby sitting on the beach smiling with the backdrop of a blue sky and turquoise sea water. I smile as I notice that I have many photos as an adult with a similar background taken on holidays abroad. My father would often reminisce to me the happy memories of my infancy in Mombasa, a coastal town in Africa. Inhaling the fresh sea breeze, laughing and chatting with one another, it had been our Sunday ritual as a family to go to the beach for an evening stroll as the sun set.

When my happy times in the garden ended, I refused to look out of my bedroom window at the uninviting concrete jungle. The message to my mind "I don't want to see that" must have unconsciously turned down my sight as it was at this time I was diagnosed with myopia: a short-sighted eye condition. I retreated within myself.

My connection to nature resurfaced years later when I left home to study at the age of eighteen. I chose universities in rural areas for both my degree and postgraduate studies. The English countryside was beautiful, so much greenery healing to my eyes. I would often skip to my lectures feeling so much joy with my surroundings.

When I embarked on my career, I became more and more absorbed in my work. The only time I really connected to nature was when I was on holiday. This was a practice I developed as an adult — my family and I did not go on holidays abroad when I was a child. Holidays became my passion, experiencing different cities, countries, cultures, and nature in its many forms. Alpine mountains, golden beaches with crystal clear blue seas, tropical rainforests, and serene lakes expanded my imagination and made my soul rejoice. I felt a sense of happy freedom when I was surrounded by nature.

In my late twenties I was regularly buried in work and heading toward burnout. My life felt like it had shrunk. I recognized that I wanted my world to include a partner and a family, but there was no time for either because of my work life. I knew inside that things weren't right and I felt from deep within that I needed to expand my world. I planned a year out of my career to go traveling to the other side of the world. I wanted to get away from everything and immerse myself in natural surroundings. I started in Brazil, spent time in Australia, and then traveled to New Zealand. It seemed my body had a compass directing me back into nature for a reset.

My lungs inflated and my heart expanded as I immersed in the ethereal landscape of glimmering snow-capped mountains, glacial-fed rivers, and rolling hills. The vibrant colors of the landscape softened my gaze. A light whispering breeze caressed my face. I was on horseback, on a slow-pace trek in New Zealand. Even though it was my first time on a horse it felt like second nature, as if it was a soul remembrance. The horse paced itself in a gentle rhythm. A deep sense of inner peace embraced my whole being. Appreciating the sheer magnificence of my surroundings fully in the present experiencing the timeless, I knew I had awakened to the power of the beauty and brilliance of nature. My soul rejoiced as I surrendered to the surreal experience. My Saturn had returned.

New Zealand opened my eyes to nature in its variety of beautiful landscapes: lakes, mountains, glaciers, national parks, and beaches. It felt like heaven on earth as I continued to have magical moments and experiences traveling — trekking, cycling, paragliding, kayaking, and skydiving.

Being in nature under the sea I discovered a whole new incredible world. The depth of peace in my whole being emanated around me as the sunlight reflected on the shimmering coral, creating a technicolor effect with the extraordinary sea creatures. I was diving in the Great Barrier Reef in Australia. Having overcome my fear of deep water just three years prior to this, I appreciated such magical moments being imprinted in my inner being.

My travels in New Zealand in particular opened my heart to nature more than ever before and that changed my life deeply. It taught me to bring nature to my world on a daily basis, not just on holiday. Upon returning to England, I started to make that happen. I upgraded to a modern apartment in a leafy London suburb with a golf course opposite. It was perfectly manicured and so green. I purchased a bike and would cycle daily to the end of the golf course declaring to myself that it was 'my garden.' That awakening I had in New Zealand would forever be etched in my soul and created a cascade of further wondrous experiences with nature and a lasting impact on my daily life back in England.

Capturing the precious moments I had experienced in nature mixed with imagination; I began to create sanctuaries in my mind. They were somewhere I could go to feel inner peace and calm when challenging times disturbed my sleep. There were three scenes that I would replay as if they were on a big movie screen. I would begin in New Zealand on a horse, then I would be in a tropical rainforest cooling down in a natural rock pool with a waterfall cascading down. In the distance on top of a mountain, my guardian angel would be waiting for me — my late grandmother. She would wrap her arms around me and acknowledge me as the Indian goddess Lakshmi, whispering "Everything is going to work out for you." I would then fly as if I was a peacock (my spirit animal) and head to the golden beach with turquoise sea, just like in Mexico, and float on my back like a starfish surrendering to the divine.

Those feelings became an integral part of my being and touched all areas of my life, including my relationship. Opening my mind to living outside of London where I could feel the essence of nature, my future husband and I looked for a home to share. My heart swelled as we drove into the main tree-lined entrance of a 72 acre, grade II registered historic park and garden. The leaves on the trees displayed pretty shades of autumn. After viewing the show home, as we drove out of the development, my fiancé and I knew this was where we would be creating our life together. My inner child exploded with happiness. I was going to live in a park! My very own wonderland!

Four years later, my husband and our young daughter are happily settled in our beautiful home. Outside, the manicured trees and shrubs lining the borders sway gently in the breeze. I water the plants as I walk barefoot through the 'garden of Eden' that my husband lovingly created for us. I feel the rich earth underneath my feet as it grounds me. I take in the tall pine tree on the far left just outside the fence above the raised flower bed. The branches bow down toward the serene seated Buddha statue in the center, which is surrounded by a variety of herbs as well as a delicate array of colorful flowers. The peach rose bush at the back smells delicious. There is a purple hibiscus tree planted on the far right in honor of my late grandmother. In front of it is a small greenhouse. It's mesmerising to observe the birds, the Blue Tits with their colorful plumages scurrying to and fro from the nest box that my daughter had made, awaiting the arrival of their offspring. In this place, my heart sings the way that it did in New Zealand. The pure happiness I receive in nature is available to me every day.

It was not until a decade later that I realized that somehow I had gotten caught up with life and despite living in such beautiful surroundings, I again felt a sense of disconnect to nature unless we were away on holiday. For exercise, I was going for a daily swim at my health club. My bike, which I had used to explore my outdoor wonderland, was gathering dust in the garage.

Time to truly enjoy the excess of our park and beyond had dissipated and I made a concerted effort to reconnect myself with all that I loved — a cerulean blue sky with fluffy white clouds, a field of exuberant gold crops glowing under the sun, the song by Sting '*Fields of Gold*' playing into my earphones. Having just walked, skipped, and run along the walking paths in the farmer's fields heading back to my park filled with majestic trees, I rejoice "This is where I live!" As I turn to my right, the field is full of green and the sun is setting serenely. I close my eyes and see hues of lemon yellow, followed by sap green then cobalt blue in waves of energy floating. The beauty activates the chakras around my solar plexus, heart and throat rotating in spirals, aligning and harmonizing one after another with the energy rising upwards. I'm singing and dancing as the music changes to a dance track. My body is moving and every cell is rejuvenated. I feel freedom and joy as I connect with my spirit in the dance of happiness.

My family's routine has been to go on a 5 kilometer circuit family bike ride in the early evening through the park, woods, and across the fields, past a stream that flows into a lake, up toward and across a bridge and down the hill and back across the fields. I collect some fresh sticky weed called *galium aparine* for making herbal tea. My husband and daughter race each other on some parts while I purposely trail behind, lost in my own world seeing the compelling wonder of nature that surrounds me with fresh new eyes with a sense of childlike wonder. The inner child offers the return of a second innocence. The child within knows the way to joy and happiness.

Spring is in the air. The sun glistens on my face. There is beauty everywhere. As I embody my surroundings, more and more there are metaphors to life in nature all around me. The birds are nestled high on the branches whistling their tunes. The delicate horse chestnut flowers on the tree congregated in a cone are delicately falling like confetti. The trees are so alluring, in so many shapes and forms. Inhaling the scent of the wood as I run my fingers along the bark of a tree, I can feel the texture as I observe curiously the intricate fractal patterns in finer detail. I am reminded that I am connected to this innate intelligence — I am filled with awe.

Self realization invited me to appreciate and delve deeper into nature — meaningfully connecting to the present moment, immersing me with my senses for a deeper healing and awakening of my spiritual being. Nature has accelerated my inner journey through the dance of a metaphoric dialogue and taught me so much about my relationship with myself and the path to my evolutionary growth. It has accentuated my creative expression devouring me with gifts of inspiration, intuition, clarity, and motivation to take inspired action toward fulfilling my dreams and goals.

Nature continues to be my guide, healer, and divine inspiration. It is consciousness expressing itself through me, a reflection where I can enter another dimension, a passageway to a sense of something much deeper. The essence and Soul of Mother Gaia is there in her many forms: ancient trees, dancing leaves, budding flowers, a soothing stream, vast open blue skies, fresh fields of emerald green leading me into the integration of oneness, allowing me to see and ultimately discover more about myself.

A couple of years ago, I was at a one-day self-development workshop, 'Big Magic,' in London hosted by writer Elizabeth Gilbert. One of the tasks we had was to write a letter from our higher selves allowing our Enchantment to voice its desire. I rediscovered that letter at the time of writing this story. I feel it is important to share my divine wisdom with you as my inner self has always recognized the importance of nature. I want you to see how powerful intuition is and how it can guide us all to our magnetic north.

Dear Beejal,

I'm your enchantment and this is what I want to tell you. I love being with you when you are in nature. I love where you live; please spend more time with me in the garden and park. I delight in watching the Blue Tits coming in and out of their nest and listening to them sing. I love it when you create — especially when you paint. I feel your peace. I love it when you play the djembe; you are so immersed in the rhythm to the beat when your eyes are closed. I am with you when you meditate every day, when you do yoga and when you hear the sound of the gong. I am filled with joy when you are by the sea. I feel so close when you connect to your hopes and dreams, and I go deeper with you into the magic that emanates as a result. I am with you when you have inspiration come to visit you so many times. I love to be with you more so you can live the life you love.

Love from your Enchantment <3

This letter was an affirmation that nature gives life to everything. My hope is as you spend quality time in nature, your eyes will begin to open more widely and the detail in nature will become more apparent to you. When you awaken to the essence of nature, it connects you to the present moment, soothing and renewing you, creating inner peace, gratitude, and appreciation. The higher vibrations of nature can raise your vibration, impacting positively on your well-being, healing and nurturing your soul as well as deepening your understanding of yourself. Go outside and seek your wonderland.

Ignite Action Steps

Connect with Nature. Go out alone, with pen and paper. Take time to ground yourself. Be still and focus on your breathing for some minutes so you feel present. Take 10-15 minutes to walk around to explore your senses deeply. What do you see, hear, feel, smell, and taste? Note your observations.

Create a sanctuary in your mind. Think of a place in nature that you visited where you felt at peace or a place you wish to visit. Imagine a movie and amplify the image so it appears on a huge screen. Visualize yourself in this place and engage as many of your other senses as you can — sound, touch, smell, taste. Add another place or two and add it to the movie. Play the movie in your mind and sense any feelings you experience in your body. This sanctuary you have created, you can visit it anytime you like. Select a song that resonates with this sanctuary to make it even more powerful.

Beejal Coulson – United Kingdom
Creator / Founder of Quantum Life Technique,
Clinical Hypnotherapist, Author
www.beejalcoulson.com

Ignite Happiness Activity

Write a letter to yourself from your enchantment. Start the letter "Dear your name, I'm your enchantment and this is what I want to tell you… "

Create something to offer Mother Earth such as a poem, some writing, a drawing, or build nature art — using only what you find on the ground. Use the following page to represent your energetic appreciation for Mother Earth in a unique and creative way.

ABBEY RICHTER

"Happiness is being confident with your own uniqueness."

My story is designed to raise your awareness about the connection between happiness and body image. It is filled with many of my heartfelt experiences to inspire you. After speaking with dozens of young adults, I have realized that having an open discussion about body image is both needed and welcomed. I want to help you be aware of how having the right mindset can empower you to love your body more.

FINDING BEAUTY WITHIN

"These are the best years of your life," is what teenagers hear from adults on a regular basis. While this might be true, there are countless difficult realities teens experience in society today that many adults either do not remember or did not exist when they were my age. My greatest challenges as a teenager so far have been dealing with societal pressures related to how I should look. Everything changed for me when I started seeing the beauty that exists within. This is the story of how that happened.

Young people today are judged in many ways, including how they perform academically, who they are as a person, and how they treat others. As a young person myself, these assessments speak to who I am as an individual and what values I implement into my daily life. Other times however, we are judged on things that are beyond our control and have no reflection on us as individuals.

One of the most prevalent and destructive ways people are judged is based on their physical appearance. With teens, this can be dramatic. Whether it's weight, height, acne, or other comparisons to conventional standards of beauty, young people around the world are faced with a minefield of judgment and criticism. The influence of social media on our lives further serves to intensify these standards. We feel pressure to conform and to be seen by the amount of engagement we get and the number of followers we have. For me, I felt a double dose of judgment — for my height and for my ongoing challenges with acne.

Even when I was younger, my best friends were always taller than me. Not just an inch or two, sometimes as much as a foot taller! Some people think it's cool to be placed in the front for every class picture, but for me, it had gotten old by preschool. Every year, the photographer would pick me to be in the front because I was the shortest. In kindergarten, I asked my teacher if I could stand on a box in the back row so I wouldn't have to be the shortest in the front again. I remember crying when she said no. Ever since that moment, I have been sensitive about my height. Each year, my friends grew taller and taller, and the gap between us got larger. In primary school, I was singled out because of my height all the time. I remember classmates picking me up without my permission, pushing me over, and making fun of me for being shorter than them.

About two years ago, I went to the doctor for my annual visit. She did a physical exam and checked my heart, lungs, eyes, ears, weight, and height. She typed it all up as I sat in the waiting room. I looked around to see other patients talking to one another and reading magazines. There was a young girl sitting across the room who looked about my age. She was engrossed in her magazine with the words "The Perfect Body" on the cover in big letters. I thought to myself, "What is the perfect body?"

After a few minutes, the nurse led us to another room where the doctor joined us. I had been hoping my doctor would tell me I had just hit my growth spurt and that I would be growing more, but instead, she devastated me by saying I was done growing taller for the most part. Each and every word the doctor spoke became louder and louder in my head. Everything in the doctor's office became fuzzy as the tears began to well up in my eyes and then trickle down my face. All I could think of was being short for the rest of my life and how my friends at school would forever make jokes about it.

I would eventually come to accept my height for what it is. I would learn that it is one of those things about myself I really can't change, so I might as well embrace it. But I wasn't there yet. I also had some acne issues to address.

One of the inevitable challenges teenagers face is coping with acne, and I am certainly no exception. I began to develop acne on my face starting in seventh grade. My friends and parents would try and talk to me about it; however, I didn't notice and I really didn't care about how my skin looked. As long as it didn't bother me, I wasn't interested in worrying about it. In eighth grade, however, I started to care more about my physical appearance. The judgment from peers and family that came along with being a teenager finally hit me at full speed.

As I got older, my acne worsened until it became impossible to ignore. It got to the point where I would come home from school in tears. It became painful to look in the mirror. I could tell that other people noticed and judged me, which made me feel even more self-conscious. This was not what happiness was supposed to feel like or look like. I was afraid to go out in public, look people in the eyes, or have conversations with my friends and family. I would pretend I was fine, but I knew deep down that I was not happy with how my face looked. It took a toll on me physically and psychologically. It began to chip away at my self-esteem. Friends would try recommending new products and although I gave them a try, nothing helped. If I described the cleansers, masks, organic treatments, and other products I have used over the past few years, the list would go on for pages. I even tried giving up dairy, which was definitely no fun!

When I was in ninth grade, I went to the mall with some friends and a lady at the makeup counter offered us a makeover. Of course we graciously accepted. After a few minutes of sitting there while she rubbed more and more powder and foundation on my face, I began to feel very uncomfortable. I let her finish my makeover and then looked into the mirror. Everyone around complimented me on my makeup and said I looked gorgeous. I didn't feel gorgeous. I knew that under the layer of makeup was something completely different. Using makeup to cover my blemishes wasn't going to make me more comfortable in my own skin. I felt like I had a mask on. I walked around for the rest of the day with the makeup applied, but as soon as I got back home, I removed it.

Normally I would try and hide the anxiety that came along with my acne. I believed if I hid my fear of being judged by people by acting confident, I would be fine. I realized that putting on a show of confidence can sometimes help; however, it's not healthy in the long-term and I can only maintain the facade for so long. Ultimately, over time, it made me more self-conscious.

One Saturday morning a few months before turning 16, I awoke earlier than usual. Saturdays were my one day during the school year to sleep late, but on this particular morning, I woke around nine o'clock and heard my mom talking outside. I went to join her in our gorgeous garden so I could spend the morning with her. My mom often travels for work, so I make sure to take advantage of the time she is home to make it special. We sat together on the patio chairs outside admiring all the beauty around us. Our backyard garden is incredibly lush and I was immersed in the fabulous feeling of being surrounded by nature. The birds were chirping, the flowers were beginning their spring bloom, and the tall trees swayed gently in the breeze. The sun was just rising over the treetops, making it the perfect time to be outside. I was feeling relaxed and carefree.

The light and colors in the garden were so vibrant that my mom suggested we take a few pictures. Without even thinking, I refused. I listed off all the reasons I didn't want to be photographed. All I could see was that my hair was messy, my acne was bad, and my body certainly didn't look good from that angle. Whatever it was, I was armed with the perfect excuse.

My mom said, "Look around you! You are surrounded by beauty; and to me, you are the biggest part of it."

As I looked at the flowers and the majestic Redwood trees surrounding us, I realized their magic was in their uniqueness. As I took a closer look, I could see their imperfections. In that moment, I had a life-changing epiphany. I could clearly see that this didn't diminish their appeal in the least.

Maybe the same was true for me. Perhaps my intense focus on my imperfections was preventing me from seeing my own beauty.

That morning, I made a promise to myself to focus on the 'whole me' rather than obsessing over small things that simply didn't really matter. I committed to being happier with my body; to appreciating it. I realized that the small flaws didn't overshadow the beautiful parts of me, like my personality and humor. The little things don't ruin us. Everyone has imperfections, like the flower with a wilted leaf or a tree with a broken branch, but those imperfections don't take away from their beauty.

I saw, for the first time, my radiance as a whole; without looking at the surface but instead looking from within.

Over the past year, I have kept my promise by developing habits to stay healthy and to improve my self-image. One of the habits I've implemented is daily exercise. Exercising regularly has made me so much happier. Originally, I was motivated to exercise so I could look like the people on Instagram™. Now I exercise to get stronger, stay healthier, and be happy. I have found that, as I have become more fit, I have more confidence in myself both physically and emotionally.

Similarly, I exercise my creativity through music and art. I'm no great artist nor a multi-talented musician, but being creative and developing my talents brings me closer to who I am and helps me feel good about myself. When I exercise and am creative, I feel more beautiful. I've come to understand when someone is confident in themselves while embracing their own unique beauty, that is beautiful. When we stop thinking about it and we naturally learn to love ourselves, happiness follows.

Today, my acne is better than it has been for several years, but it is still with me. My skin is far from 'perfect,' but I have learned the best treatments for me and how to better take care of myself. The acne still frustrates me, but I realize it is normal and most people go through this process. Through dealing with these insecurities, I've gained a better understanding of people struggling with imperfections. I clearly see now that it's best not to judge people by their appearance.

Even now, I find myself wrestling with concerns about my body image all the time. To be perfectly honest, I look in the mirror and critique myself every single day. I can always find an imperfection — my skin, my hair, or the fit of my jeans. It never ends. I have realized how problematic it is to pick ourselves apart and focus on the faults. Is it empowering? No! Does it make me feel better? No! As a teenager and a woman, I am seeing that we all need to be intentional and gentle with ourselves as we develop appreciation for our individual uniqueness.

When thinking about our body image, another perspective includes what we see as a prominent role in society for many decades, which is the observation and measure of conventional 'beauty.' While these standards existed when my parents were teenagers, the pressures faced by young people today are intensely magnified as a result of social media. Social media leads teenagers like me to compare ourselves to people with 'perfect' and desirable bodies. The images we see are supposed to be real; at best, they are carefully composed pictures designed to make the subjects look their most beautiful. At worst, the pictures are edited to promote a completely unachievable body.

When we compare ourselves to the pictures we see online, we are comparing ourselves to unrealistic and unattainable levels of beauty. The reality of social media is when someone posts something online, they generally care about how many people comment and like their posts. Unfortunately, this often leads to a very consistent image of what people think we should aspire to *look* like with less emphasis on physical and emotional growth and well-being.

There is an old saying about how beauty 'comes from within.' I've been thinking a lot about that recently, and I both agree and disagree with the sentiment. There is such a thing as 'objective beauty.' It can be measured scientifically through facial and body symmetry. We all know it when we see it. And, as I see it, life can sometimes be easier for beautiful people. People tend to be attracted to them, they want to help them, and at times, they have opportunities offered to them that the rest of us might not receive. Yet even though they often have major advantages, some beautiful people are still insecure and unhappy.

People are attracted to physical beauty. It's human nature. While physical characteristics may get someone noticed, there has to be something special behind the pretty face and the chiseled body. Regardless of what we may look like on the outside, the confidence that radiates from the inside is what keeps people interested. We all need to find our own path to unlock our individual beauty. Everyone's journey is different. When you finally find the way to tap into your core of strength inside, everyone around you will know and those physical flaws you've been worrying about all this time won't matter anymore.

My outlook from my Ignite moment has helped reframe how I see others as well as how I see myself. It has allowed me to change my perspective. I look in the mirror still, but don't pick myself apart. Instead, I see my unique beauty. I accept it as a part of me; my story. Not a flaw but a testament to who I am.

You may find faults in your body or personality, or something you don't like, but let me share that when you reframe your brain and see your faults differently, you start to embrace them — maybe even cherish them and how they got there. Often what we don't like is not going away, so turning those things into something positive will help you. You can educate others, show them how to overcome their flaws, and see flaws as a benefit rather than a limitation.

**Love the 'whole you.' Value what you have been given.
You are magnificent, and that is truly powerful.**

IGNITE ACTION STEPS

Journal Activity: Changing Mindset

Take action in creating your most powerful body image. By doing so, you will learn how to instill daily habits to create a path to your best health, mind, body, and spirit. Connect to your innermost wishes and make them come true.

- Start a journal. Pay attention to your activities for a week and list the ones that make you feel fulfilled, happy, and healthy.

- Use the list as a roadmap to create personal goals. List specific activities to help you accomplish those goals. Keep in mind, there is no right or wrong way to do this. Allow your stream of consciousness to flow.

- Begin your journey to being happier *today*. Define a small action step that you can take right now to get closer to your goal and connected to those happier feelings.

- At the end of the day, while you may have not had time to complete a goal or activity, finish your journal by giving a detailed description of how you made progress in your goals that day and how it made you feel.

- If needed, write out the obstacles keeping you from these goals, what is stopping you? Ask yourself, "How can I overcome these barriers?" and "What do I need to add or remove from my life to amplify my happiness?"

Journaling this way will help you become more aware of the things that make you happy and will bring out your most unique and beautiful self.

Abbey Richter – United States of America
Author, Speaker & Student
abbeyrichter.com

MELODY D. BYRD

*"Be happy when you start. Be happier when you finish.
Be happiest when you help others do the same."*

In reading my story, I hope you feel that we are connected by the various tests of life. View my story as an example of how good things can come to you when you commit to finishing what you started. Be intentional and unabashed about reaching your goals and watch your life unfold in all the ways you dreamed it could.

FIND THE STRENGTH TO PASS THE TEST

"What do you want to do about college?"

My mother had finally asked the million-dollar question. In angst, I lowered my head. I knew the answer but was embarrassed to say it. Growing up with a no-nonsense Jamaican mother meant you did not have the opportunity or permission to say, "Can I get back to you on that?"

Sheepishly, I answered, "I want to go back and finish." Whew, relief washed over me! Now I could release myself from the made-up story I started living over a year ago when I dropped out of college after a five-year stretch of partying and pretending to live a perfectly normal life while slowly flunking out of school.

For most girls growing up in my predominantly black neighborhood, graduating from college was not a goal. However, my mother, a college graduate, expected just the opposite from me. After I proudly graduated eighth grade as the class valedictorian, my mother mandated that I attend a predominantly white all-girls Catholic high school. On a very snowy winter day in 1979, I reluctantly took the entrance exam and, months later, I received my acceptance letter. This made my mother happy, so I was happy.

I didn't want to go, though. None of my friends were going and I was worried I would not like the other students, who did not look like me. The school was located over an hour from my home and the people who lived by the school preferred I not be there either. They showed that one day when, after making my initial tuition payment in person, the neighborhood boys taunted me and chased me away from the school. That had never happened to me before — I felt like I was in a different world. I was afraid, but that did not deter me or my mother. My fate was sealed, so I began to prepare myself for what would be a drastic change.

To my surprise, once I started high school, I began to make friends easily. Some looked like me and some did not, but I liked them all the same. I participated in several activities, including playing the cello in the school orchestra. As for my grades, they were average. My favorite classes were Spanish, English, and Algebra. I avoided classes I thought were too challenging, like Calculus and Physics, as I could not see any good reason to stress over learning things I may never use in life.

When my senior year arrived, I began preparing for graduation. In seeking some direction for choosing the right college, I made an appointment with the senior class advisor. I assumed she would steer me in the ideal direction.

Looking at my grades, Sister Alice said "Melody, I see you're an average student."

I immediately tightened up and felt defensive as I did not consider myself to be average, nor was I there to discuss my academic performance. I only wanted to talk about my college options. However, she continued, "I think it is best if you attend a school for average performers."

Becoming annoyed that I had to plead my case, I responded, "But, Sister Alice, I want to go to the University of Illinois. My best friend Kim is going. We both applied and will be roommates. My sister Renee might go, too."

She didn't budge and continued to dissuade me, noting that my grades weren't good enough.

"I am not sure if that is the best choice for you. It will be very hard."

Fed up, I ended the conversation with, "I understand, Sister. But I think I can do it. This school has prepared me for it."

I left her office with knots in my stomach. Maybe she was right, but Sister

Alice didn't know about the Jamaican work ethic my mother had instilled in me. I vowed to prove Sister Alice wrong. Within a few weeks, I confidently applied to the University of Illinois. Several months later, I was ecstatic to surprise Sister Alice with my acceptance letter. Again, my mother was happy, so I was happy.

I started at the University of Illinois (U of I) in the fall of 1983. My mom and dad, still friends though divorced, drove the two hours to move me into my dorm room. On that day, I met the men of the Phi Beta Sigma Fraternity, or 'The Sigmas' as they were known around campus. They helped with the move too. Afterward, they explained that their fraternity was an all-male social service organization on campus. They did community service work as well as held social events. They, along with several other similar organizations, were referred to as the 'Black Greeks' because the organizations were predominantly black and they used Greek letters for their names.

The Black Greeks were campus leaders and, once I learned about their reputation, I looked up to them. Next to the athletes, the Black Greeks were treated like rock stars on campus. During the rest of the semester, like a groupie, I continued to attend various events sponsored by the Black Greeks. Studying was not a priority for me, but I was happy to end my first semester with my typically average grades, again proving Sister Alice wrong and making my mother happy.

By the next semester, the Sigmas asked me to join their sister organization, Zeta Phi Beta Sorority. This, too, was a predominantly black social service organization but for women. Enthusiastically, I agreed and, soon after, I became a member. Once I joined, I immediately gained the rock star status that came with being a Black Greek. The feeling of being revered and sometimes envied became addictive.

Attending social events as a rock star began to take precedence over my studies. No one was holding me to account for maintaining good grades, not even my mother. I falsely led her to believe that I was studying and passing classes when in actuality my grades were slipping. I was worried but imma-turely did nothing to address the impending dire consequences. I was too busy partying like a rock star! Missed classes and failing grades landed me on academic probation, beginning a dizzying cycle of failing out, being accepted back, and then going on academic probation again.

The weeks turned into months, which turned into years. Normally you could find me walking right past the library and heading to a social event. I rarely studied and mistakenly began to think U of I was too hard, like Sister

Alice had said. I felt that it was more important to have fun than to fulfill the unwritten promise to my mother to get a degree and keep her happy. After five years of irresponsible behavior, U of I had enough of my shenanigans and, to my disappointment, I was booted out because of my low grades.

However, luck played in my favor before I left. U of I held an annual Black Congratulatory event for graduating minority students. I submitted my name as a graduate and invited my entire family to attend the event as if it was my official graduation. That's right — I didn't tell my family that I hadn't graduated. It was important to show my mother that I had lived up to her expectations and graduated, even if I knew I hadn't. My family was so proud of me and I was happy I pulled it off. I found out later that my mother knew something was not right, but she kept quiet. I kept quiet too, hiding the truth like the unopened textbooks I had brought home from college.

Weeks after I arrived home, my mother demanded that I start looking for employment. Every Sunday, I bought the newspaper, hoping to find a good job. I figured five years of college had to count for something, but it did not. After interviewing for several positions without receiving an offer, I discovered college attendance only counts when you graduate. Maybe Sister Alice was right. More importantly, how was I to tell my mother the truth? I didn't want her to be angry and yell at me.

As fate would have it, I did not have to tell my mother. One of her friends, Janet, knew of a gentleman who was hiring recent college graduates from U of I. He had access to the list of graduates and my mother gave Janet permission to speak on my behalf to ask for a job. When he checked the list and did not see my name, he told Janet that he could not hire me. Janet told my mother what happened and this just confirmed my mother's suspicions. Afterward, my mother finally asked the million-dollar question.

"What do you want to do about college?"

In angst, I lowered my head and in a sheepishly soft tone said, "I want to go back and finish."

She quickly responded with her heavy Jamaican accent, "Then go back and finish!"

Wow! Was that it? I was relieved and shocked, all at the same time. I expected a severe tongue-lashing ending in tears and huge disappointment. This conversation, while brief, was enormously impactful. Until then, I hadn't realized I could tell my mother the truth and choose to go back to college. I felt determination igniting in me to finish what I had started. This determination changed the trajectory of my entire life. In that moment, fear of the truth no longer held me hostage.

My mother contacted the dean and begged him to allow me to return to school. He approved my readmission. I excitedly prepared to go back to U of I but this time I was on a mission from God.

I packed very few clothes as looking good at parties was no longer my priority. My focus was squarely on graduating. I found a small apartment off campus and away from the temptation of the rock star lifestyle that I gave up. During the week, I studied, showed up to class prepared, and passed my tests. On the weekends, I worked or went back home to visit my family and friends.

Well, guess what? It worked! I was so excited to see my grades significantly improve, and U of I even recognized me for my academic performance. It was like being a 'scholastic' rock star! For my final semester, one professor recommended me for an internship at a prestigious hospital. After successfully completing it, my manager wrote a glowing recommendation letter that I used for future employment.

Eventually I received the envelope that I had been eagerly awaiting. I ripped it open, jumping up and down and screaming, "Thank God," as tears rolled down my cheeks.

When my mother arrived home, I handed her my diploma. With a broad smile I said "See, I did it!"

She just smiled and said, "I knew you could."

Thinking back now, I should have sent a note to Sister Alice letting her know she was somewhat right. Graduating from U of I was challenging for me, but not impossible. I learned that graduating college took more than going to class and studying for passing grades. It took heart, commitment, and a willingness to allow something bigger than me to take over my life as I submitted to the learning process. I had to find the strength to pass this test in my life. I learned that with my resilient spirit and strong will, I could accomplish anything. Knowing that makes me happy!

After receiving my degree in health, I began feverishly looking for a job. Within a few weeks, I accepted an offer from a small health insurance company. This began my 25-year career in the healthcare industry. Then, six years ago, I changed the trajectory of my life again and left the healthcare industry. I wanted to help others who struggled with their humanity and, like me, felt the need to portray a perfect life even when it was not healthy to do so.

Over time, I had become an expert in this type of behavior and was living proof that it did not work; nor did it create happiness. I became a certified life coach and took a job managing a technology training program for women, veterans, and minorities. I am responsible for training the program participants in soft skills like leadership, teamwork, and communication in such a way that they become polished professionals who build a strong work ethic and value authenticity.

In addition, I mentor and coach them from the beginning of the program until the end, helping them to finish what they started. I find the work very rewarding and satisfying. I like helping others tap into their internal strength to pass any test that life throws at them. I routinely share stories with my mother about how I help my students and friends. She's proud of my work and I have even heard her bragging to Janet about my success.

Some 36 years later, I am still very active with my sorority. I do much more than attend social events. After holding several leadership roles, I now train leaders as well as help raise scholarship money for deserving college students. My happiest moments occur when I mentor the collegiate members as I remember my challenging college days. I know how important it is for them to finish what they started.

As I look forward to what's next in my life, I dream of owning a coaching and training company to help adult women navigate the choppy waters of life. On the weekends, you can find me doing community service work, attending classes to strengthen my coaching skills, and speaking at workshops sharing my life's lessons.

At some point, you, too, may have to make a major decision that will change the trajectory of your life. If the action you want to take Ignites a fire in you, then you have found the way to move your life from good to great! It's not always easy to accept the elevation that will come; however, look into your heart, use your natural talents and harness your innate passion to live beyond pretense. Find true authenticity and felicity to live the most amazing life ever. You get to choose how to live your life. Tap into your inner strength to pass any test that life presents. Be tenacious about finishing the important things that you start and watch your life explode immensely, bringing happiness to your soul!

Lastly, remember to thank those who help and support you along your life's journey. This chapter is a thank you to my Mom for never giving up on me.

IGNITE ACTION STEPS

When you are ready to live authentically, beyond any pretense in your life, follow these steps to find the strength to pass life's tests.

- Reflect on the times when you stopped doing something that you now regret. These are times when you were not happy with the result and, if given a chance, you would finish it in a way that would leave you satisfied.

- Decide on your next steps to finish what you started. Then, choose to move forward. There is power in choosing the direction of your life. You are the interior designer of your happy path. You can pave it with happy thoughts, happy words, and happy actions to create your happiness rock star moments!

- Commit wholeheartedly to your action plan. Know that you can meet any goal using passion, communication, and teamwork. Avoid the "rock star temptations" that will take you off track and hamper your progress.

- Encourage yourself. This is an inside job and you must set yourself up to win. Silence the inner critic and be your own biggest cheerleader. If necessary, call me and I will have my mother talk to you. She can help you focus.

- Finish, then celebrate! Celebrate, then finish! Either way, finish! You now know yourself as a happiness rock star who finishes what you started by tackling life's tests. It takes courage to continue to move forward and tenacity to achieve satisfaction in your life. Choose — powerfully — to be happy with the results, knowing that you did your best and gave it your all.

I'm proud of you for reading this far. Now take a break and get started so you can finish what you started!

Melody Byrd – United States of America
Speaker, Author, Life Coach
www.melbyrdrocks.com

Leslie Lee

"Unattended souls will be turned into someone else's happiness."

My intention is to open your mind to new perspectives that come from having an awareness of your thoughts and embracing the circumstances that can define you. I hope to give you the feeling of truly being known. I want you to be empowered through acknowledging your triggers and using them for good. Take back your power and open yourself up to the happiness and self-love that you absolutely deserve.

It Must Be Nice

I was riding in a yellow school bus on a gravel road. It was my first day of third grade and I was excited to finally get to wear my 'first day of school' clothes. I was in my own little world, looking out the window, my feet dangling from my bench. The seat beside me was empty. The bus stopped and one of my classmates got on. I looked over at her, hoping she would sit near me, but she looked at me with disgust and sneered, "It must be nice to have your clothes bought for you! My mom makes my clothes." My heart pounded, my cheeks flushed pink, and my stomach dropped. I didn't want to go to school anymore. Her words confused me and my bashful nature kept me from asking her what she meant. I felt sheepish that my parents had bought my clothes and the excitement I had at wearing them was suddenly ripped out from under me.

Some part of myself was envious, thinking, "Wow! Moms can make clothes?" My mom had always bought my clothes, so the realization that someone else had their clothes made *just for them* by someone who loves them seemed neat to me.

My favorite childhood moments were early mornings before the sun rose. I would sneak out of my room to snuggle next to my dad and listen to him as he read the bible at the kitchen table before leaving for work. It was the only uninterrupted time that I got to spend with him, and I felt safe and seen. I figured out at a young age that if I woke up early, sat with him, and made his breakfast and lunch, he would be fully present with me. My dad worked a lot while I was growing up and for some reason I correlated my dad working to me having store-bought clothes. I didn't understand how the world worked, I just knew he worked a lot. I remember wondering if my dad would be home more if my mom made my clothes. I wished that were the case.

Even as a teen, I still loved mornings, and one morning in particular sticks out in my mind. Eager to go to my first prom, I awoke with the birds, sunlight streaming through my window. The big day was finally here. My mom gabbed with me as I sat in the chair at the salon while the hairdresser pinned up my locks and placed rhinestones in my hair. Feeling confident and pretty, I was excited to see my date's face when he picked me up. Moments before he arrived, I slipped into a white satin gown and admired my freshly manicured nails as they sparkled. I had butterflies in my stomach and I kept checking myself out in the mirror, as if I had forgotten what I looked like.

Arriving at the school, I was overcome with nervous excitement. We stood in line in anticipation of the grand march where everyone gets to show off their dresses. Groups of guys and girls were taking photos together, and since I was just a freshman, I was elated when one of the older girls asked me to take a photo with them. Beaming, I walked over to their group. The tallest girl grimaced at me and said sarcastically, "It must be nice to be thin and pretty. Turn sideways and you'll disappear." My cheeks felt warm and rosy, just like that day on the bus. I wanted to crawl into a hole — one where I wouldn't get my beautiful dress muddy. And just like that day on the bus, I swallowed my hurt and said nothing.

The week after prom, a Friday afternoon after school, I tried talking to a friend about what had happened that night. She wasn't mean, but she wasn't understanding and said nothing to validate my feelings. It felt like she agreed with them and I was all alone. Leaving school, I dashed into my house in tears. I ran to the kitchen drawer and grabbed a knife. Mom was standing at the counter making supper. I held the knife up in front of my face and said, "If I just had a cut across my face or had a scar, people wouldn't make such mean comments." I will never forget the look of horror on her face. She was mortified. Right now, writing this, I feel ashamed to admit that out loud. Who would ever wish that?

I used to wish that I didn't look the way I did. I hated being 'pretty.' I loved being thin, but hated how I was made to feel like I shouldn't love it. I wasn't allowed to like or appreciate how I was created. I heard, "It must be nice," as criticism, not a compliment. It seemed as if every time I heard that phrase, I had to apologize for being me. I could sense other people's lack, but I didn't realize it was their insecurity. I took it as if there was something wrong with me. I now realize I was playing small, but it would take me a long time to understand that.

My senior year, I had really big dreams and so did my boyfriend at the time. I wanted to graduate in cosmetology, get married, and have a family. I had no idea part of that would come true almost instantly. The world as I knew it was about to change in just one moment. I remember standing with him in the middle of my studio apartment with tear stains on my face. In the corner of the bathroom lay the white stick revealing the plus sign. He looked at me and I could feel the weight on his shoulders. He was a senior in high school with plans to go on to college. A baby was not in our plans, but it was now my reality.

Day after day, I gazed fearfully into the bathroom mirror feeling as if my perfect world was about to crumble. I knew the secret, but no one else did. The seeds of self-doubt that had been planted by everyone around me as they questioned my right to be me only intensified. "This is all my fault. I am stupid. I can't raise this baby. Maybe I should give it up for adoption. Someone else can do a better job than I can." But I knew from the moment I found out I was pregnant that I loved her and I felt even more ashamed for loving her. Listening to the voices of others echoing in my head made me question myself. Who am I? I didn't even know who I was. Who will I be? What will my body look like? What can I do with a baby? I was not prepared for this.

The first night after her birth, she cried. I remember feeling like I couldn't do anything right. The words, "You don't know what you're doing," crushed my spirit, but her father was right: I had no clue what I was doing. The birth, a c-section, had stripped me of all my innocence. Shaved, cut, and scarred in more ways than one for all the world to see; yet the words, "It must be nice that you had a c-section, you didn't do it the natural way," reverberated in my ears.

Those feelings again. I felt so hot and red, embarrassed that I couldn't even have a baby the right way. All I could think about was that I was an 18-year-old mom who now was scarred for life and my body would never be the same.

I was Mom to this blue-eyed blonde curly-haired toddler. She was energetic and sassy; spirited. One day, we got all dressed up and off we went to my cousin's wedding. The wedding ended in an argument and the words that were yelled at me forever changed my spirit. "You will never do anything and you will never make anything of yourself. It must be nice to not have a dream."

I remember feeling my cheeks get hot, but this time I felt anger and frustration. I wanted to scream back and say I have a dream and I will 'make something of myself.' Just watch me! How wrong he was! But I shrank back and held in my emotions and my words.

I did have a dream. It's just not the same dream others might have had. I had dreamed of being a mom my whole life. I was happy being a mom. I dreamed of being loved and accepted at my core. I was a very young mom worried about taking care of the people in my life and working full time as well. It was stressful, overwhelming, and scary, and I loved her so much. In the moments when those blue eyes stared deeply into mine as she whispered, "I love you, Mommy," all of the chaos in my world stopped. I was happy and content because she loved and accepted me; and at that time, it was what I needed to make the next best choice.

Despite building my own highly successful aesthetics empire from the ground up since becoming a mom, I have always felt like a high school girl. The teen mom who had no clue. The little girl with store-bought clothes. The girl who would never do anything with her life. I have avoided 'it must be nice' comments at all costs. Everytime I heard that comment, I always heard it as a negative. I'd learned how to deflect it and push aside my feelings, but the rage was building inside me, even though I kept my silence. Until, one day, I didn't.

That day, I was talking with my husband on the phone on my drive into the office. I remember him complaining about his work and how he didn't like it. It was a repeat of a conversation we had had a thousand times already. He spoke his same familiar lines and I dutifully spoke mine, telling him, "Maybe you should figure out what you like and you can do something else."

"Well Leslie, it must be nice to love your job," he snapped, and a black heat flashed through me, lighting up my cheeks. With each word he spoke, something inside me started screaming, "FIRE!!!!" All of the emotions that I had been holding in for all the years from all the 'it must be nice' comments came crashing into this honest conversation that I was having with my husband. I was raging. I went off the deep end. It was as much about everyone else who had ever said some variation of that to me as it was about him; but coming from him, it hurt in a different way. I was so tired of apologizing and being made to feel guilty for building myself a successful business that I genuinely love doing — one which was so successful that I could have the life I wanted with my children, too. I had worked so hard to get to where I was both as a career woman and a mom, and yes, it *was* nice, and there was nothing wrong with that!

"You know how hard I have worked to get to where I am! I thought you were my biggest fan. Like, what the heck?" My hands gripped the steering wheel of the car, my knuckles going white as I yelled into the hands-free microphone. "I've talked with you about all the things people say to me and how I feel about it, but you're acting the same way they do!" I'm sure I was yelling so loudly that the people in the next car could hear me. I was super entertaining for them, I'm sure, but that didn't stop the words from pouring out. "You hear people constantly making comments about how 'it must be nice' and now you're one of them! ARE YOU KIDDING ME?"

It felt like a huge release; like I was an overheated pot of water that had just let off all its steam. I felt like I was trapped in this balloon that just kept stretching and stretching and not letting me out, except I had finally managed to pop it and I was free. I hadn't realized how heavy I felt every time I had to explain the narrative of how I had built the amazing life I had created for myself, just to make someone else feel better about the things they didn't like about their own life. What had started as a familiar, comfortable morning conversation ended up as an argument. I'm not usually a yeller, but that morning, I poured out every ounce of heaviness inside me and put it on him. And he just took the brunt of my emotions and all the fire I had inside of me, even though they were not his to take on.

My feelings were *mine*. They belonged to *me*, not him. My rage was all about my uniqueness, my triggers, and my issues dealing with all those years of 'it must be nice.' And his bitter, "It must be nice," was entirely about *him* not liking *his* career and being envious that I loved mine. At that moment, although it was hard for me to hear, it made me stop and think. I realized that all the times that others have said to me, "It must be nice," are about *them*, not me. All those comments were also times when I allowed someone else to shape the way I viewed myself. Those comments created anger and resentment because I never stuck up for myself. I realized it *is* nice to be me, and I should allow myself to fully step into the joy I take from the business I have built and who I have become. I have hidden behind my failures to make other people happy, but in return, I died on the inside every time I heard those four little words. I've never allowed myself to fully step into the strong woman I am.

When I think back to that high school girl, that version of myself who hated her looks, I feel for her. I am sad that she didn't feel accepted or known because of the way she looked. I'm sad for the importance she gave to other peoples' opinions. She did, perhaps, shape the entire course of my career, leading me to love helping others feel confident and happy with their own looks, but I am sad for the way that she chose to show up as a result of what other people said. She allowed them to have so much control over who she was and how she felt about herself.

I realized I chose to be unseen and to hold my tongue rather than be unashamedly me. I chose to not show up in ways that make me happy because I didn't want to offend someone. I didn't talk about my failures and I certainly didn't talk about my successes. I shrank back if I sensed someone was uncomfortable. I didn't stick up for myself. If a waitress got my order wrong or if my food was too cold, I wouldn't complain. The only place I truly stepped into myself was at the office. At my work, I was confident and courageous. I shared my knowledge and experience with my clients, coaching them and giving them the tips and tricks I've learned that might help their business grow. My business grew to what it is today because I show up 100 percent, stepping fully into who I am and being totally unapologetic about it.

After that fight with my husband, I saw everything from a new perspective. I realized I had never said much outside of the office for fear of not being accepted. I would not raise my hand in a group of people and risk looking dumb… or looking too smart. I realized that I was not fully showing up for fear of the opinions of others. But I am learning that those four little words, "It must be nice," are a reflection of someone else's issue. They still bother me, but I have come to understand that I do not see the universe as it is, I see the universe as I am; and I choose to be happy. My life is just as amazing and wonderful as it always was, but now I don't try to hide my light to make others feel better about themselves. I am unapologetically me.

It is a tragic thing to not fully expose all of the light and all of the beautiful darkness trapped behind the fear of being known. The truth is… true happiness is using what we've learned from our own insecurities to relate to others and make them feel beautiful. Life experiences and the willingness to be vulnerable allows each of us to relate to one another. Giving the gift of revealing ourselves lets people relax into their own vulnerability so that they can meet their truest, most deeply held needs. True-found happiness is looking into the soul of another and seeing *them* for who they are — an unattended human soul with very real human emotions and a profound desire to be truly *known*. Tending a soul's innermost needs is the gift of happiness for every soul.

Ignite Action Steps

My trigger is hearing the phrase, "It must be nice..." What are some of the things that trigger your negative thinking? How can you take control of your own happiness and change the lens that you're hearing those words through? Fold a piece of paper in half lengthwise. On one half, write down any triggers you have. On the other, reframe them through a lens that will allow you to see the trigger as being a reflection of the other person and not of you.

What are some thoughts that you constantly tell yourself that you may not even know where they are from? Write them down on the left, and then reframe them with your present reality on the right.

Leslie Lee – United States of America
Founder and CEO of Aesthetic Creator
Business Consultant/Coach
www.aestheticcreator.com

Ana Maria Pelaez

"Happiness is not always easy but always possible."

For many years, I have seen people around me who are unhappy — including myself. I discovered the science of happiness and it became my passion. I am convinced that sharing my experience can change hearts, modify habits, and help people on how to be happy. . May my story inspire you to achieve the best version of yourself.

My Happiness Formula: It's All About Habits

For many years, happiness was, for me, an impossible goal to reach. With thoughts like "I will be happy the day I grow up," and "I will be happy when I find a husband," or "I will be happy when I finish my studies," etc., my life became a marathon to win, to achieve, to have. One day, while talking with my friends about life, we started sharing what makes us happy. While listening to their dreams, I realized that I already HAD almost everything THEY wished for in order to be happy.

That was an illogical and confusing moment for me. How was it possible that despite already having everything everybody else wanted in order to be happy, I was not happy?

By this time, I was 53. I was living the life of a marketing manager in a big company, living the life that was laid out for me since I was in my twenties. It was my father's company and there was a lot of expectation for me to take over and lead the company when my father left. Something about it wasn't right. For a whole year, uncertainty was my friend as I tried to find out who I was and what my path should be. My journey into happiness started that year.

My first desire was to understand happiness. I started by making a list of all the things I thought represented happiness for me, such as having a loving partner, starting a beautiful family, studying a successful career, and getting my first dream car. I wondered why, after achieving many of those things, I still wasn't happy. There were days when I came home and felt a huge emptiness. Those achievements were not enough.

Despite having fulfilled dreams and goals, deep inside I felt some things were missing. My heart, my soul, my being was not satisfied with the concept of happiness that I had always idealized with a tag: having, getting, finding. My happiness depended on external factors, material things, huge expectations, and a need for controlling everything around me.

One day, while researching in a library, wanting to know everything about happiness, I found a book, *The Monk Who Sold His Ferrari*, by Robin Sharma. In his book, he shares his story about how he got rid of his attachments and found happiness. If he could do that, why couldn't I? This was a special moment for me; an Ignite moment in understanding that happiness was possible.

I read a lot of books following that. Og Mandino, Mario Alonso Puig, and Eckarht Tolle are just some of the authors who inspired me to believe that happiness is not found in what I have or do, but in exploring my inner self. I learned how to connect with my being and how to identify those small details that would really fulfill me. I could not let my circumstances decide my happiness. I had to accept my life with what I had and change what I didn't want anymore. But dreaming wasn't enough.

Understanding happiness, was a big step but it was not enough. I needed to know how to practice it. I required an action plan. Changing my habits was my first move; now I had to master them. I wondered why so many people, including me, made huge lists of wishes, dreams, commitments, but never actually started. Achieving a dream requires clarity, an action plan, and creativity to try many paths. The world is full of good intentions. It is also full of fears that become barriers standing between us and our dreams. We have the idea, but it has to become a hunger, a craving, so that our motivation is so strong that we overcome any obstacle.

Through study and practice, I identified some of the common barriers stopping people from achieving their goals. When I want something, I ask myself the following questions:

1. Do I have clarity? If you know where you are going, the right path unfolds. Clarity gives us conviction and shows us the right direction.
2. Is it really MY dream? Or is it someone else's dream?
3. Am I being influenced by my own experience or someone else's?
4. Have I been hurt from the past, and is that holding me back?
5. Is there passion in my goal?
6. Am I willing to try different ways to reach it?

The next step I focus on is persevering and creativity. Nobody said achieving dreams was easy. Behind every big dream there are many hours of work and, when you achieve it, all the effort is worth it.

Happiness is about being able to connect with yourself, with your environment, with your community, with the people you work with. It is the attitude with which you face life's obstacles. It is the result of your good actions and choices.

Intention is the will that moves us to achieve a goal. It generates a powerful energy which invites us to take action, to do something towards achieving it or to modify a behavior. Intentions manifest themselves through thought. Thought generates feeling. Feeling generates action. When we manage to make the intention clear and we focus on our purpose to obtain the expected result, we create our reality.

After a whole year of deep introspection, I decided I wanted to start writing about happiness. I wrote my first book about what makes me happy.

People started being curious about all the changes I made in my life. "What's going on, Annie?" they asked me. Soon I was invited to speak and teach the habits I had created for myself.

I believe everyone should have their own *happiness formula*. My formula is nothing more than systems and habits I constantly repeat that keep me on the track and keep me grounded. I choose happiness and I am convinced that having my daily *rituals* will keep me on the right path.

Sometimes I forget them. That's why I invented *reminders*, little pieces of paper posted all around my house where I can see them throughout my day. This guarantees my formula of happiness to be a success. Here is the formula I created and love to share.

G - D E P T H: MY HAPPINESS FORMULA

G is for Gratitude

Human beings usually focus on what is missing. I wanted to focus on my talents, on the blessings and the gifts I had. It wasn't easy. Changing perspective on things also made me see my life in a different way. I started making a list of all the things I liked about myself, my life, my family, my work, my friends. I found myself being grateful for waking up, for a hot coffee, a soft pillow, my kid's laughter, taking my dog for a walk, for having my mom to chat with, and for my job.

Every day I find more things to be grateful for — moments, opportunities. The best thing about being grateful is that you stop complaining. If I want something, I have to work hard for it and, if I find it too difficult, I just let it go. I stopped whining completely. Appreciation became my favorite action. My choice to see all the good around me became my first and my last thought of the day.

D is for Decisions

I understood that everything that happened to me was a consequence of a decision, good or bad, but mine. Assuming the responsibility for my acts, my future, my present, and also for my past, was a liberating step. I forgave my parents, teachers, ex partners, friends, and myself. Healing the past was a blessing that let me start a new life. Today, if I make a mistake, I plead for forgiveness. I know how to repair an offense. I understood that the only way I could control anything was if it depended on me. I can't change facts, but I can always change the way I feel about them. My choices became a day-to-day challenge. Since I am responsible for everything, I am more careful and less impulsive.

E is for Environment

Who do you relate to? How much power can someone have over you? Toxic relationships lead you to toxic behaviors. Choosing the right people became one of my habits. I chose people who could understand that my life had changed and that I was now a different person. This was the most difficult decision.

Identifying who is not good for you is hard, and it is harder if it is someone close, part of your family, or a friend who you appreciate. I have seen people who become attached to their offenders. Buddhists use an expression I love: *Attachment is the root of suffering.* If you want to be happy, hang out with happy people. Surround yourself with people who bring out the best in you. If you want to be a writer, meet with writers and share with them. If you want to be accomplished, start by identifying your role models: how do they behave, how do they live, what do they read and include those habits in your list.

P for Purpose

Purpose is knowing what you are living for. It took time to understand my purpose and it took me longer to live with a purpose, Victor Frankl in his book *Man's Search for Meaning* quotes: "Those who have a WHY to live, can bear with almost any HOW." We all have a purpose inside; either it is conscious or unconscious.

In Japan there is a concept called *ikigai*, meaning 'a reason for being.' It is related to finding what you love doing, what the world needs, what you can be paid for, what you are good at. It is a mix of passion, vision, vocation, and profession. One of the most difficult things in many people's lives is discovering their purpose. Knowing it makes life filled with more joy and ease.

T is for Time for myself

Prayer, meditation, contemplation, little by little became part of my lifestyle. I understood that the first thing I should do was to love myself in order to be able to love and make others happy. I walk my dog numerous times a day. I enjoy every second. I listen to the birds. I take long showers. I read at least a book a month. I love inspirational music and movies. I enjoy cooking and inventing new recipes. I write at least one hour a week. Learning is part of the time I spend with myself. Every day I learn something new.

H is for Helping others.

The last habit in the happiness formula is helping others or doing something for others. A good action a day is a must in my life. Sometimes I do great things. Other times I simply smile at someone or I bring a cup of water or a snack to a homeless person.

Happiness is an inside experience and can be achieved using this formula. When you want a habit to be a part of your life, you have to repeat it for 21 days. Put up notes and reminders all over the house and make it a ritual. Get committed, have fun, and enjoy being happy. Happiness is just BEING happy.

I decided to write my first book because I wanted to be a Happiness-Maker. My book is titled *"Simple-mente se feliz" (*which translates to *"In the simpleness of your thoughts is happiness").* It is a profound introspection manual. My life changed completely when writing this book as it took me from dreaming to doing. I have studied a lot and trained myself to be happy. It was more about *becoming* it than doing it.

Today, I am a motivational speaker. I inspire individuals with my conversations about obtaining happiness. I have developed courses both online and for groups of people who need happiness in their lives. I work with leadership teams all over the world. I train teams who want to apply happiness into their companies. I encourage people to be *Happy*; to add Happiness Strategists in their workplace so they can gain skills and then apply them to spread happiness throughout their company.

The meaning of happiness is so vast and deep that what I truly do is show that *happiness is possible*. I know it's not easy to be happy, but it can be done. It is an inside process; I just give my clients the tools and they do the inner work.

Happiness is the path you create every day with your decisions. You can choose happiness. You can feel it and live your very best life. Happiness is yours. I invite you to make a list of those things that you think make you happy, that fill your soul. Then, ask yourself, are you really happy? When was the last time you felt happy? Is happiness in your hands or is it in the hands of an external factor you don't have control over? Take time for yourself. Find whatever fills your soul.. If you are truly happy, you will see it reflected in your environment, family, and workplace, simply because happiness comes from within.

Ignite Action Steps

Gratitude: Have a gratitude notebook. Write at least five things.

Decisions: Take a deep breath and listen to your heart.

Environment: Make a list of people you admire and why you admire them.

Purpose: Always keep your *ikigai* on hand.

Time for Yourself: Schedule at least 10-15 minutes of time for yourself each day.

Helping Others: Do one act of kindness a day.

Have you wondered what would happen if you had a goal in every situation of your life? Examine your professional development: Where are you now? What goals and dreams do you have, and how do you intend to achieve them? In your family life, ask yourself: How could you create quality time with your family members? How could you strengthen relationships with your friends? How is your health? Could you improve something? Which habits should you modify?

Once you are clear about where you want to be, visualize it and write your action plan. Work every day so that you don't lose focus. I assure you that you will see change in your life. When we find the WHAT, the HOW TO appears immediately. Once you know that, the actions can become systematic.

Ana Maria Pelaez – Colombia
Marketing and Happiness Developer
www.anamariapelaez.com.co

HANNA WICKSTRÖM

*"Every day you say no to your dreams it might
take you even longer to reach them."*

I am a person with a lot of imagination and this has given me much happiness through the years. It is what started my dream of being an author. It also helps me see the good in the simplest, smallest 'every-day' things. By sharing my story I hope that I can show you how to find happiness in many different ways in your life. Keep reaching for those dreams you have despite what people say. My wish is by reading my story you get inspired, motivated, and of course find HAPPINESS!

I FOUND HAPPINESS IN WRITING

Happiness. What is happiness and how do we achieve it?

I think it's different for everybody. What makes me happy is the small things. I have a good life, not perfect, things have happened and they have left their marks, but it is a nice life. I have my family, my horse, and my cats and I am so grateful for that.

I invite you into my story of how I found and find happiness by writing stories.

I have been writing stories since I was around 12 years old. What made me start was a project in school. We received the task to write a short story and I fell in love with it so when the project was finished, I started to write at home. In the beginning, it was mostly short stories and I didn't have big plans for them; I just loved to write them. To create stories was also a way to deal with all of my imagination that had to go somewhere.

All of my life I have had a lot of imagination and when I was little it was central to my play. I found happy times with my sister, friends, and my cousins and my creativity was always used. I came up with a lot of the things we invented and I wanted it to be as real as possible. When we played horse games, for example, I got into the project of creating the most realistic stable I could with what we had in the garden. When I got older and slowly grew out of games, I needed to give space to my imagination in a different way. The answer was writing. It was a relief and a satisfaction to get all of my ideas, thoughts, and fantasies down on paper and watch it create a story.

When I was 17, I started working on a story that I had very big plans for. I was focused on another piece when I got the inspiration. The story I had been writing wasn't going too well and I wasn't happy with it. Then, I was watching a movie about a girl who lost her family and was now living in an academy for fairies. That movie gave me inspiration for a new story so I put the story I had been working on to the side and started on the new one. I was interested in telling a tale about a girl who had lost her family. I delved into the prework of the plotline and then I hit a wall. I didn't know how to continue my outline and I wasn't writing much at all. I had gotten what we call in Sweden, 'skrivkramp' (writer's cramp). Writer's cramp is not something physical, although it might sound like it. It's called writer's cramp when you are stuck and don't know how to continue your story. This was extremely frustrating for me and for a time I was worried that I had lost interest in writing. Not being able to continue made me lose motivation and I started questioning if writing was really something I should do. I got scared that my interest had faded in something that I had loved for so many years; writing was a part of me and the thought of giving it up felt strange.

I talked a lot about my book and I wanted to continue; I just didn't know how to finish it. Talking about it but not writing anything made people think that it was all just talk. I was told by others that I had big plans but I didn't do anything to achieve them. This might have been true, but I prevailed and although it took seven years to complete my book... I did it! And all that time it took to write my book made it even better. I was only a teneager when I started, yet I developed as a writer during those years and my book developed as well. If I would have finished it earlier it might not have turned out as good.

When I was 20 years old, I wanted to find a place where I could study writing and I found Glimåkra Folkhögskola. A Folkhögskola is a kind of school that only exists in the northern countries of Europe. These schools can be found all around Sweden, Denmark, and Norway and have been operating since the 1800s, 1886 to be exact. The schools offer education for adults and most of them give the students the opportunity to live at the school. Glimåkra Folkhögskola had a one-year writing course and that sounded very appealing to me. I had my ideas for my novel, but I didn't know how to work with the story structure that I had and I wanted to be in a community of other writers. I started studying and it was motivating for my writing.

In my class, there was a boy who sometimes made me very sad and insecure. He was never mean on purpose, but I think that he didn't understand that what he said made me disappointed. I was writing my book at the time and a few days a week we had to read each other's work and give some feedback. We sent our writing pieces to all the people in the class and then we sat down in our classroom and talked about our work. This boy gave his feedback to me in such a way that I sometimes felt like quitting my writing. It wasn't really what he said; it was the way he said it. I tried to talk to him about it but I never got through to him. He told me that my characters were too alike and that my main character was a 'Mary Sue.' A Mary Sue is a character who is perfect and so competent that it appears absurd. He also said that I should use more 'show don't tell' in my writing. All that he said was good advice but he said it with a patronizing tone, like I was an idiot who didn't understand these things. I started to feel like I didn't want to send parts of my story to him anymore and I was thinking of writing something else for the feedback and writing my story in peace. However, I kept sending my story in because the others in my class didn't give their feedback like he did. One of them is a very dear writing friend and she helped me a lot during my year at Glimåkra.

Despite all this, what he said to me was very true and listening to him and taking his advice has developed me so much as a writer. I am still a little insecure when I write because of him but I try to push that away and instead focus on the actual advice he gave me, and to also take it with a pinch of salt.

The day I finished my first book is a day I will always remember. When I wrote that last word, sat back on the chair, and said to myself, "It is finished," I started crying. I had been working on that book for seven years and fighting to get it finished and finally I had done it. I still had to read through it to check for misspelling but the story was done and I couldn't have been more happy. For a time I felt like I would never get it done and I was almost ready to give up. Something in me said to keep writing and keep reaching for the dream to become a writer.

I did just that and now I have my first book in my hand. The next step is to get published and start writing the second book in the series. The series is planned to become five books at the moment. It might change to less or more but right now it feels like five. I have planned out all the things that are going to happen and it feels very amazing. I am so excited and ready to continue my writing journey.

I am so happy that I pushed on and got rid of the insecurities that threatened to make me quit my dream. What made me get rid of it was Glimåkra Folkhögskola and later Dalarna University where, at the moment, I study scriptwriting for movies. At Glimåkra I was surrounded by others who also loved writing and creating stories and that gave me new inspiration and motivation. Even now, at Dalarna University, everybody in my class is interested in movie plotlines and writing scripts. We have written scripts as school projects and I am more motivated than ever to keep writing now that my first book is finished.

Like I said, I have been writing for many years and I have always liked to create stories in various forms. Writing stories has been my salvation, especially during my early school years, but even now I can find comfort in what I write. I never had the easiest time in school. I can't say that I was being bullied, but I had a very hard time fitting in and always felt that my classmates never really accepted me. During that time, I could always find comfort and happiness in my imagination. Even now when things feel hard or I'm feeling sad I can always go to my book for comfort. The world I have created in my work is entirely my own and to be in it gives me happiness. My characters are my best friends, especially my main character. She is never a Mary Sue! Visiting her world and her friends is one of the things that gives me the most happiness. That is the best part of creating stories; I can create them in any way I want. I can design a world that is completely fictional and shape it the way I see it. My characters may be imaginary but for me they are alive — I have given them life. My main character gives me a lot of inspiration; she is something I want to be and I think that I unintentionally created her like that because of how insecure I was during the time I started working on my novel.

I get the question a lot, "Where do you get your inspirations from?" Inspiration to create comes from everywhere. It comes from beautiful nature, riding my horse, movies I watch, and books I read. When I take hikes in the woods or along the sea I am filled with happiness, and when I get home I can sit down at my computer and recall what I saw in my hike, and make it part of my story. I get very emotional, in a good way, when I come across a place where I can say, "This looks just like the place in my book." This might sound silly, but when I take my horse on a trail ride, I feel like I'm my character and I'm riding her warhorse. I feel free when I let my horse canter along the path in the woods and the wind strokes my face.

I learned one thing during the time I wrote my book and that is: "Every day you say no to your dreams you might be pushing your dreams back a whole six months, or a whole year." I don't know where these words come from; I came across them in a YouTube video and I fell in love. I try to not get affected by the bad things people say about my writing because now I know... *I can, I can, I can.*

So what is happiness? Again, it's very subjective. For some people, something extraordinary needs to happen. They may have been through something very dramatic and need a big push to get back on track. For me, it's the small things that bring happiness. Whatever it is, and there is no right or wrong here, you need to find that special thing that makes you happy. It can be things you see, things you hear, your hobby, and maybe things that make you sad but you learn something in the process. I learned how to keep at it even if I was the only one who believed in me. My Ignite moment was finishing my book even though the odds, people, my insecurities, and time was against me. Everyone has their own reason for staying committed and mine was a deep feeling of devotion to becoming an author.

I know that sometimes we focus more on what we don't have and we forget what we actually do have. When things feel hard and you are sad about something, try to find something in your life that you are grateful for. It doesn't have to be something big or extraordinary; it can be something as simple as a sunny and warm day. You walk out your door and feel the warmth from the sun. The birds are singing and the smell of spring tickles your nose.

I stayed committed for seven years to my story because the dream of becoming an author was stronger than the doubt. On a journey to dream you will always have doubts. It is the hero's journey we all go through. Ask yourself if not having them would be okay. If you can't say you want something else, then don't give up. Find the fun. Get to know others who have the same dream and be inspired by them. Tap into your inner happiness and feel the satisfaction with how it is in that moment, how things are right *now.*

You have to believe in yourself and never listen to the negative things other people say, unless it is helpful. The boy in my class at Glimåkra Folkhögskola is a good example of this. He made me sad and insecure. I am still a bit insecure when I write and do think about what he would say about my writing, but now I can wave off the emotions and take what I need from what he said. In many ways he has taught me so much in my writing process and having his voice in my head was not always bad; it made me write better.

I hope that by reading my chapter in this book you will now go and enjoy the small things in life, and find out that they are big things after all.

Ignite Action Steps

One of my teachers at university taught me this exercise and I fell in love with it, so I want to share it. It is originally meant to be used when writing stories as a way to step into your character's world. However, I'm going to change it a little so that it doesn't focus on that but rather on you.

I invite you to find a place where you often feel happiness or the thought of it makes you feel happiness.

Write it down why it makes you happy

Go to a calm and quiet place and sit or lay down if you prefer that.
Close your eyes and try to rid your mind of all thoughts.
Breathe slowly.
Imagine yourself at a place you really like.
Keep your eyes closed.
Listen.
What do you hear in this place?
Birds, people talking, wind, water, or maybe total silence.
What does it smell like?
Open your eyes.
Welcome to the place.
What can you see?
Walk around here for a bit and have a look around.

Describe everything about it: colors, scenery, people, smell, temperature, sounds... etc.

_____

_____

_____

_____

_____

_____

_____

_____

_____

_____

_____

_____

_____

This is a great way to relax and step into your feelings of satisfaction, self-worth, and personal enjoyment. See how easy it is to find happiness when you focus on one specific thing you like. It's not a big thing but a small thing. Small things can make a difference.

Go a bit deeper.
Close your eyes again.
Return to your happy place and
Imagine finding one small thing that fills you with a deep sense of peace and complete HAPPINESS!

Hanna Wickström – Sweden
Writer
hanna-wickstrom@hotmail.com

TEHNIYET AZAM

"Your light does matter; you never know whose
dark tunnel you are lighting up."

You are the epitome of Happiness and you will find it within. We keep on looking for happiness in everything and everyone when it's right there in our own self. It may be hidden under judgment, self-limiting beliefs, and fears of rejection, but it IS there. It's time for it to come out.

THE LIGHT IN THE TUNNEL

It was a crisp April morning. The birds were chirping and there were signs of spring finding its way out of the dreary and dry winter to the Chicago suburbs. She was 21, a new immigrant, and when she woke up, she felt totally displaced. As soon as she opened her eyes, she saw the four plain white walls of a room she had no memory of. There was only a small window and another girl, a stranger, asleep in a nearby bed. "What happened; where am I?" she asked herself. "Is this a dream?" She wasn't sure of what was happening so she laid her head back and tried to settle her worries. The room and the girl in the other bed didn't go away. She pinched herself to see if it was real and the pinch hurt. Just then, the other girl woke up.

"Hey, you must be Tenny? How are you feeling?" the other girl asked.

"I am okay but where am I?" was the reply filled with fear and confusion.

The other girl stood up from her bed and put her hands on Tenny's shoulders. "You are in the psych ward at Good Samaritan Hospital. You came in yesterday. I heard doctors talk about the overdose you did." She walked toward the restroom. "I heard that your mom, brother, uncle, and aunty came to see you. How lucky are you to have such a loving family."

The other girl's words made no sense. Searching her memory, she felt none of that. Why didn't she remember anything? A nurse came in, brisk and efficient. "How are you feeling today?" The nurse was a middle-aged, beautiful, smiling woman in pink scrubs with her hair tied in a bun. The nurse handed the girl a small bag, saying, "Here are the clothes your family brought for you yesterday. They were here to see you, but you were sleeping and the doctor advised not to wake you up." She then rattled off a list of activities, breakfast, group therapy, and a meeting with a psychiatrist. That's when everything hit her, the reality of why she was in that hospital ward. A bad breakup had left her feeling hopeless and without value, believing no one in her life wanted her, so she had swallowed 30 sleeping pills from her grandmother's medicine cabinet in the morning before going to school.

She loved her school. The community college was a happy place, a safe place, somewhere that was helping her transition into the American education system after she moved here from Pakistan. When she started feeling dizzy and strange in the library before speech class, her heart started beating fast with fear. She told her teacher what she had done, swallowing so much medication; her teacher quickly called for help.

That girl was me and that moment was one of the darkest realities of my life. I had just moved to the United States not even a year ago. At 21, the eldest child of three and the only daughter, I had a lot of dreams and desires in my life and I thought that this new country would give me a new start. I always felt loved and accepted by my parents, but I was aware that the society I grew up in wasn't always so kind, especially as I did not fit the ideals of beauty and passivity for women. My struggle with that affected my entire life, and still does at times even today.

In addition to my new surroundings, Pakistan also had not been kind to me, or at least, one Pakistani man had not. When I was eight years old and was visiting another city for the first time without my parents, for a relative's wedding, something happened. After the wedding, I went to stay at my dad's best friend's house for two days. I called him uncle. He loved me like his own daughter. His brother did not, a monster who saw me as meat for his pleasure, as all women should be.

No matter how much I want to erase what he did from my memory, I can't. That night, I cried, unable to sleep. My uncle and his wife did their best to console me, as I kept silent as to what had happened. They stayed with me all night with no idea of what had transpired earlier that day. But I knew. I remembered. And that incident would go on to extract a toll on my life for the next two decades.

I started to seek refuge in things that I couldn't possibly find. I started getting closer to my dad's eldest brother and his wife, my eight-year-old self thinking that maybe they could rescue me. Maybe I could tell them what had happened to me, but I could not bring myself to speak the words. My grades at school started to decline. I didn't want to study. I went from being a high-achieving distinction student to someone who was hardly passing, my already diminished self-esteem making me an easy target for bullies.

Despite everything, I always kept a smile on my face and I was the happy-go-lucky girl who was there for everyone whenever they needed. Through helping others, I was seeking that validation and support for myself. Once at university, I found my two best friends who became my strength. They were my support system. While I was there, I focused more on finding that man who could be my shield instead of getting my degree and my education suffered.

Two years after I graduated high school, my parents decided to move to the US. Before leaving, I found that man. He was everything to me. I knew that no matter what happened this man would never hurt me sexually. He was vastly older than me, our age difference around 14 years, and as he was coming out of a nasty divorce, he was not ready to get married to me. But I had made up my mind that he was the man for me! After numerous fights and breakups, five years later we got engaged, but a few weeks before the wedding, we called it off. Bereft of my support system, I felt like a bird without wings. What would I do now? He was the first and only person who I ever told about my experience as an eight-year-old. I cried, I yelled, I tried to get it out of my system, but life had other plans.

My parents and my brothers were my constant support. My family did everything, absolutely everything, to keep me happy, to provide me the things I needed to feel loved. My parents genuinely loved me, even though I sometimes wondered how they could love someone broken like me. My brothers bent over backwards to make sure I was happy. But there was something else that was bothering me, something I couldn't get rid of.

I kept on struggling but then my life changed all of a sudden. This was when I heard the first cry of my niece, Inayah, from the delivery room. Her cry sparked something in me. I still don't know what, but it gave me a rush of energy.

That's when I started looking at my parents from a different perspective. I got very close to them and shared each and everything with them, except my molestation. They became my best friends. I can recognize their support now because I removed that cover of judgment against them for not protecting me when I needed them most. It was not their mistake; they didn't know. How would they know if I had never told them?

My life started to get better. My parents bought me a ticket to Mindvalley University and encouraged me to travel to Estonia to rediscover my real self. My dad's elder brother bought me the plane ticket. Everyone thought I was going to get over my broken engagement, but I knew I was going so I could learn to forgive my past.

On my way back from Estonia, I was sitting in a hard plastic chair at the Istanbul airport and I couldn't escape the thought that I was going to go back to the US and my life would be the same. I would still feel inadequate. I would still know that I was lacking. My body was jittering and I rubbed my fingers against the palms of my hands. I kept my outward calm, but inside I felt the mirror of my life was in a thousand broken pieces. When your superheroes taint you or break your trust, it's a life-shattering experience. My cell phone buzzed then, startling me out of my thoughts. My internet was quite choppy, but I received a beautiful picture of my niece. She was wearing a dress that I had sent her before I left for Estonia. My sister-in-law texted, "Tia, look! Your baby, Eenu, looks so cute!"

My jitters melted away, a spark of energy taking their place. The hair on my arms felt electric as I felt the energy flow through each part of my body. That was the moment when I knew, THAT'S IT! No matter what life throws at me now, I will start by focusing on myself and taking care of me.

I came back home and talked with my parents about stepping back into my life and starting by taking care of *me*. They supported me like they always do. My parents took care of my bills and other material needs so I could focus on healing myself. I found a job at a call center despite my parents wanting me to just focus on my education, complete my degree, and get a good job. It was during those two years that I actually found myself. I worked on myself, I read books, I attended conferences. With every new piece, another part of me found closure and healing. Little by little, my steps became more confident and my heart more happy. With the information and knowledge I gained at conferences and from books, with each uplifting speech of the people attending and presenting, with each new healing method, my life became better and better.

Best of all were the people I met. Those friendships are judgment-free and will last for a lifetime. It's like a unicorn fest. My friends hold space for me

— the real me — that is judgment free and so very safe. I can be myself with them without fear. There are many people who have gone through so much in life, and they understand me from the inside out and lift me up when I need lifting. I chatted with my new friends about life and how to get a positive outlook on everything. I stopped looking for validation from people who were no longer serving me. I removed all the toxic relationships. I gave my life and myself a new meaning and a new purpose.

I came out of the victim mindset of "Why me," and instead I got up and said, "Try me."

I found real happiness. It was always there, but was buried under the cover of judgments, self-limiting beliefs, and the fear of rejection. I went to therapy. I still haven't forgiven my molester; I know the moment I see him, I will likely feel the need to give him a big tight slap, because it was he who destroyed my self-worth for almost 25 precious years of my life. At that time, I couldn't save myself; but now, I am the one person who can save him from me.

I started to believe in myself and think that whatever it was, everything was worth it.

When I returned from Estonia, I had a plethora of knowledge. Meditations, techniques, journaling… you name it, I had it. My time in Estonia was over-whelming to a huge extent. I didn't know what take and what to leave behind. I spent my next two years learning about me, about how to find my real self. I spent time learning about what I like and what I dislike. I read a lot of books. I sometimes did journaling. I woke up each morning with the attitude that my day was going to be amazing. I started to forgive and then believe that there was nothing that could bring me down.

Forgiveness has been a huge part of my journey. It took a long time, but I have learned to forgive myself. Growing up, if anything went wrong, it was always the fault of the girl. Well-behaved girls are quiet and compliant and always do the right thing. They look the right way, also — body shaming of girls and women is real, and colorism is too. It took a long time to understand how all of these factors affected me and how they made me think I was not pretty or worth anything. I always looked for validation from anyone — family, friends, teachers — *anyone but me*. I was always thinking about others and how I could make *them* happy. I was holding myself to untenable expectations and unable to find happiness in myself. When I forgave myself for that, when I came to truly understand what an impossible standard I was holding myself to, I felt empowered.

I have forgiven others, too. I have forgiven all my bullies, whether those were my fellow students, relatives, or my teachers who told me that I was dumb. I know now that I don't have to prove myself to anyone. I am who I am. This is me, and if you accept it, fabulous! If not, it's your loss, not mine.

I want my niece and new nephew to know this also. They should never feel that they are not enough. That moment when I first laid eyes on that beautiful little baby girl, I felt that knowledge deep inside of me — she needed me to make sure she knew how valuable and important she is to this world just the way she is. Having walked through hell to discover my own worth, I know it is on me to make sure both those children understand what took me so long to learn: that happiness lies within you.

When I look at my niece, I see life, a Universe of possibility in her. She teaches me that after every sunset is a sunrise. She was born in the middle of the worst years of my life. I had lost myself, my confidence, the love in my life, and the will to live. Looking at her as she lay in her crib, seeing the spark in her eyes and that little smile… she brought a new energy to my life. The way she looks straight at you, seeing *you*, sending silent messages with the power of her gaze… I could feel her energy, her strength, her inner wisdom even as an infant. The expression on her face when I look at her tells me, "You've got this," and I believe her.

My niece's presence has shown me that one has to look for that joy. You might be upset and in the darkest era of your life, but one tiny ray of hope can brighten up your entire future. When I look at her, I feel scared also because this world is not an easy place to live in and I don't want her to be hurt, but she won't be. I am going to make sure that she is aware of the untruths of the cultural barriers that might stop her from sharing, from being open, from understanding that she has value. She will not let anyone hurt her because she will have her eyes wide open. She will be strong. I know she will, and so will my nephew. I'm going to make sure of it.

My life's journey has taught me that I need to find myself and be okay with who I am. I need to accept myself as I stand and work always to be stronger, taller, and more of who I am. I went back to college to improve my skills. I traveled. I started looking at different aspects of life and I began to fix the things that weren't working for me. When I look back to that girl lying on that hospital bed in confusion, lost and alone with strangers, I believe that it was a good thing that happened to me. The three days I spent at the hospital were, I feel, the most transformational days of my life. I felt the importance of living from a very close distance. Years later, I have now found my happiness.

I could never have imagined it during that dark time, but I am truly happy. I have started to believe in myself and I know that whatever it was, everything was worth it. Now that I'm happy, I can count my blessings; I can find the real joy. In trying to take my own life, I learned that life is precious, and that mine is one worth living. Know your worth! Don't let the actions or judgments of others or a piece of paper define your worth. You are strong. You are resilient. And you can get through anything in this world. Have the vision to see your real beauty. Let your light shine bright and light up the entire Universe.

IGNITE ACTION STEPS

- Listen to something first thing in the morning. It can be anything. A meditation, words from the Holy Scripture, whatever gives you the feeling of being blessed, the rise of positive energy. Do it first thing when you get up.
- Look into the mirror and tell yourself how amazing you are. Words of affirmation rewire your brain from all self-limiting beliefs and fears that you might have.
- One day at a time, one hour at a time. Don't rush yourself. You will get where you need to be. Whether you follow someone else's vision and copy their version of the Mona Lisa or you carve your own original path and create your own masterpiece, the artwork that is you is worth trillions.

*Dedication: To Ammi and Abbu who believed in me when I didn't. To my brothers, Muazzam and Umar, Sil, Tooba, and my sister Saman, who loved me unconditionally despite my issues. To my best friends, Zainab, Usman, and Hina, who didn't give up on me when I did. To my nephew, Musa, who continues to bring that spark and energy in my life. To all my aunts and uncles, especially Amma and Baba, who were my unbreakable support. Most importantly, to my niece, **Inayah**, who brought my life back to me, whose existence gave me the reason to live, be strong, and be better. I love you all and couldn't have done it without you...*

Tehniyet Azam – United States of America
Organizational Development Specialist
www.tehniyet.com

SHREYA LADVA

"People who give you the 'Good Vibe' are people worth holding on to."

I want to teach you that it doesn't take much to change someone's life for the better; your caring personality can even make them feel alive. When you're feeling down, remember the good memories and moments that you've experienced where you felt dynamic and vibrant. This is called the 'Good Vibe,' so when you feel this way, try and recognize the moments in which it happens so you can repeat it again and again. I recommend that you spend your time with people who make you feel this way as well. People who make you feel the 'Good Vibe.'

GETTING THE GOOD VIBE

Pressure. I felt the weight of his arms across my chest and around my back in a warm embrace. I froze, paralyzed. I had never felt anything like this before. I had only felt the sensation of pure friendship a couple of times prior, but it wasn't like this. This was different. This time, there was true affection for one another and I melted into it.

A few months earlier, I was sitting in a small, brightly lit classroom, staring out the window with my head resting on my hand. Social studies was probably the worst class you could be in on Friday afternoon, depending on who you ask. I could barely pay attention to what the teacher was saying; listening was such a tedious task. It never occurred to me how dull it was living in a cycle.

Going around and around with no purpose, no *life*. I would repeat the same thing every day. Wake up, go to school, come home, do homework, eat dinner, shower, then sleep. And then do it again the very next day. It was monotonous. Mind-numbing. I was trapped. I had never really realized that I was in a cycle until later on. I wish I had known.

I remember a time when my routine, my cycle, had become so boring and repetitive. It was at the end of grade eight; more specifically, the last day of school and at least 10 students were moving and changing schools. Some of them, I had grown up with over the past four or five years of my life and I didn't even have the guts to say my farewell. Some of them — to this day — I have never seen again. All that I can recall is saying a quick "'Bye" to them while passing in the hallway. And that was the last of it. I realized later on that, at that point, I was utterly disconnected from people who may have made a difference in my life. I wonder what could have been if I had taken the time to leave an impression.

As a family, we decided to head into the city for a pleasant dinner the next evening. Even though I'd rather just stay in and order pizza, I didn't complain. Vancouver, a coastal city at the base of the Rocky Mountains, is absolutely beautiful. Driving into the city, I could look up through our car's sunroof and watch the tall, thin rectangles of the skyscrapers endlessly shoot toward the sun. The moments when we went into town and looked at the Vancouver skyline were the only times when I felt... alive. Connected would be the right words. I didn't know what I was connected *to,* but there was this feeling inside me. Some sort of energy, if that makes sense. While we were waiting for the food, my dad sparked a conversation about Estonia; in particular, a place called Tallinn. He then began to tell us about an event called Mindvalley University — a four-week long course that teaches people how to become better individuals and fully take control of their lives. And then he announced the big news:

"We're moving to Estonia for a month," he said. The breath stopped in my lungs, unable to get out. When I did finally exhale, I lost it. I glanced over to my brother and then back at my parents, who were beaming at me. What was there to beam about? They explained that we would be attending the second annual Mindvalley University event in Tallinn, Estonia in two months — July. We were leaving at the very end of school. Naturally, sitting in that restaurant at that moment, feeling very nervous but unable to say it, I just nodded my agreement. My brain was bombarded with thoughts that crowded into my head. My dad proceeded to show my brother and I videos of the country and pictures of what to expect in our adventure. Even though the city was beautiful, I was still skeptical of what was to come.

Two months later, it was July. My dad, brother, and I walked down the steps to the tarmac, having just arrived in Tallinn after 15 hours on a plane. It was Friday night, yet as bright as if it were still daytime. I was exhausted from the trip and just wanted to collapse on a bed. Being in Tallinn was a whole new feeling. I was away from school, away from anyone I had ever really known, and it felt like I had left my whole other life behind.

The next evening, I was getting ready for the opening party. For some reason, I wasn't nervous this time, even if part of me felt like I was supposed to be. As soon as we walked into the venue — an old power plant — I was enveloped by a new type of energy. A new sensation unlike anything I had ever experienced before. It was electric. We picked up our wristbands and headed in. My dad — the natural extrovert — started talking to strangers as if they were old high school buddies. It was insane. Meanwhile, I followed him around like a little duckling, barely surviving the social overload.

From person to person, we continued this way, until my dad introduced himself to this one particular woman. They started with the casual 'hello' and 'what's your name?' sort of thing. My dad mentioned my name and the woman looked at me. I smiled a little and introduced myself, feeling a little socially awkward, and — like a typical teen — I kept the talking to a minimum. Their conversation continued and I zoned out, hands tucked behind my back as I fidgeted. I examined the venue a little more, trying to soak in everything around me. The lady turned to me and asked, "Can I introduce you to some people that you might get along with?" Dumbfounded, I nodded and followed her into the crowd. I found three people all half-dancing and half-talking with one another. She introduced me, then left. There I was, standing in a city I had never been to before, in a country that I had never been to either, facing three strangers.

"Hi," I said. They all smiled at me.

"Hi! I'm Cassidy," the first girl said, and I smiled back.

"Hi, I'm Kaitlin. I'm going to give you a hug," said Kaitlin, and we hugged each other.

In my previous encounters with people I'd never met, not many of them were natural huggers, so this first impression was a little unusual to me. How was I feeling? I wasn't. Everything was happening so fast that I didn't know how to react to any of it. It's like when you're in math class and the teacher has already begun the lesson, and you've only just sat down at your desk. The butterflies in my stomach didn't settle until much later. For the rest of the night, we danced and shared memories. I met about 10 other teenagers and became best friends with Cassidy, a friendship which persists even to this day. I don't think that I will ever forget that night, those memories, and the friends I made. It was beautiful, like there was more to life than just what you do in your cycle. In Tallinn, I could be whoever I wanted to be.

I met people who could always bring a smile to anyone's face. The food was absolutely incredible. We lived a train ride away from the central location of the course and in the middle of the city was a place called Old Town. Old Town had a unique, archaic architecture that was littered in history. You'd see gelato shops and pubs filled with the sounds of people laughing, and European folk music and dancing in the central square. All my memories of that month overflow with joy. It was truly the best time of my life.

I remember one day very vividly. It was one teen's last day at Mindvalley and he was hugging everyone goodbye. He and I had become pretty good friends over the course of the month, so I went to his farewell. Everyone was there and it was a sort of somber moment. We didn't know if we'd see him again. Well, nobody knew if any of us were going to see each other again. I didn't know what to do to say goodbye to him, so when he turned to me, I panicked. My fight-or-flight response kicked in and I froze like a deer in headlights. So, naturally, I did what any socially-awkward teenager would do: I held up my hand for a high five.

"Aww hell no," he said, and then hugged me tightly; in that moment, I was just stuck. Frozen in time with my hand still awkwardly in the high-five position. I tensed up. I was in shock. Yes, I know it's strange that I was in shock, but the real truth? To be completely honest, I wasn't that close with anybody at school, so farewell hugs were new to me and I hadn't really hugged anybody before that, except Cassidy and Kaitlin on my first night in Tallinn. I thought to myself, "What do I do now?" For two seconds, I was completely distraught until I finally maneuvered my hands and hugged him back. I released all the tension that was rapidly building up by the second and then there was this... pressure. Across my chest and around my back by his warm embrace. I had only felt the sensation of pure friendship a couple of times prior, but it wasn't like this. This was different. This time, there was true affection for one another. This was the moment when it felt like I had been seeing gray for 13 years and now I could finally see color. A connection was established that day; one that no one would ever forget.

That particular hug was the first farewell hug I had ever had and it changed the way I looked at things. It reminded me to cherish these moments in Tallinn and spend every drop of time with these incredible people. So I did exactly that. After he left, I spent the remainder of the time that I was there — every single moment of it — with my best friends, knowing that I wouldn't see them again for an entire year.

On my last day at Mindvalley, I hugged my friends goodbye. At the start of this trip, I wouldn't have thought that we'd be so close in only four weeks, yet there we were. I can't emphasize how grateful I am for that experience and how it changed my life. It was tough to leave people when I didn't know if I'd see them again. Even now — two years later — I still haven't seen some of them in person. It hurts sometimes to know the people that I felt the most like myself around — the people that made me the happiest — are all in different cities and countries, but it's a reminder to me that they're out there.

On the flight back home, I opened the packet of letters that we had all written for each other before we left. They were called our 'Sugar Cubes' and they were filled with little notes from everyone I had met. Those little notes were like a piece of the friends I had made, and I was taking them home with me. I was taking the memories with me. I cried while taking off. It made me sad to think that I might never see them again. I read the notes on the plane ride back and just really let it burst out. I broke down every time I remembered the feeling that I wouldn't be seeing them again. You see, the people there weren't just other teenagers. They were unique. Special. Some of them traveled full-time, some of them didn't go to high school, some of them were aspiring influencers. But that didn't matter; all that mattered was who they were as a person. They were kind, selfless, artistic, bold, and in general really bright. They were the colors in the world and with them, I felt this sort of energy inside of me, the same type of energy that I felt while driving down the streets of Vancouver. The same energy I feel when I'm blasting my favorite song in the car or dancing around my room. I was really going to miss them.

Gahmya was our teen instructor at Mindvalley and our best friend. She helped me see the color inside of me and touched every one of us differently. She supported us throughout the whole month and has become a very special person in my life. She helped us uncover our passions. For me, it was writing, which is the main reason I'm here writing this today.

Two months after Mindvalley University 2018, Gahmya contacted all the teenagers about starting Zoom calls to talk with each other again. You could imagine — considering I cried while leaving them — my reaction when I found out I was going to see them again. Believe me, when I first joined that call, it was that same energy.

Since I had last seen everyone, I had been writing a lot more things and tapping more into my creative side. November 8th, 2018, was a huge day for me. That was the day I published my first article. Gahmya had been working with me to write an article about finding happiness and after weeks of writing and editing, it was finally published online. I remember that I was truly beaming with joy; then, once again, I felt the exact same energy.

When I went back to school the next fall, I was eager to take control of my life and turn it into the one that I had always wanted. I reminded myself to treasure moments and took it upon myself to put my ideas out there. This resulted in multiple bonded friendships and, eventually, farewell hugs at the end of the year.

Since I had enjoyed my time so much in Tallinn, I convinced my parents to take me and my brother to Pula, Croatia, for the next annual Mindvalley University. My first day back, there was this one moment that I remember when my best friend Cassidy came running up and hugged me tightly. The rest of the day was hug after hug after hug.

Today, I think about Mindvalley all the time. I think about my marvelous friends and how they've supported me over the past two years. All the good memories and laughter that we all shared like on the first day when we were all sitting around in a circle talking about things like old high school buddies. I also think about what my life would have been like if that one boy hadn't hugged me on his last day. Then I would have just left the whole course without wonderful friends. I wouldn't have experienced that Zoom call in September. I wouldn't have gotten in touch with Gahmya and worked on an article in November. I wouldn't have gone back the next year to see them again, nor would I be writing this now. And it's easy to say that I don't think I would've been as happy as I am now if I hadn't gone.

Knowing those amazing people and getting to talk to them every day makes me happy. The gelato runs at 10 PM, parties by the beach, group chat talks that lasted for days, beanbags and serious convos, the Good Vibe, and a *lot* of laughs. Those things give me the energy. I named the energy my 'Good Vibe' – yeah, I know, it's so original. And I crave this vibe in everything that I do and hope for it in my future. I still think about my life before — my color-less, static, motionless cycle of not having good relationships with my school friends, not cherishing moments, not really *living*. My catastrophically boring life drained me of who I was and prevented me from becoming who I wanted to be. Everything was starting to look the same, everything felt the same, but all it took was some sort of light, some sunshine to bring me into a clear patch where there are trees of green and red roses too. Where the skies are blue and the clouds are white. Where I see everything bloom, for me and for you.

That hug on that boy's last day at Mindvalley brought me toward my new friends and the life that I have now. I miss each and every one of them, but I know the next time we're able to be together will be magical. And that makes me a whole lot happier.

The smallest gestures and the smallest of hugs can make the biggest differences, so the next time you receive a hug, hug back and embrace the *Good Vibe*.

Ignite Action Steps

List 5 things you can do to make you feel the Good Vibe:

1. _____
2. _____
3. _____
4. _____
5. _____

Take five minutes every day to do one of the things on your list.

List five people who make you feel the Good Vibe when you hang out with them. Put in a little effort and take some time to talk to one of those people every day.

1. _____
2. _____
3. _____
4. _____
5. _____

Pay attention to the signals that people give you. When they reach out in friendship, take a risk — accept their offering. You never know when you're going to find your next best friend.

Shreya Ladva – Canada
Writer
https://thriveglobal.com/authors/shreya-ladva/

NICOLE ARNOLD

"With passion comes happiness."

Finding your passion can lead to experiencing sustained, satisfying happiness and help reveal the core of who you are. Discover your deepest self, outside of your social roles and cultural influences, so that you can unlock your greatest gift and turn it into a habit that will lead to a life full of happiness.

THE HAPPINESS HABIT

I was stuck in traffic. As I drummed my fingers impatiently on the steering wheel, my eyes kept darting to the clock on the dashboard, willing the numbers to slow down instead of getting closer to when my kids got out of school. I tried to push aside the guilt of being late again and focus on the audiobook that my mindset coach had recommended. I tuned in to hear the words, "Who are you, outside of your history and the roles you play?" My stomach tightened painfully in response.

What a hard question! I didn't know the answer, but I realized that at the age of 41, it was a good time to start asking. Who was I outside of a woman, mother of three, wife, daughter, granddaughter, sister, Jew, Canadian, mindset coach, and friend? What was left? I didn't know what else there was to be. I almost started crying in the car. I was trying so hard to be a superstar in all of those roles that I felt too exhausted to dig deep and find out who I was outside of them.

If I had understood that answering the question would lead to a more fulfilling happiness than I had ever known, I might have been more diligent about seeking the answer. In the end, when I wasn't expecting it, the answer found me.

Two years later, on the verge of launching my own mindset coaching business, I discovered the activity that would answer the question of who I am outside of my history and the roles I play. My kids — 14, 13, and 9 — were all in bed and, if not asleep, certainly quiet. My husband was dozing beside me on the couch as I scrolled through my Facebook feed trying to quiet my stressed-out mental list making. My eyes moved down the screen, taking in all of the family photos, pretty renos, and cries of existential angst. I stopped scrolling when I saw the ad that would change my life. Someone named Michelle McQuaid was launching a 7-day character strength challenge starting the following Monday, and it was free.

I clicked through to learn more. I needed a boost and this challenge looked like a perfect fit for me. I was launching a strength-based life coaching practice to help people remove the barriers that stand in their way of unlocking their gifts so they can live their best lives. What could be more helpful than focusing on my own strengths? I saw right away how signing up could be a double win, giving me new tools to enrich my coaching skills while at the same time helping me discover my own strengths.

I hadn't moved from the couch, but I could already feel the buzz of excitement that challenges always bring me.

I've been hooked on challenges ever since I conquered the Canada Fitness Test in elementary school. The test was a hallmark experience of kids growing up in the '70s and '80s in Canada. The actual competition took place each spring, but the brightly colored charts displaying illustrations of each activity and the award benchmarks hung like wallpaper in the gym all year round. The levels started at Participation, followed by Bronze, Silver, Gold, then the Award of Excellence. For the participation level, you received a paper certificate that got crumpled in knapsacks before it even arrived home. For the 'medal' levels, winners received thick fabric badges the size of a chocolate chip cookie. I didn't try very hard the first few years that the Canada Fitness Test came around, but in grade three, I began to pay attention to the charts on the gym wall for the first time. I wanted to move beyond the participation level. I don't remember what prompted my desire, but I had started wanting a badge — the flimsy piece of paper wasn't satisfying me. I realized that if I paid attention to the charts, I could make the next levels my new goal.

When my gym teacher took us out to the school yard to practice for the

50 meter run, I was determined to get under 8 seconds and secure Bronze or, even better, Silver. My feet pounded the asphalt as I ran as hard as I could to the line of yellow paint that marked the finish line. My new efforts earned me a Silver badge. The following year, I doubled down on the hanging bar hold, maintaining eye level and managing to keep my hands around the slippery bar, even when my whole body started to shake and my skull hurt from the intense effort. I received Gold. I felt so proud of how far I had come and set my sights on achieving the next level.

I pinned my first two Canada Fitness badges to my bedroom wall and dreamed of adding the majestic mix of blue, red, gold, and silver threads that made up the Award of Excellence. The only thing that was holding me back was a faster time in the endurance run. As I ran around the track that fall, winter, and spring trying so hard to complete faster laps, I learned that I could keep going even when I felt uncomfortable. When the Canada Fitness Test arrived that spring, I crossed the finish line with time to spare and happily accepted my first Award of Excellence. Tears filled my eyes and I felt all puffed up, like I could conquer the world. I took home my beautiful new badge and hung it on my wall to admire each morning when I woke up. That's when I learned not to be afraid of challenges — I understood them as invitations to get stronger and feel happier.

Back on the couch beside my sleeping husband, I clicked "Yes," practically holding my breath with eagerness to begin a new challenge. To get started, I needed to fill out a registration form and complete a character strength questionnaire that would give me a list of the 'positive parts of my personality.' I typed in my name and email address, and then turned to the survey and carefully considered each question. I enjoy completing online assessments, even though — like their Cosmo magazine sisters of the past — they always tell me something about myself that I already knew. The character strength report was different — it surprised me. Instead of my usual list — curiosity, leadership, problem-solving, courage — sitting at the top of my list of strengths was *creativity*. My heart beat a little faster when I saw it. Creativity. Huh? My face opened into a wide smile. I hadn't thought about myself as creative in a long time.

As a child, I had felt very creative. I wrote poetry, painted, and sketched. I started many journals that I hoped people would want to read some day when I was a famous author. I submitted poems to a local children's magazine and was ecstatic to see them in print. In my teens, I shifted from thinking about myself as a creator of art to a consumer of art. I can't explain where my insecurity about my creative abilities came from, but it had something to do with how inept I felt adding my school reports to the pile of papers on the teacher's desk when my cover pages lacked the beautiful pencil-crayoned work I saw others submit. There was also the feeling of woeful inadequacy every time I shakily performed a scene in my high school theater program. By university, I was happy to read the books that others wrote and attend the plays that others created. I no longer had dreams of being an author and acting on stage. I didn't mourn the loss of these aspirations; I hadn't even noticed that my dreams had died.

Sitting on my couch in the darkness, my eyes connected to the word 'creativity' perched like a crown atop the list of my other strengths and something stirred deep inside of me. I felt a thrill run through my body like an electrical current, creating a tingling sensation from my scalp to my toes. Suddenly, the strength challenge felt like a whole different kind of proposition. It had become an invitation to create. The stress I had been feeling earlier in the evening about launching my business faded into the background of my thoughts. Instead, I felt focused and alert with the prospect of exploring and engaging my creativity.

The next form that appeared on my screen guided me to design a strength habit for the week — a 10-minute activity that could engage me creatively. With a nod to maximizing my time, I gleefully created a task that could help me develop my coaching practice. I would use the time to brainstorm solutions I could offer to organizations. I thought about this activity as *creating* solutions. I decided to start writing each morning, after the kids left for school, when I sat down at my kitchen table with my coffee. Even though I rarely wrote on paper, unless I was keeping score in a card game, I opted to use pen and paper rather than typing on my laptop. I had a wistful sense that I would tap into a different level of creativity with the tactile experience of pressing pen to paper.

The first morning, I carried my coffee mug over to the table and lined up my pen and paper before setting the timer on my phone to 10 minutes. I wrote furiously for about five minutes and then paused. More ideas came and I wrote again. And then again. At 10 minutes, the chimes sounded, and I put down my pen. Pure joy was spreading through my body like a warm wave. I could feel the stretch of my cheeks from the huge smile on my face. I must have been smiling the whole time. I felt so happy. I liked the ideas that I had come up with, but most of all, I loved the satisfying feeling of conceptualizing and then transferring my thoughts to the page. I enjoyed the interplay of the flow of ideas and then the challenge of staying focused when my thoughts slowed down. Buzzing with good feelings, I turned my attention to developing my website, feeling focused and motivated.

The next morning, I rushed the kids out the door for school, eager to start my writing session and bring forth the same satisfying feelings as the day before. I wasn't disappointed — I lost my awareness of sitting at my kitchen table and just felt the ideas flow from my mind to the pen as my hand quickly moved across the page. The week went on and every day I moved eagerly to my chair keen to dive into writing. The words poured out of me. Each time the flow subsided, I could feel my brain engage and revel in the challenge of creating. My 100 minutes went by quickly and when the chimes sounded at the end, I found myself wanting to write more. I had never felt so confident before, so sure that I was in the right place, doing the right thing. My eyes were wide open and the hairs on the back of my neck tingled with pure excitement.

By the last day, I understood what had happened. The strength challenge had awakened the writer in me — the writer I hadn't even known was still there. I like to think that until that week, the creative spirit that I had felt as a child had been resting quietly within me, silently taking in stories, expressions, emotions, and sensations. Practicing creativity for 10 minutes each day for a week awakened this spirit, Igniting a fierce desire to write.

After the challenge was complete, I kept writing in the morning. I began to produce more sentences than I had in my life. I started with writing all the copy for my website and then I worked on developing positive psychology-oriented articles, posting them on my business blog.

At the end of that year, I traveled to Amsterdam and Israel and felt inspired each day to post journal entries online about my personal adventures. Four years later, I continue to post regularly to both my business and personal blogs. I've also begun a novel, a short story collection, and a non-fiction book. From those first mornings of creation during the Strength Challenge, I have formed a daily writing habit that makes way for the wellspring of good feelings that emerge when I am developing stories, articles, and journaling. I continue to use pen and paper. I've become hooked on the almost magical feeling of watching the ink bleed onto the crisp whiteness, revealing my thoughts and ideas as I move my pen across the page. Writing has become as important to me as being a woman, mother, and coach; it has become a core part of my identity.

Since I created my writing habit, I see the world in a different way. I observe more and talk less (even though I still talk a lot). I notice so much more of the rich and sensual detail of the world in everything I do, sinking into tasks that used to feel mundane. When I make dinner, I'm more aware of the firm and slippery surface of the onion as I slice it and the popping sound the garlic makes when it meets the hot oil in the pan. I can almost see the scent of the onion and garlic wafting toward my nose before it engulfs me like the music in a symphony, taking over all my senses. In those moments, I feel so connected to the world around me. Writing connects me to people, too. Through writing, I share thoughts that I could have never spoken out loud, allowing people to know me in richer and more meaningful ways. The more I write, the more I am slowly, but surely, learning my voice.

The intense desire to write has uncovered the wholeness of me — childhood, adulthood, and every part of me that has no category. My new sense of knowing and connection helped me answer the question I had pondered in traffic so many years before: who am I outside of my roles and history? Now I know — I am a writer. When I said those words at my first writer's retreat, I could feel the truth reverberate throughout my body, bringing hot tears to my eyes. That's how I knew without question that being a writer comes from the deepest part of me; the part that exists outside of my history and the roles that I play. I am a writer. Knowing this gives me deep joy. Pure happiness.

It's no wonder that I feel so happy. The very act of writing contains the elements that are scientifically linked to happiness, including curiosity, joy, openness, accomplishment, connection, and the search for meaning. When I write, I bring these feelings to my life and the lives of those around me. I really feel the boost that writing gives my happiness levels. Sometimes that lift translates into the compassion I need to parent three teenagers. Sometimes it's the extra fuel I need to make a nourishing dinner or go for a run. Other times, my increased happiness comes to me as calming words inside my head that I never used to hear before — it is the sweet voice reassuring me that I'm doing the right thing; I'm on the right path.

We owe it to ourselves and the world to accept the opportunities that come our way and invite us to get stronger and feel happier by discovering the very best of who we are, so we can start applying those strengths to the challenges in front of us. It's always the right time to start that journey.

If you're trying to be a superstar in all the roles you're playing but regularly feel like you're missing the mark, I recommend finding an activity to practice that Ignites your passion and sets you on your path to living your best life. Once you've identified it, then give yourself a chance to experience happiness every day by creating a habit where you practice your passion. The happiness that you feel from doing what you do best will give you the boost you need to follow your dreams. Say *yes* to your next challenge — it could lead you to finding your passion and the greatest happiness you've ever known.

Ignite Action Steps

1. Complete a strength assessment like the VIA Character Strengths Survey (free). It's available for adults and youths (10-17), and provides a report about your strengths and the positive parts of your personality.

2. Choose a strength that feels exciting to you and design an activity that you can do for 10 minutes each day for seven days. Anchor that activity to a daily habit like sitting down with your morning coffee to help you remember to do it each day. When the 10 minutes is complete, take a few minutes before moving on to your next task to assess how you feel. Alert? Excited? Relaxed? Savor those feelings.

3. Repeat for seven days and then reflect on how your happiness was impacted over the week from practicing your strength.

Nicole Arnold, MA (Psychology) – Canada
Mindset Coach
www.positivelymotivating.net

SIMONA SABBATINI

*"It's not what happens, it's how we react that makes the difference.
Life is a great opportunity; grab it!"*

Life is an incredible adventure; a fascinating journey. Hard moments can lead to great opportunities and happiness. I wish for people to feel inspired by my story, understanding that the way we react to life events can change our entire future. We can choose to be happy and cultivate positivity. Daily happiness is a priority and gratitude for what we have is a daily exercise.

HAPPINESS IS A CHOICE

You open your eyes and you feel grateful, serene, and ready for the new day. What a great feeling! I know it because it's what I feel the majority of the time. It doesn't matter if it's a sunny day or a cloudy one; the emotions of harmony and happiness are inside me before the day begins. My life is full of ups and downs, critical issues, and challenges — exactly as yours and everybody else's in this world. Sometimes things go well, sometimes not. I discovered that happiness is a choice. We can build it (I purposely use build) one stone on top of the other, one step at a time. It took effort to achieve this result as everything started during the most painful moment of my life.

I was born in the 1960s during a financial boom in Italy, the first born of a highly educated couple from two different backgrounds, one side professionals and the other side businesspeople. Following in their own parents' footsteps (who married very late because they wanted to choose the right person), my parents married in their thirties — something unusual in that period. When I was born, I was the first child for my parents, first grandchild for all of my grandparents, and the first niece for my only aunt. I really didn't lack love, care, or affection at all. I enjoyed the loving attention a lot and it was the root of my strength when things suddenly changed.

I still remember the nice, lovely feeling of being cared for and the happiness I felt when I was with my grandparents. They shared many fascinating stories about their lives. My grandfather was a great storyteller, able to explain life experiences in such great detail that I felt as if I was right there. His stories inspired my sister and me a lot.

One such exciting story was about my grandmother riding an untamed horse in the early 1900s, a time when girls were supposed to be quiet at home and marry as soon as possible. Others were about our great grandfather, the mayor of the village, who refused a bribe with a famous quip, *"What my son's ears can't hear also, mine cannot."* My favorite one was related to poor people he helped with some loans. These people were unable to pay the money back and when my grandfather understood how difficult it was and that the situation could harm the good relationship they had, he decided to cancel all the debts.

My dad was a playful and creative person. He was an entrepreneur who worked hard and spent very little time with us, but when he was around, he was able to transform our days. I still recall a time when we planned to go for a picnic, but when the day arrived, it was raining heavily and it was not possible to go. On seeing our sorrow, Dad came up with the idea to hold the picnic in our dining room. We were so excited and happy!

Mum was more practical and very strong. She was such an open-minded person and always available to talk with us. My curiosity was (and still is) endless, and I was fascinated by the possibility of discussing everything in depth with her. Mum's answers were never yes or no; it was always, "Yes, because..." or "No, because..." and she always gave us the opportunity to reply with our own opinions. This feeling of being free to say what was on my mind gave me a great sense of closeness to her and built my confidence.

One day when I was six or seven and coming back from grocery shopping, I asked for a sweet. I was a tiny girl who didn't eat a lot. My mum kept walking, refusing to stop and buy one because it was already lunch time and it could compromise my appetite. I replied that I could eat it after lunch. A few steps past the shop, I remember my mum pausing and turning to look at me. She bent down, looked me softly in the eyes, and apologized. She told me that there was no proper reason that she could give me to explain why she didn't want to buy me a sweet. In a loving voice, she told me that while we were already ahead of the shop, we weren't going back. She said to take it as a lesson: *Sometimes in life there is a 'no' without a reason.* I understood this as best a young girl could, but I had no idea how much this lesson was going to serve me over the course of my life.

The two most impactful aspects of my childhood were the time dedicated to me and my sister and the stories that were told to us. Our parents and grandparents spent hours playing with and talking to us. They paid attention to our ideas and gave us the freedom to express ourselves. I still remember long nights sharing with my mum, silence around us, only me and her talking about many issues. They were Magical moments. I was happy and excited. I know that in reading this story it looks like everything was perfect, but it was not. Challenges and difficulties were there, but I remember what I consciously decided to keep with me: the nice memories that helped me to overcome the worst pain in my life, the loss of my beloved Mum.

One Sunday, when I was 16, we were in the countryside, spending the weekend at our vacation house. It was Mother's Day and while Dad was at home doing some renovations, Mum, my younger sister, and I went to church. I had some money that Dad gave me to buy a cake to celebrate Mum. My sister and I were excited thinking about how to prepare something special for her and we had some nice ideas. Suddenly Mum started feeling unwell. She stood up in church and then sat again several times with apparently no reason. She would sit when everyone in the congregation stood and stood when everyone sat. We were a bit embarrassed by this behavior, not understanding what was going on.

At the beginning, our biggest concern was why she was behaving like that and what people in church were thinking. After a few minutes, Mum told us that she needed to go back home but was not feeling able to walk. I stood up, ready to run home and call Dad, but she asked me to remain with her and sent my sister instead. From that moment, everything became like a movie.

Dad arrived with the car, assuming he would just be taking her home, but he immediately understood that the situation was critical. We were not very familiar with the area and had to ask several people along the way for directions to the hospital. When we finally arrived, I remember running after the nurse when I heard her saying that my mum had high blood pressure, I shouted "It's not possible, she has low pressure!" The nurse asked me if I was sure. The whole family was aware of my mom's low pressure, so obviously I was sure.

Our anguish grew as we waited for doctors to give us feedback. When they finally talked to Dad, we didn't understand what was wrong. I knew it was something bad because they didn't allow us to see her. I remember staying outside the Intensive Care Unit just waiting and watching the nurses and doctors going in and out. Nobody talked to us; they just said we had to wait. I felt like going crazy, but I immediately thought that I had to be strong and not show my pain to my younger sister. We didn't see Mum again. After five long days, she passed away from a stroke in her brain. Her passing left us shocked, in grief, and unable to understand why. She was only 49 years old.

I loved my mum deeply. She was my best friend. With her, I was able to be myself and talk about everything. And she was always there, listening to me and involved in what I was willing to express. I felt lost and alone without her. The grief and despair seemed to hold my heart tightly, giving a feeling of physical pain. Coming back from the burial, the house was empty but for the three of us who didn't know how to cope with our feelings and go back to 'normal' life.

At the beginning, everything was in a fog with people coming to visit us every day and a lot of condolence messages waiting for a reply. I experienced new and different feelings and emotions. Sometimes I thought that it was just a nightmare — it was going to pass and Mum was coming back — but I knew it was not possible. Sometimes it felt like she was around. I could almost feel her next to me and it scared me. I was unable to understand or accept my loss, nor manage all the deep and difficult emotions. It was hard to go on. Dad was lost in his grief, unable to accept what happened and manage two young girls experiencing their own devastating loss. But one step after the other, we restarted our daily activities; we went back to school and Dad to work.

Looking back at that period, I see that it was the starting point of my new life. The following events helped me to overcome the grief and become the optimistic, happy, and positive person that I am.

Most of all, our grandparents' reaction was a source of inspiration for my sister and I. They faced the loss of their sole beloved daughter with deep sorrow, but they also showed they were able to accept what was impossible to change and focus on what they could do — take care of us. My sister and I admired their strength. They helped me to focus on life, not death, and to do what I could to feel better while helping my sister and Dad, too.

I began doing what I imagined would have made Mum proud of me. Behaving well, looking after my younger sister, and talking with her for hours about our grief. Those talks gave us the understanding that, sadly, our grandparents were the most affected ones. Losing your sole daughter in your 80s must be truly terrible and our compassion for them helped us to handle our own mourning.

Discussing our feelings helped us cope with our sorrow. I felt stronger talking with my sister as Mum had with me.

When the question, "Why did this happen to us," came to my mind, I was able to recall Mum's lesson: *Sometimes life says no without reason.* Many years after our conversation about the candy, I understood Mum's lesson: There was no reason; it happened and I had to accept it.

Early in our mourning period, I remembered two girls in our neighborhood who lost their mum just a month before me. That fact helped me to realize I was not the only person in the world facing such a challenge. Their sorrow and mine were the same. Anything can happen to any of us at any time. It was a difficult period with many days spent in despair and worrying that something could happen to my dad and sister too. Real nightmares. To overcome these feelings, I started to appreciate every day. Every morning I was grateful for my sister, my dad, and grandparents for being alive; it was a daily source of consolation. When I recall that period and how difficult it was, I always feel gratitude to my family because they gave me tools to overcome this trauma.

I believe that this sad experience is the last gift I received from my Mum; the chance to understand what's important in life and live accordingly. From the moment of her passing, it became very clear to me that nothing is permanent and that the majority of our daily issues are very petty things. Sometimes my friends are annoyed, worried, or demoralized for nothing. To me, most of the things are very simple. Either you change it or you move on. Inside myself, I feel that I experienced the only thing you can't change: the loss of somebody you love. Everything else, you can manage. Understanding that death is part of life and can occur any time, I developed the capability of appreciating every single moment of life.

Nowadays, after a long journey reading and studying, it is easier to identify priorities and understand what is indispensable and what is not. As a self-employed entrepreneur, I've worked hard while always trying to balance and pay attention to what is most important to me: my beloved ones. Daily happiness is a priority and gratitude for what I have is a daily exercise.

Feeling that I am a lucky person, and understanding the big role my family played, my mission is to give back to others. I want to show that we all have the tools we need to face life's challenges. Sharing experience, knowledge, optimism, and positive thinking, I try to support the personal and professional growth of others in my profession as a coach, all over the world, and pro bono with organizations that support particularly vulnerable communities in countries such as Kenya, Uganda, Azerbaijan, and Georgia. I try to teach everybody to look at what they have and not what they are missing. I empower people by helping them leverage their internal strengths and recognize what they already have within. When we all do this, we gain the tools to understand that happiness doesn't depend on external factors. Instead, we cultivate it in our heart, accepting everything life gives us and doing everything to change what is within our power.

Every time I'm looking for a solution or a better way to solve an issue, optimism and harmony are great magnets. It seems that they attract energy that helps me to identify priorities and get the best possible solution based on my values and principles. All this comes from the way I react when presented with a situation that I can't explain. What happens is just the starting point of a long journey. It is the way we react that gives direction to our life. When things are difficult, the nice memories and good feelings of the past help us to get the energy required to face the challenge.

Everywhere I look, I see things that make my heart leap. I am grateful for the recognition I get in my profession. In my private life, the strong bonds with my husband, my son, my stepchildren, and my family at large are a daily source of happiness and love.

Every day, I live the life of my dreams. I don't expect big things to happen; instead, I enjoy the simple things that life offers me: the smile of a child, a walk in the forest, the magic of waking up alive. We can all manage difficult situations and get the best out of them. You can decide to live and love your life fully with acceptance and optimism. It is not what happens; it is the way you react that makes the difference. React with love, positivity, and your eyes wide open to your dreams. Stay focused on what makes you happy and simply *enjoy* your life.

IGNITE ACTION STEPS

Building happiness and positive thinking is a journey. A simple morning routine as soon as you wake up can change your day and your life. If you live with somebody (partner, children, roommate, etc.), please inform them that you need a few minutes alone before breakfast, with no disturbances. It's your moment before the normal routine starts.

- Look for a quiet place and start with a '5 x 4' breathing exercise. For each of the four parts of your breath, count to five. Breathe in for five, hold the breath for five, breathe out for five, hold the breath for five.

- Immediately afterward, think about three nice things that happened the day before. Recall them vividly. Try to go back to the feelings you had in those moments. Ideally, recall one related to a situation, one related to a person, and one related to the purpose of your life. Write them down. The key is to recall the emotion you had and feel it to the deepest level, savoring it. Nice moments are our harvesting time. We need to collect everything nice and store it in our brains. Whenever hard moments come, we have our store full of positive emotions and memories that will help us to manage challenges in the best possible way.

- Focus on what you accomplished the day before (it doesn't have to be a big thing).

- Before you end the exercise, say, "Whatever will happen, the day will be fine."

Simona Sabbatini – Kenya
Personal and professional development coach
www.desiredecidedevelop.com

5 Action Steps are from me, choose from this book other 5 Action Steps that you prefer, write them down and try to implement them every day.

If you do them you score 10 points, if you don't it's 0, if you do it half you give the correct value.

Give yourself a Goal in terms of points and a reward as soon as you'll get there

Action Steps	Points	Day	Day	Day
I recalled 3 POSITIVE EMOTIONS	10			
Got ENGAGED in what I was doing	10			
Had a nice moment with a PERSON I care	10			
One thing that gave MEANING to my day	10			
I acted according to my daily focus	10			
Daily Total				
PREVIOUS WEEK POINTS				
TOTAL of the WEEK				
TOTAL				

Desire Decide Develop

Day	Day	Day	Day		Total	My Goal

WD-TH-WL-01

ALEX GONTKOVIC

*"If you follow through in all that you do, you can
achieve great heights and great happiness."*

**My wish is to give you a reason why you should follow through with your
intentions and goals, especially when things start going wrong. If you do,
you will learn and gain a lot. It's all about your dreams, your attitude, your
mindset, and the way you follow through to reach the goal.**

MASTERING THE UNEXPECTED

It was a wonderful morning, the air was filled with a nice thick fog, heavy
with expectations and importance. I woke up and looked over at my roommate.
He was still sleeping soundly, as always. I completed my morning routine,
just in time to get ready for breakfast. The smell of freshly-made croissants
filtered up throughout the whole building, right into my large room. I had a
great room with a wonderful view of the church that was right across from
the camp's dormitory. I cracked open the window to let some fresh air in, and
the smell of the sea, quickly replacing the smell of breakfast, woke up my
roommate with a startle.

"Sleep well?" he asked.

"Yeah, I am just a little nervous for tonight," I replied anxiously.

As he got ready to head out to the canteen, I made sure I had everything for
my day at camp. When the counselor finally rallied the troops, together with
the guys, we went to get breakfast. As we entered the hall, the sound reminded

me of what I loved about this place. It was bustling with people, ready to get to know you and be friends. I was excited to meet everyone, but I already knew some people as I had met them at last year's summer camp and they also came to this one. I was excited to see that Anastasia was already sitting at our table with the gang. I was happy to notice her there, to be honest. I was due to perform on stage later in the day and I was nervous about it. I knew that she and my friends would reassure me and calm me down.

The one thing that I have always enjoyed throughout school has been acting. I love it and I find that it is an amazing way for people to express who they are. When I am playing different characters, I can reveal myself in the character's expressions, mannerisms, and actions. It is something rather amazing. I had fought for the chance to be the master of ceremonies for tonight's talent show. I did it last year, and I knew that it was going to be an awesome experience.

After breakfast, we all dispersed from the dining hall to our individual camp electives, mine was Pre-IB (International Baccalaureate) which I took alongside my good friends, Martha and Sasha, among others. Today we were preparing for a large essay writing project that was meant to teach us how to research. The topic that I chose was the Rwandan genocide. I have always found history to be something that I enjoy and like to pursue. I chose the Rwandan Genocide because when I first heard about it as a 14-year-old on a trip around Africa with my parents and some family friends, I gained a lot of interest in the subject.

To complete this project to the fullest extent, we worked on it in the famous St. Andrew's University Library near Edinburgh in Scotland. I love St. Andrew's so much. It's so pretty and felt so homey, despite being an extremely cold library as I remember. But then again, scientists say that the cold is good for learning as it wakes you up, so I guess it did help me remember to some effect. Nonetheless, I thoroughly enjoyed working on the essay in that historic space, losing myself in the sources that I found and also what I learned. Gaining understanding about what the Rwandan Genocide was, and why it happened between the Hutus and the Tutsis, was somewhat of a steep learning curve for me. The intensity of the sadness I felt as I dove deeper into learning about these tragic events was reinforced by the emptiness and the lingering fog of a seaside city and the empty library.

As the day went on, I realized that maybe rice and potatoes was not something that I was looking for in my lunch. I snuck away from the group and bought myself a big and rich salad from a small store in the main street. I was rather proud that I had something light for lunch, as I knew that the real stress was just beginning, and I did not want to eat something heavy before it. The reason for all my anxiety was because I am a person who is outgoing, but I don't believe that I am an extrovert. It takes me a few days to warm up to people, whether it is at school, or at camp, or even as a master of ceremonies. This barrier is not something that I am proud of and I use experiences like these to push myself and break through my personal boundaries. This summer would let me explore who I am and how I can work on some of my weaknesses.

After I consumed my salad, it was time to work on my fun and interesting film elective. I had the opportunity to film a whole day in the life of our camp. My team made sure to capture everything. From the beautiful views when you wake up, to the wonderful gelatos you eat in one of the main attractions: Jannetta's Gelateria. I am especially proud that I had the opportunity to be part of the team that created the best film produced this year. But we didn't win. We used a little footage from the camp photographer which really elevated and sealed the deal on our film but wasn't permitted. Working on that project, filming, consolidating, and debating about what the next steps were and how we should take them was the best part. I loved getting to know the people who I worked with. I found that the most creative work often came when we had gelatos in hand and a few laughs beforehand. I am no stranger to procrastination, but in this group, we didn't hesitate to complete it.

When I arrived at my elective I was so excited to work on the film scene because it was the scene where we got to film the gelato and how we ate it. I found my favorite ice cream of all time there. First off, I would ask for a passion fruit scoop, in an ice cream cone, that was halfway coated in a sort of blue, sour sugar substance. Then I would ask for the whole ice cream scoop to be coated in sprinkles. It was my go-to ice cream to the extent that the servers almost knew my order by heart.

When we got to the shooting of our scene, I was ready. First, we ordered, then put our two actresses into position to get close-up shots and headshots of them eating and enjoying the ice cream. It took us some time to perfect it, but eventually we did. It was a nice smooth shoot that zoomed in, and some would say invaded their personal space, but I believe that some would call it an extremely attractive food porn. Not only in the end did we get some great shots, but we also attracted people to the ice cream shop as a film crew in front of it was definitely some unexpected advertising. We worked together to make it happen. It was tough at the start, but we got through it in the end.

After our little film experience, I was happy to realize that I had some time before dinner to prepare for our talent show later that night. I went through my mental checklist of what I needed to prepare and do for the talent show, such as shower, get dressed, and go down to the theater before anyone else to make sure that I was ready. After a quick dinner, I made sure to shower and put on my infamous red pants. I love fashion. I really enjoy everything to do with clothes and personal style, and my signature look my whole life has involved red pants. They are a statement that I love and treasure as the color red has always been something close to my heart.

As I headed out to the theater, I tried to calm myself with a really good psychological breathing technique called the Square Breathing Method. I first discovered it when I needed to take an MRI for my jaw. It works on the principle that you breathe in for four counts, hold for four counts, exhale for four counts, and hold for four counts. It is a method that has not only been tried and tested by doctors, but also by me. It helped me slow my heart rate, calming me down in situations where I was extremely nervous, like this one. I personally believe that it has helped me get through a lot of different performances as it really settled me and made sure that I was not overthinking too much.

As I strolled to the theater, the sun was setting which cast a beautiful orange hue over the whole town. The seagulls were chirping and flying over my head, out to sea to get their last meal of the day. I met with the head of the camp and she passed on a clipboard that had all of the acts and teams that would be performing in the talent show. It was quite an extensive list, and I wanted to start as soon as possible to be able to get through the whole set.

As the campers started to pour in with their counselors, I started using my breathing method again, feeling the heaviness of the expectations that lay on me. Even though I have grown up on the stage, I still get stage fright very easily. I take it as a part of working and being an actor.

The first act up was the counselors. They had an energetic song that they filmed and that they would dance to in real life as it played in the background. I introduced them, their song started to play, and they approached the stage, getting to their places, but then the music stopped abruptly. After a few seconds of awkward silence, I jumped out on stage and just did what a real master of ceremonies does — I controlled the situation. I apologized for the technical difficulties and then I went along and talked about my day — about the filming that had taken place that morning, what flavor of gelato I had eaten, and with whom. Then I got the go ahead from the tech booth that the situation had been resolved, so I gracefully walked off stage.

The song started up again, and then just a few seconds into it, the same thing happened! The silence cut through the air like a knife sliding through freshly baked cake. The realization that I would need to calm the audience down washed over me and I stood stiffly as nervousness was rising in me. Once again, I left the safe shelter of the curtains at the side of the stage and walked back out into the spotlight. I drew deep within me, reaching for the confidence that I must have stored somewhere for emergencies, and asked the audience, "Who knows a good joke?" That lasted a good 30 seconds before I got the go ahead again. I told the audience, "See you soon," and walked off stage once more. I was feeling very content with everything that I did.

The third time that the music stopped working, I felt a plunging sense of doom settle into the pit of my stomach. I dragged myself up on stage again and just stared at the audience for the space of a long breath before saying, "Well, I'm back, and it seems I'm going to be the only entertainment you have tonight."

The audience roared. Their annoyance with the whole debacle was quickly and cleanly washed out of their systems. I was flooded with the relief that I did everything I could to make the best of a bad situation. I was glad that I could do something to take people's minds off the technical difficulties that we had and proud of myself for doing it so gracefully despite my inner nervousness. This experience made me realize that there is no need to be stressed. A person can achieve anything; they just need to understand that they should proceed with a calm mind and positive attitude to reach their goals.

As the music ended up working, the talent show ended, the audience slowly started to trickle out, and the performers left the stage to go and meet their friends. I made my way down through the empty theater and reflected on the entire show. I was able to look back and understand that although the audience was happy, I still needed to work on my nerves. I needed to be aware of my feelings and fears that are not exactly reality-based. I understand that there are people who are scared of public speaking and who are not sure exactly how to do it (and by public speaking I mean in front of a class, audience, or even your friends); it is a very common and somewhat natural fear, in my point of view. I acknowledge that I still fear it, even though I have done it many times. The only way I will get over this fear is by practicing, which is exactly why I sought out this experience, even though it was frightening and somewhat challenging for me. And, having done it so brilliantly that night, I knew that I had it inside of me to conquer any challenge I put in front of myself.

On stage, I had been very nervous, especially as I had to unexpectedly go on stage multiple times and did not have anything prepared. On my way back to the dormitory when people congratulated me about my success on stage and how natural it came to me, I found it to be a huge relief.

I never want to seem inauthentic, especially on stage, and I was glad I had succeeded that night. This and other experiences like these have taught me that when faced with the unexpected, all you have to do is set a goal and follow it. I am persuaded that there is no better way to proceed in life.

As my friends and I left the theater, we had an opportunity to run to the store. Tesco™ is really close to our dormitory and that's where we get all of our snacks. A favorite snack among everyone was these thin cookies that were coated in chocolate. They would be shared among the counselors and campers, a ritual food that I was a huge fan of, and I truly enjoyed eating them. I jogged over to the store to pick up some of them so that I could enjoy them in the evening, while also making sure that I got back in time for curfew. Knowing that no matter what, my friends would always be there for me, no matter how I did on or off stage. My performance on stage showed that being yourself is the most important part because this is one of the easiest ways to forge connections with others. It also reminded me that, as an actor or MC, I will always have a few tricks up my sleeve the next time I have to go and perform.

Overall, it was a successful day. It taught me a lot and showed me that there is always room for improvement in my life. Since that day, I always look for ways to step into those places that I need to improve, realizing that no matter what I do, and especially when things start going wrong, I need to follow through with it until the end. Every time I do, I learn and gain a lot. It's all about your dreams, your attitude, your mindset, and the way you follow through to reach the goal. If you follow through in all that you do, you can achieve great heights and great happiness.

Ignite Action Steps

Sit down, take one piece of paper, and write down the goals you have in mind. The purpose of this activity is to see and remember the goals all the time, so that you can implement and manifest them into your life consciously and also subconsciously.

1. The first step in achieving this is to write all of your goals down. You should then narrow them down to three goals overall. This is to create a stronger focus on them and so that you can devote your energy and time to them.

2. Next, write your goals on different pieces of paper and stick these pieces into the places you frequent the most, like the mirror in your bathroom,

above your coffee machine, on your desk, etc. Make sure you can read these goals and see them clearly even if you are not focused on them.

3. Afterwards, you can start to use the Law of Attraction that is described by Rhonda Byrnes in book and movie *The Secret*. I truly believe these laws can be beneficial to everyone, so devote some time and energy to investigate what the movie explains about the concept.

4. Lastly, when faced with adversity, remember to breathe squarely. By breathing in for four counts, holding for four counts, exhaling for four counts, and holding for four counts. It is very easy to remember and is an effective way to calm yourself down so that you can face any challenge head on.

Remember: No goal is too small or too large for you to achieve.

Alex Gontkovic – Slovakia
Passionate actor and future entrepreneur
@alex.gontkovic
@alex.gontkovic
@alex.gontkovic

CLAUDIA PATRICIA PÉREZ DELGADO

"Embracing vulnerability and practicing forgiveness takes us on a pathway to a happier life."

There are many ways for you to build beautiful and healthy interpersonal relationships no matter what you have experienced in the past. Through forgiveness and empowerment, you can Ignite your inner Happiness. My story will show how the moment you let go of your past and practice forgiveness, you can achieve true happiness.

FORGIVENESS AND HAPPINESS

It took a 29-word sentence, a firm, brave voice, and the determination of an 11-year- old girl to free me and my sister Ana of childhood sexual abuse. This was my voice.

I am that girl.

This is the story of me, a Colombian and American citizen with multicolored green and honey eyes, and very long, light hazel hair. My mom and dad were teenagers when they married and had my beautiful and huge-hearted older sister, Ana. A year later, they had me. They divorced when I was a 1-year-old baby and I can't blame them — they were still children themselves. My sister and I lived with my angel-look-a-like mother, Maria Teresa.

Our father, Eduardo Fernando, loved to travel. He loved gambling and women even more and wasn't exactly present as much as any daughter would like. He was a very educated and intelligent man with a good heart, but at times disappeared from our lives for two or three years without even calling. I loved my dad Fernando very much and the times we were together enjoying each other's presence and laughter were so much fun, but he just wasn't someone we could count on in our lives.

Both my parents remarried. My mom, only 22 and with two young daughters, married my stepfather, Esteban, a rather good-looking Catalan/Colombian who was well-educated and an eloquent speaker, and he came to live with us.

Most of the girls at my school had their mothers with them at home all the time, but not us. My mom was an international flight attendant for American Airlines and had to travel for a living, which meant she was away from home 80 percent of the time. When she traveled, she left us with Esteban, the husband she trusted.

My stepfather was the closest thing to a father figure for me and was someone I, at the tender age of 11, loved and trusted. It was another cold and cloudy Bogotá night when my stepfather knocked on my bedroom door, as he would often do, and whispered in Spanish against the door, "*Chinita estas dormida?*" ("Sweety, are you sleeping?")

But this time, I replied, "My mom comes back tomorrow night and if you come into my bedroom again, I will tell her everything about what you do to my sister and me." I used my voice that night to stop the child abuse and the disgusting behavior of this 38-year-old man, the very man who 'took care of' my sister and me. From that moment on, my sister Ana and I were suddenly — just like that — free of his abuse. At last.

In school, I did well. I had good grades and my mom and I were told often by my peers and teachers that I was a very sweet girl. I admired, respected, and deeply loved many women I had known, especially my paternal grandmother, Leonor, and my mother. They were strong, sweet, hardworking, generous, empowered, and loving women. They most certainly had a positive impact on me and my sister.

However, in my early teenage years I started showing signs of rebellion. Yes, the anger and bitterness I felt from the years of child abuse at the hands of my stepfather started to resurface, along with the hormones of becoming an adult.

I dressed in a rather tomboyish fashion, covering up entirely with a gothic style of mostly black with some subtle touches of red, not wanting to be seen much or to seem 'sexy.' I listened to a lot of Beethoven, especially the *Symphony No. 9*, Bach, grunge, classic rock, punk music, and Colombian or Cuban salsa were played very loudly for hours in my locked room. I was keeping the childhood abuse a secret and I felt unconsciously angry. How could a 14-year-old girl express herself? How or when would I tell my mother? I talked to my sister Ana and told her we needed to tell Mom, but she replied, "I love Mom so much and she seems to be happy with Esteban. It will destroy her if we tell." So we didn't.

Although I didn't tell my mom, I desperately wanted her to know. I was angry at my mom for not seeing the cues, for not divorcing her husband, the seemingly charming, well-mannered, well-spoken pedophile she had married. My mom became the punching bag of my outbursts. I was screaming at her from the inside! *"Mami! Mirame!"* (Look at me!) "Ask me the right questions now!"

I wanted her to ask me, "What is going on Claudia, *mi amor*? Is everything okay at home when I'm not there, *mi amor*? Why are you so angry at me?"

But she never did.

On December 20, 1995, when I was 18 years old, my mother died in an American Airlines airplane accident. She was only 37 years old. We found her body three days later and buried her on December 24th at 7:30 PM. Now I wasn't ever going to be able to tell her, and the lack of closure haunted me until my mid 30s. My dad, unfortunately, died from a heart attack two years after my mom's death. Both of my parents were gone before I got the chance to tell them.

In my late 20s, I was an accomplished trilingual attorney with a Master's degree in International Law from Panthéon-Assas, Sorbonne in Paris, and another post-graduate degree in French Literature from l'Institut Catholique de Paris. I had traveled and studied in Paris with a full scholarship, and was working in UNESCO headquarters as an international consultant for higher education.

I had landed the 'dream job,' was living in the 'city of lights,' and everything seemed to be just fine, but my personal life and my relationships with wonderful men didn't seem to be a priority. In retrospect, some of my radical and at times even erratic decisions in my relationships seemed to be from being unconsciously resentful toward men. While I received marriage proposals, I simply didn't or couldn't commit to marriage. I was afraid of experiencing the failed marriages I had witnessed as a child. The two fatherly figures I had growing up weren't exactly the best examples of men to admire. The irony is that the other 90 percent of men in my life were wonderful people, to me and to the world.

I married on August 11, 2004, at the age of 27. Philippe was a scientist and book nerd, an irresistibly sexy Colombian/Belgian marine biologist, master scuba diver, university professor, and founder of an organic pesticide company. He had long, thick light brown hair, a full beard, and lived in Miami, Florida, in the United States. We met at 35,000 feet above ground on an international flight from Bogotá to Miami.

Philippe surprised me with a beautiful engagement ring only three months after meeting me and I said "Yes!" for the first time. The passion we had for each other was insurmountable, something I had never felt before. We would salsa late into the night in the Parisian-Latin clubs, surrounded by friends, lights, and the delectable smell of Colombian food. During this time, my beautiful deep-blue-eyed son Sebastian, was born — a nearly 10-pounder, a size that almost killed his Mom at birth! Sadly, the dancing and the marriage lasted only three years.

The passion was alive in our relationship, but moving from Paris to Miami and not being able to work in my profession left me feeling miserable. I didn't like living in Miami; it didn't feel like home. I had sacrificed everything and was so unhappy. Although no serious fights had taken place, I left my husband. I moved out of our apartment and rented another one in the same building a few floors up. My son was a chubby, cute, blue-eyed 2-year-old baby and I was still breastfeeding. My deepest desire was to go back to Paris. Phillipe was eager to reunite, but I wasn't. However, I wanted to keep an amicable relationship for our co-parenting, so I asked him if we could go to France and base our lives there together. He declined, saying that his company and his life were in Miami.

This started a very contentious four-year-long divorce battle in court. My ex-husband was hurt and in love. I was young when I had moved from Paris to Miami, and four months pregnant, so I knew basically no one in this southern city. It's called the 'Sunshine State,' but for me, it was anything but sunny and oh so different from my beloved France. I was left with confused feelings. I felt lonely and was struggling with the hormone changes that come with breastfeeding a newborn baby. And I was far from my friends and family, all of which made me very unhappy.

I needed to heal. I worked on myself, on forgiveness, and on understanding that happiness is an emotion — a mental state not found outside but found solely within me. I knew by then that Happiness was 100 percent my responsibility, and I made it my mission to re-Ignite it.

I dedicated myself to my precious young son and started working as a French teacher for young children in a French language school, *L'institut Français*. Shortly after, I was offered a job as a full-time French teacher in a private all-girls Catholic school in a lovely European-style neighborhood in Miami called Coconut Grove. It had big old trees and groves everywhere, and even during the very hot Miami summer, the trees offered a constant breezy shade. The school's location right on the bay with uninterrupted blue ocean views made it a magical place. At Carrollton school, I saw just how much I loved working with young girls. It was pure love, joy, and Happiness.

After a few other jobs as a researcher and attorney, and now that my son was 10 years old, I had saved enough money to focus on a project I had in mind. In 2015, I created and funded a non-profit in Bogotá, Colombia, along with my foundation partner, my childhood dear friend, the beautiful-hearted and very talented dancer and actress Andrea Castaño.

Our not-for-profit *www.educationmatterscol.org* is aimed at empowering and renewing the life projects and dreams of a population of teenage girls who have been victims of childhood sexual abuse, abandonment, and/or orphaned as a result of the internal Colombian violence with the guerrillas and *paramilitares*.

Ever since I started mentoring the 100-plus teenage girls who come from underprivileged homes, unimaginable past abuse, and traumas, I noticed most of them were angry at their abusers. They would tell me they 'hated men' or whoever had caused them such pain as young girls. For them, men were monsters and they saw no other way. Their frustration and pain were hindering their happiness.

I came up with more ideas for our mission to help these girls smile again, find self-love, increase their self-esteem, give them hope, and sustain their joy. With Andrea and our wonderful co-founder Fernando (the foundation's pro bono accountant, sponsor, and sweetest soul), we set up and gathered a complete team of psychologists, social workers, and theater, dance, and music teachers for the healing of the heart and mind. We also provided English and history classes, IOT (Internet of Things) courses with Cisco and Google, and computer skills for their education, IT training, and empowerment. I had found my purpose. Through my personal experience of sexual abuse as a child, I knew exactly how to talk to them, help them heal, and overcome their anger. I told them how important it is to forgive, to dispose of any venomous and toxic emotions they could be carrying, and re-Ignite their childhood happiness! And oh boy, when these girls understood that happiness is a destination and that it's their sole responsibility, that's when they started healing and smiling again. This made me so happy!

I told them as a mother of a boy and as a woman who had the good fortune of having wonderful partners and boyfriends in my life, I had at times taken the fabulous men in my life for granted. I had not prioritized my personal love life with a man. I believed it was due in part to my past childhood sexual abuse. I figured, well, I'm surrounded by other types of true love: the love of my female friends, chosen family, my sister, aunts, and my black and golden labradors. They all make me happy, but I continued to take for granted the love of my male partner.

I'm still healing, but being able to forgive was essential for my own happiness. I'm aware there are plenty of fabulous, caring, loving, honest, feminist men out there. If we express our emotions, use our voices, and allow ourselves to experience true, simple, raw, and innocent love again, free of resentment, we can re-Ignite Happiness in our lives.

Love does come in different forms and shapes. Our partner's love can become a positive, healing force if we allow ourselves to go beyond the pain of our past. Show up in your life renewed and refreshed. Hug your loved ones long enough and often enough to show them your 'Gratitude attitude.'

Roses are like people; they are all beautiful, but they have thorns built from difficult situations. These thorns can prick you at times, but they can also help you be more diligent, more careful, and have a deep empathy for other roses like you.

As I tell my teenage girls, "To obtain equality and more peaceful societies, we need to educate our children at home. Men and women must unite as a common front to overcome the paradigms, unconscious biases, and stereotypes that have been instilled over generations and move forward to a new male and female collaboration. We need to appreciate the human connection and recognize what 'happy' feels like. I got 'unstuck' and so can you, my sweet, precious warrior."

IGNITE ACTION STEPS

- Take 100 percent responsibility for your Happiness. Ask yourself and answer honestly: What is happiness to me? How can I live a meaningful and happier life? How can I live a life with purpose? Why is forgiveness a key element to happiness? If this were my last day on Earth, what would I do to make it a great and very happy one?

- Even in times of difficulty or past trauma, we can make it through, stop for a second, and say to ourselves, "Look at where I am now!"

- Move past the anger trap and move forward. Map out what you wish to become. You will get there with self-love, pursuing a meaningful life, and living joyful moments.

- Give open-heartedly to others. Don't expect to receive anything in return; the simple act of giving is in itself reward enough.

- Encourage and educate healthy stereotypes. Teach your young ones at home, and your nephews and nieces, that they can be anything. They can choose to wear any color clothes they like or choose to be anything they want to be in life.

- Talk to your children. Ask your daughters and sons questions regarding their private parts. Educate them and make them aware of the fact that their private parts are *not* to be touched by anyone else besides themselves or the pediatrician in the presence of Mom. As a mother or father, be attentive to the red flags and warning signs. **Communication with your child is very important — it can save their lives as adults.**

Real conversations with some of my teenage girls in the not-for-profit:

"So sadness is a place, Claudia?" Jeannette asked.
"People sometimes live there for years," I said.
"And happiness is also a place?" Jeannette asked.
"Yes!" I replied. "I can assure you that I, myself sometimes have been standing in this place of sadness, in this forest of sorrow, but I moved on long ago, and I know you can too. I know exactly what you're going through. I've been there, where you are standing now. I wish this will bring you hope and you can re-Ignite peace, joy, and Happiness in your young life."

Claudia Patricia Pérez Delgado – Colombia, United States of America
Attorney, Universidad del Rosario, Master's in International public Law,
from Panthéon-Assas, Sorbonne, Paris, France, Degree in French literature,
CEO www.educationmatterscol.org
@klauditadelgado
Non for profit @educationmatters
www.fundacionfuncionesperanza.org

MEGHAN HUTHSTEINER

"Inspire people by how you deal with your imperfections."

My hope is that you find meaning and purpose among the challenges you see and feel everyday. If you can control your mind, your body will follow. Guarding your mind and choosing wisely what you allow to feed it, will help you gain wisdom and discernment. Believe your existence is a perfect intentional design while acknowledging and owning God's promise, "If God is for you, who could be against you?"

CHEW THE MEAT, SPIT OUT THE BONE

I've enjoyed not fitting in with any one particular group. In order to avoid feeling the harsh rejection of not committing to one particular stereotype, I would attempt to please everyone. It served others fairly well, but in the end, I had lost myself. I didn't know who I truly was anymore because in my desire to appease society, I ignored my core being. It frustrated me, angered me, and made me feel lost and hopeless. I awoke to the slow fade that I had allowed this to happen over the decades I've lived thus far and realized I had actually been mourning the loss of myself for years.

I had a rather idyllic early childhood. I had amazing childhood friends and always had my mum around anytime I needed her. We were blessed with a home that had lush green grass and a beautiful oak tree where I spent many of my days climbing and swinging. I grew accustomed to hearing from friends and family, "When I'm in your house, I feel an overwhelming presence of love." My mum was such a loving and giving person. Her energy touched everyone. My heart was always comforted by the roaring thunderstorms of spring. When the power went out, my dad would play his guitar and we all danced and sang in the candlelight. I especially enjoyed tubing down the creek with my brother and best friends, catching fireflies, and stargazing under the night sky. We didn't have much in terms of material things, but we had each other and all lived contently.

Even though I was young, I already had a plan for what my life was going to be, and it was magnificent. I was already living my dream of becoming an Olympic gymnast. I ate, slept, and drank gymnastics — it was all I thought about. People could only talk to my feet because I spent most of my elementary school days walking on my hands. I knew that if I were to make a difference in the world, I had to "do it right" and "do it with a joyful heart or not do it at all!" — those were the words my mum often told me and they inspired my spirit. If I wanted to be someone esteemed like an Olympic athlete, I had to intentionally focus all of my energy.

Life was just beginning when, unbeknownst to me, God had given me my first preliminary wake-up call. I was run over by a bike and broke my leg in two places. It ended up changing the entire trajectory of my life. Breaking my leg destroyed my Olympic dreams and interrupted my academics, as I was held back a year. As a result of being so far behind in reading, taking tests became paralyzing for me and I soon felt the hurtful labels of my peers — real or imagined — sticking in my heart and forming a belief of worthlessness. The damage was huge.

I had massive amounts of imagination, but my teachers labeled me as a 'daydreamer' and it became a shameful thing for me. I can remember episodes of standing with my hands on my hips, staring fiercely at their authority and almost daring them to tell me again how I was not good enough. I knew I would show them one day. How? It didn't matter; I just knew I had something and if I was given the opportunity, I would prove it.

Life lessons had no bias toward age and showed up once again in the fifth grade with my parents' divorce. The day my dad left would be the last day I had a father. Mum became a single working mother and I was forced to leave my childhood heaven behind. Life as I knew it would never be the same. I didn't know what I did wrong, but I felt I was surely being punished.

My struggles in school weren't any better. Regurgitating what the system deemed to be truth in certain subjects did not hold strong value for me. Teachers serving as police guards to 'discipline me' and 'straighten me out' coupled with less than satisfactory grades reinforced the promise of not being successful in life if I didn't adjust my thinking to align with theirs. Despite my strong will, I still always had something lurking in the back of my head telling me that I was truly a counterfeit. I set out a plan to get through life by doing any job that 'graded' me solely on my physical abilities. That was what I could quantify as *real* abilities and skills because I could actually *see* what I had to adjust and more readily believe in the results.

My mother, with her blind faith, moved our family to Buffalo, New York. The bittersweet promise of a new beginning offered me glimmers of hope. The day before my new school's yearbook pictures would be a day that yet again altered my life's plan. I was just a teen trying to create a new me when fate stepped in.

A good night's rest was just what I needed and off I went to dreamland. A few hours later, my dream-self threw the covers off my bed as the house suddenly felt like a furnace. I laid on the bed, listening...

My dream began with my mum, in the kitchen, yelling at my sister Becky. I stirred reflexively in my sleep, the smell of burnt bologna invading the air. Why was I smelling burnt bologna? And why was Mum yelling at Becky? I heard mum yell out, "Fire!" To rationalize that cry, I imagined Mum grabbing a towel to take a cast-iron pan off the stove and the towel catching fire. My dream-self thought I should scold them and tell them to go back to bed! I had school pictures in the morning for goodness sake! My sister screamed in horror, "Meghan, FIRE! Get up!" Her cries pierced my awareness and I woke from my dream to an actual nightmare playing out in real time.

I ran to my bedroom door and found my sister standing there right in front of me, holding her hands to her face as a shield. Out in the hallway to the right, the flickering glow of a merciless fire made my skin feel like it was melting. Already past its kindling point, the full-blown and ferocious heat was accompanied by the horrifying snap–crackle–explosion of windows shattering. The temperature of the tiles beneath our feet reminded us to expedite our escape down the stairwell. Becky and I stood at the bottom of the stairs, frozen in terror.

Looking through the kitchen into the dining room, I stood mesmerized by the flames' unforgiving fury and compulsion for destruction.

My 6- and 9-year-old sisters, for whatever reason, had demanded to sleep with my mum that night, which brought them to immediate safety standing securely next to her in her bedroom doorway. Mum ordered me to take my sisters out the side door and go to our cousin's house next door to call 9-1-1.

We were quickly ushered inside and watched the fire from their couch as if it were a drive-in theater. Their massive bay window was the perfect windshield that provided front row seats to my life going up in flames. Time stood still watching life happen without an ounce of power to control it. I watched every stud burn and the furniture disintegrate. The fire laughed as it overtook the kitchen where my mum had poured her love into creating a happy home for her kids. It was beyond belief. Everything was truly gone, with nothing left. You would think that I was disturbed by the new and profoundly changed life I was about to embark on, but I wasn't. I felt the natural emotions of loss, but I had far more overwhelming feelings of joy and gratefulness that God had spared each one of my sisters, and that my mum had escaped unscathed.

The fire department came and put out the fire within 25 minutes. They asked us if there was anything inside that we might like them to try to salvage. The only thing that mattered to me after 14 years of life was my flute and the 4x6 photographs that captured my heart up until that day. A fireman walked up and handed them to me so kindly that I can still feel the comforting hope he restored in me that night. The firemen said it was the worst smoke they'd ever seen. They were in disbelief that we had no smoke detectors and that we had even woken up, because if we were in there even four minutes longer, we all would have died from smoke inhalation.

In that instant, we had become homeless. People saw the struggles that my mum was going through and their solution was to help her by telling her she needed to put her four kids in a foster home because she couldn't handle everything that was happening to her. Luckily my mum is one fierce God-fearing woman. There was no one on this planet who was going to take away the most precious things she loved most in this world: her girls.

On my first day returning to high school after the fire, I wore an adult men's shirt donated by the Salvation Army — one of those button-down flannels that I tried to rock and make cute to divert undeserved attention. I guess I didn't do too good a job because upon walking into English class, one of the popular girls sneered, "Why are you wearing your father's shirt?" I felt humiliated in front of the whole class. The pains of beginning at a new school kindled the embers of buried emotions from my dad leaving.

I function best when I am challenged. I've always been in competition with myself. Many days, I came home from school with no food in the house, no heat, and no electricity because mum had chosen rent as priority. Instead of cursing the life I was living, I started brainstorming what actions I could take to overcome these unmerited obstacles. My mum always reminded me that one gift that suited me well was my ability to sell ice to the Inuit. The only thing that I had that wasn't going to cost me a penny, was... yep, to sell myself... hahaha, noooo, not my body — my wits and my will. I may not have been able to test and prove my intelligence on paper, or even spell intelligence, but I had the unwavering certainty that if there was a will, there was a way. And if God was for me, who could be against me?

I got out there and started promoting myself. I decided to take up dance after high school and was accepted into the dance program at university where I studied a dual major. This gave me courage to compete in Miss New York and Miss Nevada USA pageants where I was seen dancing and was recruited to cheer in the NFL. I found the courage to try for the big screen and felt disbelief when I started getting multiple casting calls daily. I supported myself in Beverly Hills as a celebrity stylist. It helped that I carried myself with such certainty that business owners thought I already embodied what I was setting out to do. Having positioned myself with such high standards forced me to hold myself accountable to those standards. I felt the responsibility to be a stand-up person in society and took on the conviction that my actions mattered. It would be a disservice to all those who believed in me if I didn't do what I set out to do.

By the time I was 28, the success I had set out to achieve and taken so long to build was extinguished because I started allowing negative thinking to take over my mind. How had I gotten to this point only to lose it all in an instant for the umpteenth time in my life? I had to ask myself, what was my purpose in life? Did joy and happiness lay in what I had acquired and achieved up until now? Having already experienced a tenacious fire that engulfed my life and now experiencing my life going up in flames a second time, it felt like my childhood plans were no match for God's plan. Little did I understand in the moment that my materialistic purpose was not God's purpose.

Coming to that understanding saved me years of being held back from growing and molded me into letting go of the fear of losing something that may have never been meant for me. It's one of the most beautiful metaphors I can call my own. I've learned now to take in the good and spit out the bad. The journey that I continued to embark on slowly and surely revealed to me my *true* purpose in life. I surrendered my will to God and cried out, "If you are for me, then just show me. I am tired of trying to figure this out on my own. I want your will, not my own!"

I felt like God was sharpening his sword to reveal more of His design: the design he had for me. A new fire was kindled inside to allow God to create HIS purpose for my life! I didn't put my faith and trust in any material thing anymore. I discovered that being honest with myself in moments of hardship was the real beauty and happiness that revealed my earthly purpose. And along the way, I experienced moments and seasons of utter happiness, even amidst the storms!

I know circumstances don't have to define you. Rather, we are what we think. I've lived a lot of my life trying to plan out every detail and I find that setting a goal and having a target has served me exceptionally well. I think there is something utterly wise about being brutally honest and clear on what you want and why, and then letting God take the wheel to reveal the purpose of it. Have faith that He is *for* you, not against you.

John 14:13 "And whatsoever ye shall ask in my name, that will I do, that the Father may be glorified in the Son." My understanding of this is that God gives us the desires of our heart for certain things and when we ask God to reveal them to us, he is faithful and willing to reveal them. That is where my relationship and faith began, when I started seeing doors open and close that I felt could never be opened otherwise. I take away so much more than just what I asked for! I get joy, comfort, wisdom, and peace that goes above all understanding because I acknowledge God and he made my path straight and my purpose more clear.

Let your thoughts focus on your goals. Know that you will become what you think you are. Faith is believing, not seeing, and there is an element to life where you just have to let go and believe.

It's perplexing that success can feel scary, but when we're called to something larger than ourselves, keeping faith can bring so much happiness. As I search my heart and get brutally honest with myself, I know that God can take what I thought was meant for bad and turn it into something even more beautiful and full of joy than my little ol' planning could've planned. It's the learning we receive in these moments that creates space for connection and happiness in our lives. What a gift!

Happiness isn't just the longevity and duration of blissful times frolicking in the green meadows and living wealthy without a care in the world. It's not about ensuring we escape hard times and basking in the happiness rays. If that is your definition of happiness, you've already set yourself up for failure. It is inevitable that we will experience pain and suffering. If you step over the fundamentals of learning how to explore the person you've been so perfectly designed to be, you may experience the superficial misguided 'happiness' and fall short of the utter joy of letting go of every fear and finding peace in knowing you are exactly where you're supposed to be. Allow yourself to journey without fear. I allowed happiness to *become* me in those moments. In doing so, I found that I'm not alone. Where I thought I was alone in misery and agony, sharing with others and trusting in God's will has opened me up to healing and happiness.

There is a verse that comforts me and I hope will comfort you as well:

For the Spirit God gave us does not make us timid, but gives us power, love and self-discipline. (2 Timothy 1:7 KJV)

IGNITE ACTION STEPS

Make your bed first thing in the morning — It's the first program in my head for completing a task. Feeling like I have completed something starts my day off right.

Be grateful for as much or little as you have... your thoughts will soon become you.

Give thanks even when you don't feel like it one bit. Your brain doesn't know the difference between reality and what you are telling it, so tell it to be grateful often. That gratitude will bring you peace that goes beyond your understanding.

Give and accept forgiveness — Don't let your mistakes linger in your heart and poison your thinking. If we ask God for forgiveness, then we are called to be like Him and forgive ourselves as well. Work on your mental hygiene.

Ask yourself, "What am I willing to do?" — Figure out your interests and pursue them. Take on challenges that will bring you closer to your end goal. Ask yourself, "What do I procrastinate about, and why? What am I unwilling to do? What do I dislike about myself?" If you're willing to get 1000 percent honest with yourself, you'll discover your potential as you find out who you are. There's real helpfulness in uncovering the beautiful parts of yourself and awakening your potential for joy. It can make you decisive; someone who can say no when you need to say no and yes when you mean yes. It can help you avoid unnecessary conflict and see your own goals flourish. These incredibly complicated questions are the beginning of a beautiful mountain to climb.

Meghan Huthsteiner – United States of America
Nutritional Therapy Practitioner/ Clinical Esthetic Medical Assistant
linktr.ee/circadianhealth

Pooja S. Lankers

"Having the right mentor is like crossing the ocean
by boat instead of swimming alone."

Happiness is our birthright and we are all entitled to live it. After working for decades with people unleashing their potential, I'm more and more convinced that this is really true. The question is how to get there? With a full heart, I want to invite you to explore the essence of your *Being*, which is pure Happiness. How? When I ask myself what truly helps me the most on my path of realizing Happiness, I get a clear answer: having a mentor. A person who has already realized a higher state of Happiness than me. Someone who can guide me faster, safer, more directly, and sometimes even beyond my imagination in all areas of my life. I want to share with you the story of finding my spiritual mentor and the way Happiness transformed my life.

Get Your Guide — The Magical Journey to Happiness

Imagine you're going on a long awaited journey. You know that once you arrive at your selected place, the best guide ever is waiting for you — someone ready to introduce you to the deepest secrets and treasures of that place. After you give that teacher your trust, your entire experience will transform. This is the power and the path of trusting a mentor.

Trusting a guide may sound simple, yet it's one of the most fundamental secrets to happiness. But how do you find such a person? Word of mouth? Intuition? A Google™ search? To shed some light, I'd like to tell you how I found my guide to happiness; the person who helped illuminate my journey toward the essence of myself. Through this experience, I've become convinced that we each need someone to help us blaze a path to our inner depths and reach the happiness at our core.

Have you ever felt that you are here on earth for a reason? From a very young age, thoughts about why I am here came with acute emotions. It was quite a roller coaster. Sometimes, I was convinced that it would come naturally; but most times, I would become devastated with the fear that my purpose would not come to me and that my life would be worthless.

Growing up, the drive to become happy, to be free, and to help others feel happy was strong inside me. The call for freedom was perhaps the strongest of all, which is why my 20s were full of travel and constant motion. I was living in the 'new' Berlin in the early '90s, which was a symbol of freedom after the long separation. The city at that time felt exciting, creative, and free. We were a huge community of young people living our dreams. I was a young entrepreneur living an 'amazing life,' yet inside I felt miserable even though I was 'healthy and rich.' Despite meeting many people, I felt disconnected. I was alone even in the company of close friends. I felt desperate to change, but how could I explain that to others when everything looked so great? Where did I start?

To handle my inner despair, I stayed constantly in a 'creating' yet 'distracted' mode. The stress peaked with panic attacks and anxiety, leading me to feel paralyzed. Eventually I became burnt out. It was obvious that I had to change if I wanted to live the happy life I was yearning for. The panic attacks forced me to a turning point because I couldn't go on the way things were. The realization hit me: all the success, friends, and possessions I had gathered were not enough. I had to change something inside of me.

I stepped out of the tech start-up, founded a creative community in an old factory, and bravely began something that was very new to me: *inner transformation*. I knew I was disappointing many people by taking this step, yet I felt compelled to continue.

My inner journey started as a 'road trip' toward my soul. I stopped at many stations while searching for fulfillment, exploring methods from both the Eastern and Western worlds. It was exciting and brought me closer to myself. Yet an impalpable feeling was still there telling me that something wasn't on track. As I met beautiful, interesting people, I felt as if I was running around without a map, always searching. I thought to myself, *I have to belong to something.* I tried buddhism. I tried shamanism. Art. Dancing. Psychotherapy. Acting. As you might imagine, this didn't work out well. My curious, dynamic personality was leading me to explore all these areas, but I was only seeing the surface and not the depth. It was, somehow, the same pattern I lived before. I was running again. Only later at the start of my 30s did I slowly begin to understand why this method didn't work. In each and every wisdom tradition, it's said that you must give your full commitment in order to experience the depths of your being. I was behaving like a 'surface' traveler, going to many different places but never staying and committing to go deeper.

Everything changed when I had my baby girl. The physical challenge of motherhood brought me to the great Ayurvedic Dr. Pankaj Naram who later became my Ayurvedic teacher and mentor in the art of ancient healing. I had been feeling very low in energy since giving birth and that was compounded by the burnout that I had experienced before. I was looking for healing and a new dimension in my life. I will never forget the magical moment when Dr. Naram put his hands on my forearm to read my pulse. He told me, "I can help you," and I felt in my heart that these words were true.

Full of hope, and with the certainty that something profound was going to happen, I went next to his master student Suyogi Gessner who was doing the diet and lifestyle consultation. Wow! I had never met a woman like her before. She was grounded, practical, loving, and at the same time so open to spiritual wisdom. When I found out that she lived in Berlin, I knew immediately that I had found a road map through Ayurveda and a mentor who could guide me to becoming healthy and happy.

I saw Suyogi frequently as an Ayurvedic doctor, which gave me the opportunity to come to know her better. She taught me to listen to my heart and commit to a deeper journey. My health improved. The signs of burnout disappeared. I felt strong and clear like never before. It took me about a year and a half to understand the next secret wisdom: the value of asking the right questions.

One day, I was finally ready to ask Suyogi why she is the way she is, shining from within, stable, open, capable, and happy. She instantly answered, "Because of my spiritual master. I owe him everything." Oh! That wasn't the answer I had been expecting and I felt a new inner dimension open. Some years ago, I read the book *The Autobiography of a Yogi* by Paramahansa Yogananda. It was one of Steve Jobs' favorite books and a beautiful inspiration to so many people. From the first page, I loved the Eastern concept of self-realization Yogananda shares in his book. It resonated clearly for me. I had always felt there was a huge treasure of true love within us and the idea of unleashing it felt so true. I don't need to love myself; I am love. Previously, I had experienced alternate states of being with my soul and leaving my body during deep meditations, but these moments often scared me as I didn't feel protected in those vast unknown spaces. I felt a very different energy coming from Paramahansa Yogananda. His energy came from having a guide whom he could follow with full trust and devotion. I felt this same energy the moment I heard Suyogi's answer. A grounding, calm, loving, and peaceful energy. That energy of surrendering from within my heart affected me deeply.

Within seconds of hearing Suyogi's answer, all these thoughts were running through my mind. But having a living master? That was so new to me. My rational mind considered people coming back from India with a new name to be a ridiculous concept. But my soul was shouting "Yes!"

A minute later, Suyogi showed me a picture of a beautiful Indian saint, P.P. Hariprasad Swami. As I looked into his eyes, I suddenly felt my inner eyes open. It was an awakening; a recognizing. I remembered that I had dreamed of him before. It was always the same dream… I was walking on a familiar track behind my childhood home when, far away, I saw someone standing. As I came closer, my heart started jumping with so much joy, happiness, and bliss — an overwhelming feeling of meeting my best friend again after being apart for so long.

The memory of the dream touched me deep in my heart, but what happened next transformed me. Suddenly the feelings of insecurity and the constant search for happiness from my childhood disappeared, all stopping at once. I felt as though I was at home and on the right road to happiness and freedom. P.P. Hariprasad Swami gave me a soul path and became my master guide; a mentor showing me the next steps and preparing me to travel my path toward true love and happiness in a wonderful way.

From that moment on, my whole life changed. I finally understood that happiness is the most adventurous journey of our lives, one filled with so many facets to explore. I believe that happiness is our reason for being here on Earth; for having the gift of a human body and life. Today, I experience this most amazing, surprising, and fulfilling journey carried by the two strong, living lineages of great mentors.

The spiritual journey with my master mentor that started 15 years ago is unimaginable. I could never, ever have thought about, visualized, or manifested what happened to my life. It's out of my vision and limits. My life is the path of surrendering to the divine and diving deep into the true state of happiness within — a free, calm, stable, clear, fulfilling river full of love and understanding.

There is a beautiful story in the ancient scriptures about the happiness of the divine. The energy is so powerful that it's said a human body can't carry it. It's like the milk of a lion. The milk is so strong that it destroys any vessel that contains it except one made of gold. This is my path: to become a golden vessel in which the inner happiness of the divine can start to flow. But to become this golden vessel, there is some work to do.

Through the unique opportunity to connect with this wonderful Indian saint, I full-heartedly said, "Yes," to this relationship. A master-devotee relationship is one of the oldest, deepest relationships in human history. From the wise to the young, it unlocks the transfer of wisdom. Embracing this connection was the most profound and transformational decision of my life.

There is an interesting concept to unleash the true Happiness of the Soul in our spiritual tradition: the six layers that cover the soul, hiding its light. If you have ever had a luminous light experience while meditating, you have received a glimpse of your soul. When our inner egos are calm, we realize what is true. This truth is always there, but for most of us, the reality is that once we close our eyes, we see mostly darkness. We can't see the light. The reason for the darkness lies in the layers around the soul. These layers are built out of "I" and "me" — stubbornness, jealousy, greed, lust, and anger. To become aware and separate from these traits is the journey to the happiness of the soul leading to the union with the divine. Asking our spiritual mentor what Happiness truly means, he answers, *to see love, to hear love, to speak love, to think love, to be love.* This is the happiness map given to me by my wise mentor.

As part of my happiness journey, I have taken the opportunity to go to India and meet profound professional soul scientists in a monastery. Their purpose is the salvation of their soul, which means being free of these layers and being with God in eternal unity. Interestingly, one core principle of this spiritual tradition is to have at least six mentors to make the journey powerful — two nuns as mentors plus four more-advanced devotees — an example of how essential it is to have a support system (and similar to how I was supported during my writing process with the the editors at Ignite).

I have devoted 15 years to the deep study of ancient secrets. The study of Ayurveda has taught me about the happiness of body and mind, which stems from being in balance, connection, and alignment. I was very fortunate to learn the art of transformation from the greatest teachers and soon found my professional purpose in supporting people on their transformational journey toward discovering their true being.

Ayurveda gives us deep wisdom about being human. Once I detoxed, nourished my body, and cleared my mind, my inner wisdom naturally opened my heart and the path to my soul. A natural intelligence awakened within me and helped me uncover my full potential. My true Identity. My divine being. What an inspiration! I found many systematic approaches and methods to both experiencing and guiding a happiness transformation: a true metamorphosis leading to the power of the soul — the seat of absolute joy, bliss, happiness, and divinity.

I find such deep joy from working one-on-one as a transformational coach and mentor on Ayurveda, spirituality, and Rapid Transformational Therapy (RTT). After 10 years, I even went back to the entrepreneurial world, starting a happiness company based on the essence of Ayurveda. I teach that the more we are in our being, the more happiness is revealed to us. With the right tools and mentor, this transpires naturally.

After all these years of being full-time busy seeking to understand the happiness of body, mind, and soul, I have realized that having, accepting, and growing with guidance through a mentor is the deepest, most sustainable empowerment asset. It's a gift, an opener, a true treasure, and a big challenge. The principle of mentoring became deeply ingrained in my system. I'm using it for my health, for my career, as a mother, and for my relationships and spirituality. I became a mentor myself and recently started an organization that trains mentors in the corporate field.

I hope my story is encouraging you to listen to your intuition and to open your inner eyes to the signs of your path of Happiness — a path of enjoying the miracles that are happening in your life. Having the right mentors is like crossing the ocean by boat instead of swimming alone. My wish is for pure happiness to be revealed to you in its most beautiful and radiant colors. I truly hope that, while in our happiness, you and I cross paths one day.

Ignite Action Steps

Search, find, and prove your mentor.

Call out that you're longing for guidance. Be as clear as possible about what you are searching for. I did it in the form of prayers. It's also possible through visualizations, affirmations, and words.

Once mentors appear, you can follow the deep wisdom of Indian philosophy, which is reflected in the language of Sanskrit. Look first toward the person who gives you facts and advice before you become attracted. Is this person really the one who lives happiness? Does this happiness resonate with you? Do you feel more true, natural, peaceful, and clear when you are with this person? Does this person embody the aspects of happiness? Can they Ignite happiness within others? Prove it to yourself with time, honesty, and deep reflection. Listen to your heart.

Make a decision and commit to going deeper.

Once you feel sure, make a strong decision. Ask the right questions. Say "Yes" and give your best.

Accept and trust your mentor full-heartedly.

The deeper we trust, the more we open our hearts to grasping and implementing the wisdom of our guide. Trust is the accelerator in our relationship with our mentors. Trust makes for a very powerful connection.

Have more than one mentor.

Be aware of the different aspects of your life. Don't confuse your mentor relationship by expecting everything from one person.

Honor your inner practice.

Take your daily reflection and celebration time to connect to your inner treasure of happiness and to think, in gratitude, about your mentors. It's our responsibility to care for these relationships as they are like diamonds in our lives.

Pooja Lankers – Germany
Transformational Mentor, Coach and Entrepreneur
www.pooja-lankers.com

Margie Abernethy

"Happiness is not a destination — it comes from adjusting to detours and learning to make lemonade out of lemons."

It is my hope that in reading my story, you realize that you can have the life of your dreams. Even if you struggle with anxiety and PTSD — as I do — it's never too late to start over. Redefining what matters and accessing what makes you happy and Ignites your soul is always available to you.

A Lesson In Gratitude

It's been four years now since that fateful day in September. It was my birthday and my husband Dave was in Chicago for work, but he was scheduled to fly home in time to arrive for dinner when we'd celebrate. I remember enjoying Sunday morning coffee with new neighbors on Conifer Mountain, then planning an afternoon trail ride with a friend through the golden aspen trees. It all sounded so simple. But that day would change the course of my life and help to set me on a completely unexpected route to greater joy and happiness.

On that trail ride, the horse threw me off, breaking my hip. A hip fracture can be fatal, and I suffered three fractures! That was without a doubt the lowest point of my life — I was 50-something, 40 pounds overweight, in debt, unemployed, and trying to save our house from foreclosure. And now I was seriously injured. I didn't know how my life had gone so wrong.

In my 20s and 30s, I felt on top of my game. I had done well in school and enjoyed a successful and rewarding career in healthcare sales and marketing.

My jobs ranged from selling cosmetic skin care to plastic surgeons, to marketing fertility treatments to infertile couples, and selling concession stands for movie theaters. I had a few fancy titles and I traveled extensively for work. It was fun, it was exciting and I felt valued as an employee and a leader at the organizations where I worked. But the good times weren't to last much longer.

My 40s were tough years. I lost almost everything I had, including a pregnancy, most of my family of origin, several jobs, financial stability, a house, and even my physical and mental health. My downfall coincided with the Great Recession of 2008, which compounded my struggles. I started to believe that bad things happen to good people, that life was full of suffering, or maybe I was just unlucky.

Almost like a crescendo, the decade of strife ended dramatically with the dull cracking sound of my pelvis breaking against the hardened mud. A trail ride had sounded like a great way to score a little 'me time' before I had to ramp up and find a new job, but my vision of a peaceful trail ride through the golden aspen leaves was not to be. Soon after we set out on the trail, the horse bucked like a bronco and I was thrown onto the ground like a rag doll. My body hit with a thump that rattled me from head to toe. A wash of pain spread through my lower body. Something was wrong, but I didn't know what. I managed to get up, but I couldn't walk without assistance. I had no idea what was wrong with me, but I knew I wasn't right.

My Ignite moment took place in an orthopedist's office several days after the accident. The doctor was grandfatherly-like; his white beard and moustache reminded me of Santa Claus. He spoke sternly, telling me that I was a very 'lucky lady' not only to be alive but because despite my pelvis being fractured in three places, there were no displacements. The breaks were all aligned properly. This meant that my injury didn't require surgery, just bed rest. I was lucky to not only have survived this injury but to have the best possible outcome!! Lucky indeed. It was then that I realized how very lucky I am, not just because of the fracture. I have always considered myself to be lucky in so many ways, but I started feeling unlucky in others. In light speed, I saw all my mistakes and bad choices — it woke me up and served to stir my soul, Ignite my desire, and rattle me free to be the person I was meant to be.

I came out of that office visit with some much-needed perspective. I suffered a fall that could have killed me. It could have been so much worse than it was; I could have suffered a traumatic brain injury or screwed up my prior back surgeries. I knew I was injured, but I could recover. I was so incredibly grateful that it wasn't even worse.

From that day forward, I realized I had a second chance at life. If I was going to achieve what I wanted, I needed to take charge and forge on with determination. I vowed to move forward and to prioritize my health as the great asset that it is. Despite my detours and mistakes, I was proud of who I had become. This shift in perspective and focus on realigning myself made a huge impact on my life, health, and relationships.

At my age, it is rare that life circumstances provide you a block of time to focus on your priorities. My blog, *Happy Healthy Over 50*, is the result of this unanticipated time.

I wanted to share my experience and deliver the two most important lessons that I have learned during my recovery process:

1. *Be grateful to be alive and for the health that you still have. No matter how dire your situation may be, there are always others who are way worse off than you.*
2. *Be opportunistic. Seize opportunities that may come to you disguised as rotten luck.*

I spent most of October, November, and December of 2016 on my butt. With extra time on my hands, I also noticed that houses were selling well in our neighborhood. Fast. And often well over asking price. During the winter and at high altitude with extreme winters.

Living as we did, on top of a mountain, you have to sell when you see the chance. Snow seasons are longer and peak buying season is shorter — between March and May so that families can be settled in by the start of the school year. By December, we had a listing agent and by the following February, our home of 20 years was sold for $18,000 over asking price on the first weekend it was listed. Our new home was only 11 miles away, but we couldn't move in right away, so we stayed in several vacation rental properties until we could finally move into our beautiful new home.

My first attempt at a blog, called *Margie's Mountain View,* went live during my recovery time. *Margie's Mountain View* was intended to provide a window into the beautiful mountain town where we intended to live — in our new dream home in Evergreen, Colorado. Only, the Universe had other plans.

By the time I figured out how to send out my first newsletter, we had up and moved to Sarasota, Florida, from our new home in Evergreen, Colorado, just two months after we moved in. *Margie's Mountain View* became *Happy Healthy Over 50* as I chronicled my health journey and we started a successful vacation rental with the furnished house. And I learned to pivot by turning the Evergreen home into a full-time vacation rental and moving to Florida. It wasn't my first choice, but it was an awesome and life-changing choice, so I decided to gratefully accept it and enjoy the experience.

We enjoyed our short time in Sarasota and we met a ton of cool people, but both Dave and I longed to be back in the mountains again. So in August of 2019, we moved 2,456 miles from Sarasota, Florida, to our new hometown of Livingston, Montana. Livingston is a beautiful mountain town with world-class fly-fishing (as depicted in the film *A River Runs Through It*), fascinating history, and a true sense of community nestled between the north entrance to Yellowstone National Park and Bozeman. It is my kind of heaven.

This whole experience of being willing to start over and move across the country has opened my husband and me to a future we couldn't otherwise have imagined. We now share the best of all worlds by dividing time between Colorado, Montana, and Siesta Key, Florida. We plan to expand our vacation rental business with another property in Montana, in partnership with my sister Kathy, and perhaps another in Sarasota, Florida.

In hindsight, I recognize that all that has happened in my life — the good, the bad, the painful — has combined to bring me where I am today. I had lessons to learn — tough lessons about loss, grief, family, relationships, and brokenness. And starting over. I'm grateful for it all. Grateful for where I've been because it led me to where I am now. I'm grateful for our health, for friends and family, and for our fledgling businesses — a vacation rental in Evergreen, Colorado, and a blog named *HappyHealthyOver50.com*.

I no longer take my health for granted. Daily movement is a necessity for me these days as it helps me to keep the anxiety at bay. I am committed to staying as healthy as I can for as long as possible and often remind myself of these words by Buddha, *"To keep the body in good health is a duty... otherwise we shall not be able to keep our mind strong and clear."*

My personal growth has also positively impacted my relationships — my marriage, friendships, and family. My sister and I reconnected after a 35-year hiatus; we lost touch after our parent's divorce. Kathy and I hope to make up for lost time and to love and support each other for whatever time we have left. She's a gift in so many ways and she always reminds me to "Keep on laughing."

As for my husband Dave, it hasn't always been easy. We are fortunate that we have grown together. We sometimes still have our struggles, but marrying him was one of the best things I ever did. He and I have been through so much together, and he's been a supportive partner who is eager to learn and to be better. Neither of us came from intact homes, so it was the blind leading the blind, but we muddled through somehow and we wound up creating a beautiful marriage together. We've both worked on ourselves and our relationship and it's truly paying off. I'm a lucky woman to have found such a supportive and caring husband.

I started my blog, *Happy Healthy Over 50*, to encourage people to make their health a priority and to help people easily live healthier lives. I share my journey to my ultimate physical, emotional, and spiritual health, and I hope to share stories of inspiration and timely information to inspire others to follow a plant-based diet for their health and the health of the planet.

Many people my age struggle with knowing how to take control of their weight, not just because we're growing older but because there has been a mass of often conflicting nutritional information during our lifetimes. So many people are confused. Since I believe that your happiest Self includes vibrant health, I want to help people find information and inspiration so they can be more proactive with their health.

Observing my parents' declining physical and mental health had a huge impact on me — and forced me to face the fact that I have several unpleasant genetic diseases in my family history, including heart disease, diabetes, and cancer. I needed to do something to avoid a similar fate as my parents, so I adopted a whole food, plant-based (WFPB) diet as a means to mitigate my risk of those inherited diseases and to better manage my weight. Even just reducing your meat intake can substantially decrease your risk of obesity, diabetes, and some kinds of cancer, as well as Parkinson's Disease and Alzheimer's Disease, which run in my family too.

Happy Healthy Over 50 was born from my vision of sharing my journey to my ultimate physical and emotional health. My hope is to help other middle-aged women who may feel stuck with their weight, confused about what is healthy, or may be dealing with a chronic diagnosis. I share tips on healthy living, including following a whole food, plant-based (WFPB) diet which is demonstrated to reduce disease, and other scientifically-documented wellness techniques such as yoga and meditation which have been proven to offer benefits.

As it turns out, laying in bed for three months was the key to my slowing down long enough to get crystal clear about my goals and dreams. At times in my life, I knew more about what I *didn't* want than what I *did* want. Many of us don't stop to think about how to find our ultimate joy and happiness. I did only when I broke my hip. My priorities are in much better alignment with my values now; it's only four years later and I'm astonished at how happy I am.

As someone who has struggled but recovered to a wonderful place in my life, I hope to inspire those challenged with mental health issues or those that may just feel stuck, as I did. In hindsight, I realized I was only imprisoning myself to that corporate life that I grew to dislike. I needed to create a whole new narrative — so I did.

The man who started Kentucky Fried Chicken™ thought he was a failure and he considered suicide at age 65. He held a number of jobs in his early life, such as steam engine stoker, insurance salesman, and filling station operator. But nothing stuck until he started selling his fried chicken from a roadside restaurant in North Corbin, Kentucky, during the Great Depression. During that time, Sanders developed his 'secret recipe' and his patented method of cooking chicken in a pressure fryer. Sanders recognized the potential of the restaurant franchising concept and the first KFC™ franchise opened in South Salt Lake, Utah, in 1952. By age 85, he was a multi-millionaire. It is never too late to start over. Never give up on your dreams, or your life! You never know how good your life might turn out.

IGNITE ACTION STEPS

When you do start over, I highly recommend a book called *The Miracle Morning: The Not-So-Obvious Secret Guaranteed to Transform Your Life (Before 8AM)* by Hal Elrod. In it, the author describes how he puts himself into a 'peak state' by performing a series of tasks and rituals every morning. I liked it so much that I shot a video about it; you can find the link in the resources section.

In the book, he makes you consider the days at which you felt your best — recreate the actions that helped to make it the best day. I have come up with a daily list of 10 rituals that I do every day, to put myself into a peak state in order to optimize the day.

Think back on your 5 or 10 favorite days — of your whole life. What do they all have in common? Was it where you were, who you were with, or how you felt that day? What are the things important to you that set you up for feeling your best on those days?

Tony Robbins starts every morning with an 'adrenal support cocktail,' a 'priming' meditation exercise, and a workout involving a 'torture machine.' I feel at my best when I've walked a dog, done meditation, and done something for others. What are the things that help you to feel at your peak?

What if you made being in a peak state a priority?

What if you literally needed to operate at peak levels on a daily basis in order to achieve your goals? What if that was your standard?

Being in a peak state means you're operating at the level you want to be so that you can achieve ambitions beyond anything you've done before. If you're not currently pursuing something you've never done before, you probably don't need to have regular peak experiences. But if you're in a state of growth, you'll need to position your life to have peak moments more frequently.

Even more — you need to set your trajectory from a peak state because how you start something is generally how you finish it. If you start wrong, it's very very difficult to get things right, but if you start right, you'll usually be able to stay right.

Margie Abernethy – United States of America
Health & Wellness Blogger
www.HappyHealthyOver50.com

ANA CUKROV

"Be a happy pebble causing the ripple effect in the ocean of life."

There is immense beauty and perfection both inside you and all around you. Happiness lies in the way you perceive your life journey, not in the journey itself. There is always something to be happy about. Whatever happiness means to you, I wish that you discover, accept, and cherish that feeling so that it can be your source of joy to hold, keep, nourish, and celebrate. Make happiness your daily choice and practice a lifestyle of joy!

A PEBBLE IN THE OCEAN OF LIFE

A happy life is the only one to live. Creating a life that fulfills us and makes our soul sing and dance is, to my way of thinking, the most important destination and obligation. Otherwise, we can't truly call it living. When we feel unbalanced or oppressed — when we do only what is expected from us or what others decide for us — we are merely getting by. Our life may consist of many successfully completed goals and still be substantially unhappy. Despite being surrounded by caring people, we might not feel joyfully loved. Starting with the way we see and decode the world around us, and finishing with the meanings we give to situations and the choices we make, our happiness lies in our hands.

What does happiness mean? Where can we find it? These are questions we all ask ourselves. I believe we can look for happiness in tranquility or in activity; in peace or in dynamics; in solitude or in unitedness; in nature or in academic achievement. We search for happiness on the outside, in the love and acceptance of a partner or child, in success through a job or hobby. We pursue what we believe will make us happy. Unfortunately, we can't use outside resources for long; they wear out quickly. It is not until we reset ourselves, until we find our purpose and our peace of mind, that we settle into happiness.

When our soul comes to this Earth, it's similar to a pebble being thrown into the sea. It's perfect and firm, whether round or pointed in shape, smooth or rough on the surface. It always has a form, a structure, and a direction. Once the pebble meets water, it makes an impact, influencing the existing surface. Then the waves come, creating a ripple.

At the start of our lives, we encounter our parents, siblings, and close family members. Then our friends, lovers, and colleagues. Eventually, we grow to touch many more people the same way others touch and influence us. There is a lot of activity in the ocean of humanity. If we learn to dive in and let go, we can spread happiness and create a life of joyful influence. Unlike the pebble, we have the ability and freedom to choose the kind of impact we make. I'm dedicated to joy and its importance in the world. If my story lights up at least a sparkle of joy in you — if you feel more connected to the essence of life — my work will be done and my own happiness will grow.

The splash a pebble makes is awesome. It happens fast and the amplitude of the wave is significant. The water flies high in wonderful shapes and amazing colors, each drop reflecting heaven in its perfection. Each new life born to the world likewise makes a splash, changing its surroundings, fast and strong.

As a child, for me, there was no other way to truly *be* but *happy*. Being open and free was the best place to be — the state of innate delight, innocence, and hope. I loved being me. I loved my joyful, enthusiastic self. I was one of those children that enjoys the game whether they win or lose. A kid who wants to bring joy to every person and who finds a reason to smile in every little detail. Everything was beautiful and precious. I really, truly loved life.

But it's not only about the kind of pebble we are. It's also about where we fall and what kind of surface we crash into. Our family, our legacy, and our history determine how the water of life envelops and absorbs us. We might bounce off the surface, sink quickly to the bottom, or float gracefully down. How we arrive in this world, whether in rain or in shine, whether we are welcomed or cause turmoil in our family, creates the way we feel about ourselves and forms what we believe happiness is.

The first thing I can remember is being accepted and satisfied. I was grateful, loving the world around me, loving life for all its richness and beauty. My parents and grandparents provided a vast wellspring of joyful resources. They took care of me, protected me, fed me, hugged me, loved me. With Mom, I laughed, giggled, joked, and played games. Protected by Dad, I explored the world. Grandpa told me stories and took me on trips while Grandma bathed me, combed my hair, and cooked my favorite meals. Like a rainbow-colored oil slick glimmering on a puddle, I reflected their emotions and modeled their reactions. I grew up understanding the habits of how to feel happy, maintain positive moods, overcome low moods, and support others when they are down.

What I really experienced early in life, though, was *unitedness*. Happy me meant happy you, and vice versa. I am an identical twin, so I spontaneously mirrored myself in my sister. Soon I developed the habit of uplifting my twin Ivana, comforting her and cheering her up the same way I did myself. This came so naturally to me that I still try to make her happy in everyday conversations almost half a century later. In a way, that interconnectedness caused a confusion of boundaries between us, as often happens in twins. It took me a while to learn that my happiness is *my* responsibility and *her* happiness is hers. Questioning the uniqueness of my identity along with my tendency to merge got in my way in later relationships. Clearing up the confusion was needed for love, parenting, friendship, and business.

As close to the pebble as the first rippling circle is, it's not the pebble itself. They share the splash, the time, the place, and even the impact of it, but are made of different matter. Sometimes several pebbles drop in together or close to one another, their impact interconnected as they form a specific pattern. It's interesting and wonderful, but let's not mistake them for one. Each of us has a unique mission.

Blessed with a gift of optimism, I was certain that life is a miracle. I carried a huge smile on my face and my heart on a platter. Over and over again, I would warm up my soul just by witnessing happy moments. As a person next to me started to glow, to energize, to smile, I felt at home. In that instant, I knew she or he had reconnected with herself/himself and with all of creation. Our loving God made us as His reflection, glowing, celebrating, and praising. That's why we can reach that joyful place while we dance, sing, kiss, tell jokes, or simply hug. That is the truth of life — we are all one.

Some 30 years ago, I fell in love. It was the pure teenage kind of love and for many years, my happiness was anchored in that love. We met by the sea and he wrote me a song. It was very romantic and nothing could lift me higher. He was from Italy and I was from Croatia, so after our Mediterranean idyll, we exchanged letters. My happiness was rooted in the anticipation of each letter's arrival. Then the war came and separated us, but I do know that I have met

Love. As Victor Hugo said, "The greatest happiness of life is the conviction that we are loved; loved for ourselves, or rather, loved in spite of ourselves." Maybe the enduring echo of my romance by the sea is why I like spending time at the beach so much. Water is healing. Water is there in conception, childbirth, and tears; in cleaning, cooking, drinking, and baptizing. It's the symbol of life.

When a pebble makes a splash, each expanding circle in its ripple is a bit larger, although lower in amplitude; wider in reach but diminished in strength. As many coexisting ripples, we teach one another and learn from each other. The souls we touch appear in a certain moment; some of them touch us back and lift us higher. Our family and friends meet each other and form new structures. Still, our essence remains the same; we leave traces of our passage everywhere we go.

My soul was always connected to and colored by joy and happiness. As a youngster, wherever there was a party, there I was. I felt safe and secure that way and I didn't need to question the sadness yet. As time went by, my eyes were opened to the difficulty others have staying positive. I couldn't make them smile, no matter what I did. I felt helpless. Sometimes, even though I tried, people would be disappointed in me. I've been corrected. I've been rejected. I've been labeled and called stupid, naive, and childish. That left marks on my soul. I tried to adapt, to be accepted, to earn my value. On a social level, I did everything I was supposed to. I studied well, visited relatives, acted polite. I felt happy to please others; it made me feel great. We are wired to help each other, after all. But what if, focusing on the outside, we lose contact with our core? Energy flows where focus goes, and my focus was on love.

As the pebble slowly sinks down, new ripples appear representing spouses, family life, careers, and hobbies. There are high points and low points. As the base of each wave in a ripple is lower, it may seem it doesn't matter as much as the peak of the wave, but it is equally important and there is no movement without it.

I fell in love again. We got married quickly and I didn't know what hit me. The high points gave me immense pleasure and the low points introduced me to the dark side of joy. Tears of joy. Tears of pain. (There's always water involved.) I started projects and businesses, gave birth to one child after another, and we moved a few times. So much to do, so much to learn! There was a lot going on for over 20 years and through it all, I kept pushing myself. What I needed to learn is that if I wanted to get to really know someone, I should pay attention to the way that person reacts to my happiness. My husband wasn't really supporting me. My sister had her own family and a lot on her mind. My parents and extended family lived in another city. Most days, I wasn't getting enough support, and I burned out.

Although already close to the bottom of the sea, our pebble's influence continues. Our ripple spreads. In the outer circle, far from the center, we don't see the effect we have. Maybe it's better that way. Otherwise, we wouldn't be humble.

Like most people in my generation (and many before), I was taught to listen and obey. To play by the rules and follow the leaders. To let go of my power and my sense of being *me*. Slowly but surely, that wore me out. I've been on the low side of the wave. I expected love and respect from my husband and kids, and received less and less of it. In the pursuit of happiness, I was everything to everyone, giving more and more, juggling faster and even faster. I felt doubt, despair, and abandonment. My cries for help brought only more deep loss. Then solitude. Apathy. Guilt. Shame. Turning around, all I could see was pain and misery. I lost my job. My husband left me, breaking the family apart, taking some of our children and confusing all five of them as well as myself.

The more I tried to understand what was going on and save it all, the less I used my natural navigation. I got lost. I needed to come back to the immense and everlasting source of joy. To that place I knew so well when I first came to this Earth. The place where we never run out of happiness. That's when I met Jesus. And that's when, slowly, acceptance began. Solitude started being my friend.

I was sad. Very sad. A waterfall of tears kept pouring out. There was too much sadness inside and it needed air. There is no happiness without it. "Those who have sorrow are happy, because they will be comforted," says Jesus to His disciples on the mountain (Matthew 5,4). I returned to the beach. To the healing of water. To the only place where I could stop trying to understand; the only place I could breathe deeply. As I lay there, I could feel my heartbeat thumping under my fingertips; I knew I was still alive. I would find my balance and peace in the contact with nature, with God's creation. The vast surface of the sea was so comforting, so stable, so accepting, so promising. It was my compass, it reoriented me. When I felt ready, I decided to let go. To accept my life — all of it. To accept my family members the way they are, as well as their decisions. To accept the liberty we all had. It gave me peace and I have found deep happiness within.

I decided to do less of what is *expected* of me and more of what makes me happy. Fewer cultural, religious, and family pressures; more free choices. I chose to stop pleasing everybody else; to be still long enough to find my inner peace. Returning to the beach day by day, I was more peaceful and happy. My gaze followed the waves, my moods corresponded to the tide, and my thoughts were lighter. I started to form new goals, recreating my life from scratch, honest and simple like a seagull's.

Your life is like an ocean. Some people are like a seagull flying above the waves, just observing — you never really get to meet them. Others are like stars reflecting on the surface in the night or a feather drifting down to the surface — gentle in contact, but not following us down to the bottom.

In my prayers, I had fewer demands and tears, and more praise and gratitude. A long line of loving and kind people, situations, words, and blessings kept emerging. From that place of peace and appreciation, I found the never-ending happiness within.

Throughout all the pain, my core kept voting for one thing: my basic state of happiness. I know now that my joy can be diminished over and over but never extinguished. My wish was to be joyful and complete, as I used to be: simply happy to be me.

Happiness is an inside-out job. An inside-out task. An inside-out reality, inside-out lifestyle, and inside-out choice. *We have to be the happiness we seek.* We have to remember where we came from and who we really are. Happiness doesn't depend on the circumstances of our lives; it lies in the way we perceive and interpret the experiences we go through.

Mother Teresa said, "Spread love everywhere you go. Let no one ever come to you without leaving happier." This is why we are here: to be the happiness we seek; to spread love, light, and joy. My ripple reaches far by writing, lecturing, or giving testimony. As I speak my truth, I see my inner world reflected by the audience — the very proof of the unitedness of humankind. My life stream meets the pulse of the group, my message spreads, and a wave of understanding and appreciation comes back to me. Furthermore, when giving my blessing, praying for someone, or simply sending positive vibrations, I can be the unknowing instrument in the arms of our Creator.

Even if we are the smallest of pebbles, even if our splash is tiny, it's great to know that we are important. We sink to the bottom, returning to the security of firm ground. As we find peace and meaning in that new surrounding, the effect on the surface still occurs. We merge with the ocean of life, being one with it, as we are meant to be.

We are given this wonderful gift in life: the ability to be immensely happy. The whole Universe is designed to be happy, so shouldn't we be happy too? If we respect happiness as our birthright, we are going to feel it. And if we see the happiness of others as the journey, we can truly live as a global family.

Speak your truth. It will never run out. It's a vast and infinite body of water. Whatever happens, remember that your dignity isn't negotiable. Your values are sacred, your dreams and desires are important markers on the journey toward your calling. As ripples together, we can rejoice as brothers and sisters and choose to live in simplicity, gratitude, and praise. There is always enough happiness when we are connected to our source of life. I am a pebble and my mission is to make a splash. The ripples of my passing must wash over sadness, loneliness, boredom, despair, pain, and confusion so that both myself and my close ones can find immense joy in the very living. So that we can track God's love that never ends. So that we can keep enjoying more and more happiness.

IGNITE ACTION STEPS

- **BRILLIANCE**: Your happiness is your task and your responsibility. Let each drop of water reflect the ocean of happiness within you. Let it shine brightly — daily.

- **COURAGE:** Be brave in living. Pursue what makes you happy. It's *your* life.

- **HONESTY:** Live and speak your truth. Be open so the force of life can run through you.

- **ACCEPTANCE:** Accept a full range of emotions. Accept every experience and every person. All is good.

- **MODESTY:** Focus on reality and be present. The less you expect, project, or interpret, the happier you will feel.

- **GRATITUDE:** Praise, pray, journal, and congratulate freely so the joy can lift the energy of the planet higher.

- **SUPPORT:** Be there for others as much as you can so they can be happy in their own way. Give, love, and praise, and your fulfillment will grow accordingly.

Ana Cukrov – Croatia
Psychology Professor

TRACY STONE

"You can't have it all, but you can have what you want."

My greatest wish for you is that you will find choices where you thought there were none, purpose where it was missing, and the ability to free yourself into your best limitless life.

CHILDHOOD OVER: HOLDING MYSELF ACCOUNTABLE FOR MY CHOICES

I flew out of Ireland and the nest of home on a rainy Saturday night in June at the tender age of 18 to live with my wonderful sister who had moved to England a couple of years before. I had just completed a secretarial course in Dublin because, in my mother's words, "You'll always have work." That Monday, I walked into the temp agency and, after a brief typing test, was sent out to work the very same day. Something about the suddenness of my launch into the working world felt like I was a lemming falling off a cliff. After a few mind-numbing temp roles, because for me there is little joy to be extracted from manually typing an endless ream of purchase orders every day, I finally accepted a permanent role and so began my unintentional corporate career at age 19. It was very much at the bottom of the totem pole. At that point in my life, I was so devoid of direction that I didn't even realize I didn't have one. Like the child I was, I didn't understand the importance of having a direction and was simply following the instructions I had been given, as I had been accustomed to doing.

I was a diligent and hard worker with positive energy to spare so I rapidly moved from administrative roles into marketing then into business process reengineering, becoming a master trainer and practitioner in Six Sigma, Lean, and a number of other methodologies designed to drive efficient change. I was advancing all the time but not because of any kind of plan, just my ability to say 'yes', to work hard, and be a people pleaser.

It was exciting, even spine-tingling at times, and I began to feel that I was making a difference, contributing in some positive way to the business, my colleagues, and our customers through my work. Being recognized for my new skills meant plenty of globe-trotting, which only a year or two prior had been nothing more than a fanciful dream. It was mind-blowing that I was now regularly visiting new countries and breathtaking cities, meeting new people, learning about culture and how it affects business and our lives. Lots of exotic airports, thousands of air miles and sumptuous hotels. Endless miniature shampoo/conditioner/body cream bottles that I would take home and share with my sister.

My role required me to be parachuted into a part of the organization to work with the local teams to help them achieve process efficiency in order to meet our customers' needs better and faster. Around twice a month, I grabbed my thoroughly-stamped passport and found myself in another corporate office in another country helping teams to achieve not only their business objectives but also greatly reducing the pressure they all worked under. I felt exhilarated and lighter jetting away after a successful week knowing I had helped people make their own lives easier, often reducing their work days by several hours. We would celebrate the end of these full-on workshops with a big team dinner. It was clear to see how engaging the people I worked with in this incredibly positive and active way gave them, and therefore me, an injection of happiness. Helping them get to that celebration point always left me high on my own release of dopamine and serotonin and left the endorphins simply racing through my system.

Without deliberately choosing it, I found myself living a life in which I was traveling constantly, eating dinner most nights in hotel restaurants, sitting with a book to hide behind as I ate alone, not wanting to attract attention. All the time hearing the constant corporate battle cry, "*You can have it all. You can have the big career where even the sky isn't a limit, the amazing husband, the perfect children. Damn it, you can also ski in skiing season, hit the best beaches in the summer, become a wine connoisseur, have a perfectly toned body, read a book a week, network like a beast, and basically have it all.*" This notion of having it all was, in many ways, alluring, empowering, and choc-full of 'I am woman, hear me roar!' In fact, it was not just alluring, it began to feel like a challenge which, if I didn't rise to it, would prove me to somehow be a failure.

I found myself growing increasingly conflicted between enjoying the work and an evolving unsettling feeling, which was for now, unclear, wordless, and not fully formed, that something, somewhere within me was missing or just wasn't sitting right. I couldn't quite put my finger on it but that unsettling feeling was peeping out from behind the onwards momentum I was sailing. Still, I both comforted and berated myself with 'Remember, you can have it all.'

I greatly relished working with teams from every continent on earth. I felt privileged to see new countries, cities, cultures, and people. I loved being good at what I did and at the top of my game. I enjoyed receiving award after award for both the results I delivered and the appreciation of the teams I worked with. But, at the same time, this hollowness continued to gnaw at my conscience day after day. I felt lonely and was anxious that I was never going to find the family life that I knew I really wanted. I began to wonder if I had missed that happiness boat entirely. I pushed the thoughts down, telling myself yet again, 'Remember, you can have it all.'

As the stock market crash of 2008 strangled the world financially and for many years to come, I inadvertently became a corporate enforcer, driving efficiency often at an increasingly high human cost. My particular skills were in great demand to help the company become more efficient by making processes more lean. One of the inevitable impacts of creating lean operations is that the company would no longer require the same amount of people to get the work done. There was a tangible shift that materialized within the teams I was working with and it troubled me deeply. The emotional climate had changed from people being eager to work together and welcoming me into their fold, to meeting with people who were afraid of losing their jobs. Despite the clear organizational need for efficiency, the work didn't feel as good as it used to and I had a nagging sense that the balance of helping the business and the bottom line had shifted the focus dramatically away from the people and not for the better. My personal happiness quotient took a hit.

I began to take my foot off the gas of my career path. It wasn't a conscious decision; it just happened. I could have pushed myself much harder, gotten involved in so much more, received more awards, and risen higher. I had the potential to touch the stars, put them in my pockets and reap the corporate rewards, but somehow my heart and soul just weren't in it and I felt like I was going through the motions. This felt strange because I loved the people I worked with, respected and valued them. I looked around me and saw how we can easily become hamsters on a wheel, working crazy hours, missing time with friends and family and not taking the time to find that husband or have those children. No matter how hard I worked, I always needed to do something more in order to grab that top rating out of the hands of someone else.

My internal voice was quietly screaming that there had to be something more. I was great at what I did but would it really matter if I disappeared one day? The business certainly wouldn't stop. So, despite being talented, experienced, and respected, the recurring question in my heart kept asking if I was doing what I was meant to be doing. If I had a dollar for every time I was told how lucky I was to have a great job in a global bank, a manager I respected, exciting work, a big salary and benefits, well, I would have a lot of dollars. But this just made me feel ungrateful and guilty when I dared to silently reflect on whether this made me happy.

I remember my tipping point so clearly; it was right after starting a new high-profile project at the bank. This required me crossing the Atlantic from London and boarding a tiny twin prop plane which bobbed its way from JFK westwards and eventually over hundreds of miles of seemingly endless flat fields in exquisite hues of green, yellow, purple, and snowy white, until we arrived in a picture perfect Midwest city of considerably less than 200,000 people. It was the kind of place where people grow up and stay. A place where you live near many generations of your family and where you stay in touch with the friends you went to school with. I, by contrast, had moved several times in both childhood and adulthood, and had lost many childhood connections. This was the kind of place where you leave school and start working for one of the few major employers in town. Meeting my new colleagues, who I would lead through a workshop that week, was eye opening in terms of their legacy and feeling of family and community within the business.

Introducing ourselves on the first day of our workshop, I realized that the baby of the team, the newest one on board, started there 16 years ago! Whole families worked there. They loved, respected, and dedicated themselves to the business. This *was* family to them.

However, we were together for a reason. There was a need to drive efficiency, to cut costs. Everybody knew that. These amazing people were still totally dedicated in their open contribution to our work that week, knowing it might bring major and unwanted change to them, their colleagues, and their town. This was a heavy weight to carry and the impact of my work on their lives hit me harder than ever before. I would go back through the several inches of deep snow every night to my hotel room and cry. I felt so bad that my work, my skill as a facilitator, as a problem solver, my ability to connect with and get the best out of people, was going to result in a huge number of them either moving into jobs they didn't want or, even worse, losing their jobs completely.

I left at the end of the very productive week with a distinct heaviness in my heart. Where would people go? They had grown up 'man and boy' in this business, given their time, energy, skills, and hearts. How many other major employers were there to go to? Not many, perhaps two or three. I understood the business need; I truly did. But this wasn't New York, London, or Delhi where people could easily walk into another like-for-like job. As much as I had fallen in love with the beautiful town and its people, I couldn't wait to get back on the tiny plane again, headed for my connection in JFK back to London.

The weight of the week was crushing me. Looking out the window and down at the endless snow-covered farms only made me feel worse, knowing how the people I had just left truly were a local community who would be hit hard by the changes to come.

On my long journey home I had a lot of time to think as sleeping like a baby is only for the innocent. I didn't feel so innocent just then. What kind of person uses their superpower to impact others so negatively? But what could I do about it? This was my job. It was what I had a great depth of experience in: solving problems, creating profitable results, making things work better, driving change, and whipping people up in the excitement of the change journey.

I had spent decades refining and honing my skills. The niggling voice coming from somewhere deep in the back of my head (or was it my heart?) was fighting its way through a jungle of logic and fears to provoke me into considering that some kind of change was needed in my own life if I was ever to get back on the happy train. But how? There were so many reasons not to change anything: the salary, bonus, benefits, colleagues, and a great manager who I valued and enjoyed working with, not to mention the years I had put in to get there. The other internal voice was saying, "Don't be ridiculous, change is bad, change is scary and hard, just keep your head down and press on."

The realization hit me like a freight train that, actually, you *can't* have it all. Something has to give. You can't have the brilliant, stratospheric career without it coming at some kind of cost. Perhaps the cost of finding the husband you long for or having children. It may come at the cost of spending time with them when you find them. Whichever way you cut it, there are only 24 hours in a day. You have to choose how you fill those hours and whether those things will bring you happiness.

It's staggering how complacent we can become, aimlessly following an accidental and unintended path, as I had found myself on, assuming we must continue on exactly that path, swept up in a momentum that assumes and rides on the back of our compliance. That complacency stifles our innovation, our personal growth and potential, the ability to meet our core human needs, and ultimately our ability to be happy and sprinkle a little happiness on those surrounding us.

Isn't it funny though how things just seem to come along at the right time? So, there I was in the Business Class cabin of the overnight flight home. The perks of the corporate world can become like a drug, so easily claiming ownership of you. Who doesn't love to be elegantly ushered up to the top deck or told with a warm smile to "Turn left and help yourself to champagne." Despite the comfortable surroundings, I was distinctly not comfortable and I certainly couldn't sleep. Change was in the wind.

My thoughts were a tangled mess of spaghetti. My heart was so heavy it felt tight in my chest and my eyes instantly gave away my emotional state. I felt so bad for all those colleagues I had left back in that beautiful, snowy, tight-knit community. No amount of self-pep talking along the lines of "It would have happened with or without you… You had a job to do… It was what the business needed" provided any consolation.

A fitful seven hours later, the pilot deployed the landing gear, wheels made contact with terra firma and we all began to reconnect to our mobile services. After letting my infinitely supportive partner know we had landed and I was looking forward to seeing him in the Arrivals hall, I did something I very rarely did. I opened my Facebook™ app. Seriously, if I did that three times a year it was deemed a busy social media year for me. I didn't even need to scroll. It was right there. A sponsored post which must have been eavesdropping on my troubled thoughts. It was asking me if I wanted to have a fulfilling and rewarding career helping people to solve their problems as a Rapid Transformational Therapy Hypnotherapist, under the expert tuition of one of the world's most recognized and celebrated hypnotherapists, Marisa Peer. "Hell, yes!" was my instantaneous response which echoed through every fiber of my body.

I mean, I have been a professional problem solver for 30 years but this somehow felt more human, real, authentic, and right. It quite simply fit me like a glove. I was already starting to feel light-headed with the potential of what this was offering. That night, lying in bed, regaling my partner about the emotional roller coaster of a week, I also showed him the advert which had offered me a potential solution to my unease. "Sign up for the call; find out more," he said. So I did exactly that. And in that moment I realized that I had a choice. I could choose to change nothing and stay the course I had found myself on or to take a purposeful leap headlong into being accountable for my decisions and where they led me. I launched myself with new energy and no short measure of 'Go get 'em, tiger' attitude into the latter.

For the first time in a very long time I felt I was in control of my own life. The feeling was a heady mix of excitement, a renewed lease of life, and the tantalizing carrot of untapped potential all wrapped up in the softest cashmere blanket of the innate knowledge I gave myself permission to possess that this was simply right.

I've always believed that there are no coincidences in life. How can anything be a coincidence? You had to make choices, decisions to be in that place at that time, in the relevant headspace in order to be open to seeing the 'coincidence.' These things aren't accidental. Neither are they preordained. I prefer to believe they are the result of choices made and acted on. That very belief offers me control over my own life, direction, and happiness. That day I allowed myself to be in the headspace which opened me up to no longer following a career aimlessly. I was awakened to change. More specifically, I chose to see the incredible potential for a change which would affect my life in ways I couldn't have imagined. I felt lighter. Happier.

Opportunities are always out there — it's our sensitivity to them that changes. Far too often we walk around with blinkers on, restricting our vision or perspective of what's available to us in life. But, that day, in that moment, I had been blinker-free, open to potential, and gave myself permission to have a choice. *I chose to take action, to take accountability for my own happiness!*

In what felt like the mere blink of an eye, I was a trained, certified RTT™ Therapist and a Coach, helping people all over the world to change their lives through powerful individual therapy and coaching sessions, exciting transformational group hypnosis events, and focused corporate group workshops. Now, I'm using my superpowers for good, helping people to quickly overcome their limiting beliefs in life and business, enabling them to step into their own limitless potential.

I am finally being true to myself, holding myself accountable for my choices and working with great purpose and boundless energy toward my goals. Freeing myself into the space where I'm good with knowing that while I can't have everything, I definitely and most absolutely *can* have what I want.

I sincerely wish the same sense of purpose, fulfillment, and deep happiness for you through finding and making brilliant choices. Start by choosing happiness. Then fuel your mind with brilliance and let your words guide you toward your greatness. Your own words are your programming and they give you the power to achieve whatever you want. Give yourself permission to follow your dream.

Seize the truth.

Everything you want is truly available to you.

Ignite Action Steps

All too often we are passive reactors to our own life journey and choices. In fact, this can become such a habit that it can seem like some kind of divine truth that we have no choice in what happens to us. This limits our life in so many ways: love, relationships, career, finances, purpose, fulfillment, and our happiness.

1. Have a totally honest conversation with yourself. If it helps, imagine you are having that conversation with your nearest and dearest, imagining them to be in your situation, and that you are giving them advice on how to overcome their blocks to happiness.

Ask yourself:

- *What would make me happier right now and a year or even three years from now?*
- *What's stopping me from having or doing that?*
- *What are the steps I need to take to have or do that?*
- *What will my life be like when I have taken these steps and have or am doing what I always wanted?*

2. Am I willing to do what it takes, to put in the time and effort to have what I want?

Hold yourself accountable for your choices and actions by creating a 90 Day Personal Contract. Grab a single page and write a title of '90 Day Personal Contract' then capture the following:

- *My objectives or goals, make them SMART (Specific, Measurable, Attainable, Relevant, Time-bound)*
- *The actions I am going to take over the next 90 days (it helps to make these time-bound also)*
- *How I am going to invest my energy and passion into these actions*
- *How I will celebrate success*

Actions truly speak louder than words. Releasing these thoughts out of your head and capturing them on paper makes taking action so much easier and totally doable. Make your greatest wishes come true and fill your life with limitless happiness!

Tracy Stone – United Kingdom
Advanced Rapid Transformational Hypnotherapist & Coach
www.LimitlessPotential.co.uk

90 Day Personal Contract

First, you need to know what it is that you want to achieve. Start by having a very honest conversation with yourself asking:

- What would make me happier now and a year or even 3 years from now?
- What's stopping me from having or doing that?
- What are the steps I need to take in order to have or do that?
- What will my life be like when I have taken these steps and achieved my greatest dreams?

Then capture and describe your short term (1-3 months), medium term (1 year) or long term (3 years) brilliant **'SMART' objectives** in this table.

'SMART' OBJECTIVES		
#	Make it Specific *What my objective is*	Make it Measurable *What it looks like when done*
1	Eg. Be able to present or talk to a group with confidence	Present at 2 monthly team meetings and at global annual conference

Now that you have described what you want to achieve, it's time to identify and hold yourself accountable for the actions you need to take in the form of a **90 Day Contract** with yourself.

90 Day Contract

Over the next 90 days, I_____, will take the following actions to pursue my objectives.

Obj. #	Actions I will take	How to fill it with energy and passion
1	Eg. Secure a mentor or coach to help develop my presentation and communication skills	Create a short presentation for the coach/mentor to show my objectives & commitment

The only permission I need to follow my dreams is my own!

Make it **A**ttainable *How I can make it doable*	Make it **R**elevant *Why this is important*	Make it **T**ime Bound *When I will complete it*
Allowing 5 months for skill development, practice and feedback	This is a requirement for my current role	25th January 2021

When I will start and complete it	Progress notes	How I will celebrate success
S – 07/27/20 C – 08/20/20	Created document to share with mentor. Identified 3 possible mentors to ask. Sent request for mentorship with document to preferred mentor and requested call to discuss.	Buy a new brightly coloured notebook to take notes in my mentoring sessions.

Aurelie Busollo
- Writer and Life Adventurer
- www.facebook.com/aureliebusollo

Abbey Richter
- abbeyrichter.com

Albert Urena
- To read more about my early life, the death of my father, and my involvement with street gangs, you can read those parts of my story in *Ignite Your Adventurous Spirit* and *Ignite Your Warrior Within.*

Books I recommend:
- *Innercise* by John Assaraf
- *Abundance Now* by Lisa Nichols
- Neale Donald Walsch - Author of Conversations with God

Alex Gontkovic
- The summer camp that I attend in St. Andrews, Scotland: www.issos.com
- The infamous Gelateria located in St. Andrews, Scotland: jannettas.co.uk

Bela Fayth
- Loving What Is: You Are Enough - Bela Fayth

Claudia Patricia Perez Delgado
- @educationmatterscol.org
- Core Woman.org
- United Nations
- UNESCO
- @the_female_lead

Books I recommend:
- *The Moment of Lift* by Melinda Gates,
- *Becoming* by Michelle Obama
- Oprah Winfrey

Joye Madden
- Follow me on Instagram @joyem1973 or on Facebook Joye Coons Madden.

Kristin Kurth-Koelzer
- For information on fostering and adoption in the U.S. see: www.child-welfare.gov/nfcad/
- The Legend of the Guatemalan worry doll: www.commonhope.org/the-legend-of-the-guatemalan-worry-doll/
- You can request your own worry doll by making a $25 donation to www.commonhope.org and writing "worry doll" in the donation comments.

Margie Abernethy
- I highly recommend a book called *The Miracle Morning: The Not-So-Obvious Secret Guaranteed to Transform Your Life (Before 8AM)* by Hal Elrod. In it, the author describes how he puts himself into a 'Peak State' by performing a series of tasks and rituals every morning.

I liked it so much that I shot a video about it: https://www.facebook.com/HealthyHappyOver50/videos/705302746962600/

Meghan Huthsteiner
- King James Bible Cambridge

Melody D. Byrd
- www.melbyrd.com

Nicole Arnold
- The Via Character Strength Survey: www.viacharacter.org/survey/account/register

A book I recommend:
- *The Middle Passage - From Misery to Meaning in Midlife* by James Hollis

Rebecca Blust
- www.positivethinkingrevolution.com

Simona Sabbatini

Books I recommend:

- *Positive Psychology* by Prof. Martin Seligman
- *The 7 Spiritual Laws of Success* by Deepak Chopra
- *Intentional Change Theory* by Richard Boyatzis
- *Plato not Prozac* by Lou Marinoff
- *The Middle Way* by Lou Marinoff
- *The Art of Happiness* by Dalai Lama

PHOTO CREDITS

Aurelie Busollo - *Victor Finkel*
Beejal Coulson - *Cat Lane*
Bela Fayth - *La Vie Photography*
Claudia Patricia Pérez Delgado - *Diego Zamora Melendez @ diegozamorafotografia*
Hanna Wickström - *Selina Malik*
Janice Mulligan - *Marcia Siggins Jonas*
Jason B. Flores - *Kelli MacTaggart*
JB Owen - *Paul Wozniak*
Kristin Kurth-Koelzer - *Marilyn Isaac Photography*
Melody D. Byrd - *Darryl Hammond*
Nicole Arnold - *Emily D Photography*
Sarah Cross - *Lenka McCarthy Photography*
Simona Sabbatini - *Leni Frau*

Afterword

Prof. Martin Seligman gave us the recipe to create and maintain Happiness; it's called P.E.R.M.A. It means:

Cultivate **POSITIVE EMOTIONS**

Feel **ENGAGED** in what you do

Create nice **RELATIONSHIP**

Get a **MEANING** in whatever you do

Be sure to recognize your **ACCOMPLISHMENT**

Thank you

A tremendous thank you goes to those who are working in the background editing, supporting, and encouraging the authors. They are some of the most genuine and heart-centered people I know. Their devotion to the vision of IGNITE, their integrity, and the message they aspire to convey is of the highest possible caliber. They all want you to find your IGNITE moment and flourish. They each believe in you and that's what makes them so outstanding. Their dream is for your dreams to come true.

Editing Team: Alex Blake, Andrea Drajewicz, Jock Mackenzie, Nicole Arnold, and Chloe Holewinski

Production Team: Dania Zafar, Peter Giesin, and JB Owen

A special thanks and gratitude to the project leaders, Stacey Yates Sellar and Sydney Schubbe, for their support behind the scenes and for going 'above and beyond' to make this a wonderful experience by ensuring everything ran smoothly and with elegance.

A deep appreciation goes to each and every author who made Ignite Happiness possible — with all your beautiful stories embracing this powerful idea of the modern goddess found within each and every one of us.

To all our readers, we thank you for reading and loving the stories; for opening your hearts and minds to the idea of Igniting your own lives. We welcome you to share your story and become a new author in one of our upcoming books. Your message and your Ignite moment may be exactly what someone needs to hear.

Join us on this magical Ignite journey!

Leading the industry in Empowerment Publishing,
IGNITE transforms individuals into
INTERNATIONAL BESTSELLING AUTHORS.

WRITE YOUR STORY IN AN IGNITE BOOK!!

With over 400 amazing individuals to date writing their stories and sharing their Ignite moments, we are positively impacting the planet and raising the vibration of HUMANITY. Our stories inspire and empower others and we want to add your story to one of our upcoming books!

If you have a story of perseverance, determination, growth, awakening and change... and you've felt the power of your Ignite moment, we'd love to hear from you.

Go to our website, click How To Get Started and share a bit of your Ignite transformation.

We are always looking for motivating stories that will make a difference in someone's life. Our fun, enjoyable, four-month writing process is like no other — and the best thing about Ignite is the community of outstanding, like-minded individuals dedicated to helping others.

Our road to sharing your message and becoming a bestselling author begins right here.

YOU CAN IGNITE ANOTHER SO JOIN US TO
IGNITE A BILLION LIVES WITH A BILLION WORDS.

Apply at: www.igniteyou.life
Inquire at: info@igniteyou.life

Find out more at: www.igniteyou.life

CPSIA information can be obtained
at www.ICGtesting.com
Printed in the USA
LVHW071616290820
664533LV00046B/1070